The Complete Idiot's Refere

Ten Ways to Improve the Odds of L

1. Know well the person you are moving in with!
2. Allow your love relationship to develop to a meaningful, committed level before you share a home together.
3. Do not move in with someone who is down on his or her luck, is recently divorced, or has a history of live-in lovers.
4. Only move in with someone who can contribute equally to the live-in relationship, emotionally and financially.
5. Before you and your love interest move in together, make sure you share similar long-range romantic agendas.
6. Solve major differences *before* you move in together, not after.
7. Be honest and open with yourself and with your would-be live-in.
8. Dispense with hidden agendas.
9. Carefully plan and discuss your live-in arrangements until they are satisfactory to both of you.
10. Expect to treat one another with love, respect, consideration, courtesy, and kindness.

alpha books

Ten Myths About Living Together

1. A live-in relationship and marriage are more similar than they are different.
2. Children with two cohabiting parents fare just as well as children in a married, two-parent household.
3. Living together is a way to test marital compatibility.
4. Live-ins are just as committed as marriage partners.
5. Most live-in partners eventually marry.
6. The financial assets and contributions to the household made by live-in partners are protected by law.
7. Live-in partners who have a child do not need to establish the father's paternity.
8. Living together promotes sexual fidelity.
9. Sex is better among live-in partners.
10. It isn't possible for a live-in partner to hide his or her true motives or character.

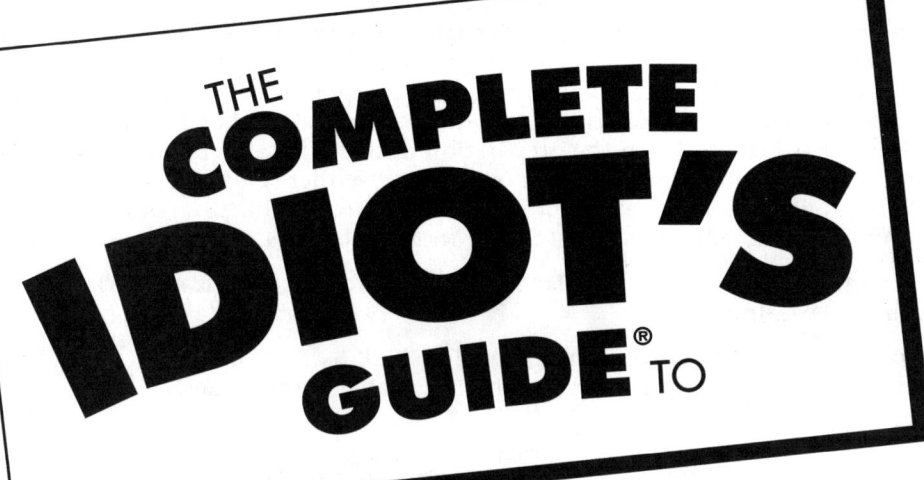

Living Together

by Rosanne Rosen

alpha
books

Macmillan USA, Inc.
201 West 103rd Street
Indianapolis, IN 46290

A Pearson Education Company

Copyright © 2000 by Rosanne Rosen

All rights reserved. No part of this book shall be reproduced, stored in a retrieval system, or transmitted by any means, electronic, mechanical, photocopying, recording, or otherwise, without written permission from the publisher. No patent liability is assumed with respect to the use of the information contained herein. Although every precaution has been taken in the preparation of this book, the publisher and author assume no responsibility for errors or omissions. Neither is any liability assumed for damages resulting from the use of information contained herein. For information, address Alpha Books, 201 West 103rd Street, Indianapolis, IN 46290.

THE COMPLETE IDIOT'S GUIDE TO and Design are registered trademarks of Macmillan USA, Inc.

International Standard Book Number: 0-02-863928-6
Library of Congress Catalog Card Number: Available upon request.

02 01 00   8 7 6 5 4 3 2 1

Interpretation of the printing code: The rightmost number of the first series of numbers is the year of the book's printing; the rightmost number of the second series of numbers is the number of the book's printing. For example, a printing code of 00-1 shows that the first printing occurred in 2000.

Printed in the United States of America

Note: This publication contains the opinions and ideas of its author. It is intended to provide helpful and informative material on the subject matter covered. It is sold with the understanding that the author and publisher are not engaged in rendering professional services in the book. If the reader requires personal assistance or advice, a competent professional should be consulted.

The author and publisher specifically disclaim any responsibility for any liability, loss, or risk, personal or otherwise, which is incurred as a consequence, directly or indirectly, of the use and application of any of the contents of this book.

Publisher
Marie Butler-Knight

Product Manager
Phil Kitchel

Managing Editor
Cari Luna

Acquisitions Editor
Randy Ladenheim-Gil

Development Editor
Joan D. Paterson

Production Editor
Christy Wagner

Copy Editor
Diana Francoeur

Illustrator
Jody P. Schaeffer

Cover Designers
Mike Freeland
Kevin Spear

Book Designers
Scott Cook and Amy Adams of DesignLab

Indexer
Angie Bess

Layout/Proofreading
Angela Calvert
Svetlana Dominguez
John Etchison
Mary Hunt

Contents at a Glance

Part 1: Thinking About Living Together — 1

1. The State of the Union — 3
   Discover the up-to-the-minute status of matrimony and the future outlook of this established institution.

2. The Scoop on Live-In Love — 17
   Learn the inside story on who is living together, when, why, and how well.

3. The Facts and Fictions of Living Together — 31
   Sort out the truth or consequences of moving in, and decipher the level of your relationship commitment.

4. Special Risks for Women — 45
   Uncover the major risks women face in live-in love and what scenarios pose the most danger.

5. Unique Concerns for Men — 57
   Be privy to the stories of men who were undone by live-in love, the women who took advantage of them, and situations to avoid at all costs.

6. Playing It Safe — 67
   Determine where your safest road leads and how to avoid slippery slopes or dangerous curves.

Part 2: Coming Up with a Decision on Live-In Love — 81

7. Devising Romantic Motives and Lovers' Agendas — 83
   Become acquainted with the art of good romantic decision-making, sound romantic motives, and sensible relationship agendas.

8. Sizing Up Potential Gains or Losses — 97
   Figure out whether moving in is an opportunity of a lifetime or a losing proposition.

9. The Power of Love — 109
   Scrutinize the power of love and the hold it has over you or your romantic partner.

10. Is It Love? — 119
    Identify your romantic style, measure the depth of your love, and determine the impact of both on a live-in arrangement.

11. Partnership Potential — 133
    Size up your compatibility, sexual heat, and communication capabilities.

Part 3: Getting Ready to Move In — 147

12. Pre-Empting Disaster — 149
    Head off trouble at the pass by evaluating love histories, making a mutually agreeable live-in deal, discussing important issues, and dealing with doubts.

13 The Cohabitation Agreement and Other Sticky
   Legal Issues   161
   *Understand the implications of the law and whether or not a
   cohabitation agreement meets your needs and protects against
   future legal battles.*

14 Drawing Floor Plans   171
   *Figure out the best place to live, and draw up financial and
   family agreements that may prove to be life-savers later on.*

15 Finding the Best Building Materials   185
   *Locate the tools and sharpen your romance repair
   know-how.*

16 Beware of Poor Foundations   195
   *Steer clear of unions between mismatched lovers that set poor
   precedents.*

Part 4: Living Under One Roof   205

17 A New Lifestyle Vocabulary   207
   *Commit to memory "we," "ours," "couple," and
   "interdependence."*

18 Living-Together Etiquette   219
   *Adopt the etiquette that makes living together fun, easy, and
   enjoyable.*

19 Smart Moves   231
   *Read about the do's and don'ts that equal smart moves in the
   direction of live-in success.*

20 Keeping Love's Embers Warm   241
   *Unravel the secrets of love talk, romantic overtures, dormant
   emotions, and responsive love acts.*

21 Sex, Sex, Sex   251
   *Become a sexpert! Learn to turn-on and become more
   orgasmic.*

Part 5: If the Roof Caves In   263

22 Sensing Trouble in Hearth and Home   265
   *Keep tabs on your live-in happiness and unearth signs of pos-
   sible trouble.*

23 Household Survival Tactics and Patching Materials   277
   *Improve your household atmosphere by using objectivity and
   creativity.*

24 Getting Out the "For Sale" Sign   287
   Say good-bye in a timely and noble fashion.

25 Avoiding Moving-Day Disaster   297
   *Move out without creating a nightmarish separation and ugly
   departure.*

Part 6: Moving Toward the Altar   **309**

    26 Marriage Material—His, Hers, Theirs   311
   Determine which live-in-lover is or isn't a likely matrimonial candidate.

    27 The Transition from Live-In to Marriage   321
   Approach important junctures and critical transitions with all the expertise you can muster if you are looking for marriage protection insurance.

    28 Newlyweds and Marriage Management   333
   Open your eyes to newlywed risks and heed valuable marriage management advice before the merry-go-round stops. Apprise yourself of the techniques that will best afford you and your love partner the greatest chance of success in matrimony.

Appendixes

    A Men Who Abuse Women   345
    B Stress Busters   347
    C Premarital and Relationship Courses   349
    D Glossary   351
       Index   355

Contents

Part 1: Thinking About Living Together   1

1 The State of the Union   3

A Quickie Look at a Century of Matrimony 4
The Strong Winds of Social Change 5
   The "Postponed Generation" 5
   The Economics of Becoming Mr. and Mrs. 6
Marriage in the New Millennium 7
   Matrimony's Gloomy Forecast 7
   A Sunny Forecast for Matrimony 7
Controlling the Winds of Change 9
Champions of Marriage 10
   Educating for Marriage 10
   Legislating in Favor of Marriage 11
   Marriage Covenants Enter the Picture 12
   The Feds to the Rescue 12
Times Are Changing 12
   The New Family 13
   A New Greeting Card Family 14

2 The Scoop on Live-In Love   17

A Bit More History 17
The Climate for Change 18
   Sex Without Marriage 19
   Delayed Marriages 19
   Working Women 19
   Prevalence of Divorce 19
Serving Live-In Love 20
From Hollywood to Hoboken, Guess Who's Moving In 20
   Personal Profile 20
   Impersonal Stats 21
International Appetites for Live-In Love 22
Why Joe and Jane Are Moving In 22
   Marriage Seekers 22
   Mutual Users 23
   Romantic Roomies 23
   Serious Pals and Lovers 24
   True Believers 25
Do Live-In Lovers Find Satisfaction? 26
How Live-In Love Impacts Family and Kids 27
   Trouble for Kids with a Capital "T" 28
   When Joe Doesn't Want to Parent 28
A Forecast for Live-In Love 29

3 The Facts and Fictions of Living Together   31

Truth or Consequences, a Self-Test 31
Commitment with a Capital "C" 33
   Joint Investments 33

The Complete Idiot's Guide to Living Together

    Trading Assets, Making Concessions *33*
    A Tale of Commitment *34*
  Marriage, Living Together, and Commitment 35
  The Great Debate 35
  Differences Between Marriage and Living Together...36
    Similarities Between Marriage and Cohabitation *37*
    Does Living Together Have to Look Like Marriage? *38*
  If It Isn't Marriage, What Is It? 38
    Living Together Is Not *38*
    Living Together Is … *39*
  Dispelling Fictions 40
  How Significant Is a "Significant Other"? 41
    Insignificant Others *41*
    A Checklist for a Significant Other *42*

4 Special Risks for Women   45

  Women at a Disadvantage 45
  Self-Testing Your Risk Factor 46
  Desperation, an Element of Probable Risk 47
  Low Self-Esteem, an Undeniable Risk...48
    Madge, Not an Exemplary Example...*48*
    How's Your Self-Esteem? *49*
  Reported Risks 49
  Risky Scenarios 50
    The House with No Windows *50*
    The Case of the House with the Locked Door...*51*
    The House with the Trapdoor *52*
    The Rebound Duplex...*52*
    The Dangerous House on Main Street *54*
  One Last Warning 55

5 Unique Concerns for Men   57

  Separating the Boys from the Men 58
    Additional Warnings *58*
    Men Who Are Successful Live-Ins *59*
  For Divorced Men Only 59
  Sex on the Mind 60
  Women Who Spell Trouble 60
  Men Who Have Been Had 61
    The Runaway Mutual User *61*
    Jumping Over the Threshold *62*
    The Knight in Shining Armor *63*
    Dumped at Bedside...*64*
  Men as Serial Live-Ins 65
  Learning to Evaluate Risk 65

6 Playing It Safe   67

  Playing for Marriage 68
    Theoretically Speaking *68*

Realistically Speaking 68
Avoiding the Slippery Slope 69
Playing with Finesse 69
Cohabitor or Marriage Partner? 70
Which Cohabitors Become Marriage Partners and Why 71
Factors That Promote Conversion to Marriage 71
A Factor That May Inhibit Conversion to Marriage 72
Games You Don't Want to Play 72
The Cat and Mouse Chase 72
Sweeping Issues Under the Rug 72
Substituting Complacency for Answers 74
Misunderstandings: Innocent and Intentional 74
How Misunderstandings Develop 75
How to Prevent Romantic Misunderstandings 76
Detecting the Lying Game 76
Safest Calls 77
What Makes These Folks Special? 77
The Best of Live-In Love 78

Part 2: Coming Up with a Decision on Live-In Love   81

7 Devising Romantic Motives and Lovers' Agendas   83

Learning to Make Good Decisions 84
Good Decision-Making Techniques 84
A Handy Tool, "Reversibility Thinking" 85
Applying Good Decision-Making to Love Relationships 85
Decision-Making for Two 85
Implications of Romantic Partnership Decisions 86
Deciding on Romantic Motives 86
Listing Your Romantic Motives 87
What Constitutes a Good or a Bad Romantic Motive? 87
The Art of Agenda Making 88
Managing Love's Growth 88
The Best Romantic Agendas from Start to Finish 89
Agenda Tips 90
Uncovering Your Partner's Agenda 90
Is Moving In on Your Agenda? 91

8 Sizing Up Potential Gains or Losses   97

Creating a Menu of Opportunity 97
Opportunity Qualifiers 98
Are You Astute Enough to Evaluate an Opportunity? 99
An Exercise in Opportunity 99
Opportune Moments 100
The Underside of Opportunity 102
Getting Out of a Live-In Relationship 102
When Moving Out Turns Ugly and Spiteful 103
Testing for Potential Losses 103
Minimizing Potential Losses 105
Tools for Rethinking a "Golden Opportunity" 105

9 The Power of Love — 109

Love, the Big Motivator 109
Uncovering Cupid's Secrets 110
Growing Into Love 110
  Love's Nutrients *111*
  Love's Rewards *112*
  Love Issues *112*
  Cupid's Crooked Arrow *113*
The Fatal Attraction 113
  Limerence vs. Romantic Love *114*
  The Obsessive Lover *114*
Love's Unrealistic Idols 115
What Is Love at Its Best? 116

10 Is It Love? — 119

Identifying Love Styles 119
Love Style Choices 120
  Gender and Love Styles *121*
  A Typical Ludic Eros Lover *121*
Finding Out Your Love Type 122
A Trio of Reality Checkups for Love 123
  A Checkup for Beginners *124*
  A Checkup for Intermediate Lovers *126*
  A Checkup for Advanced Lovers *128*
Mutually Exclusive or Mutually Necessary? 130
Coming Up Empty on the Love Front 131

11 Partnership Potential — 133

The Compatibility Factor 134
The Core of Compatibility 134
  Empathy and Understanding *135*
  No Substitute for Respect *135*
  Passion, the Love Potent *135*
  The Compatibility of Daily Living *136*
  Summing Up Compatibility *136*
Sexual Compatibility: You Gotta Have It! 136
  Room for Misinterpretation *137*
  Test Your Sexual Compatibility *138*
  A Tale of Sexual Incompatibility *140*
Putting Out the Brushfires 141
Communicating with Purpose 142
  An Indispensable Communication Tip *143*
  Greasing the Communication Wheel *143*
  Clogging the Communication Wheel *144*
  Attention Grabbers *145*

Part 3: Getting Ready to Move In — 147

12 Pre-Empting Disaster — 149

Your Relationship Histories—Past, Present, and Future 150
Charting Relationship Histories 150

Your Partner's Historical Love Graph *150*
Interpreting Your Partner's Historical Love Graph *151*
The Suspect Under Suspicion *151*
Some Things Never Change *152*
Are Some Historical Facts Better Left Unsaid? 153
The Art of Making the Deal 153
Rules of Engagement 153
Driving a Hard Bargain *154*
The Matter of Ultimatums *154*
Ultimatum Guidelines *155*
Important Discussions You Just Can't Afford to Put Off 156
Readiness Quiz 158
Cold Feet 159

13 The Cohabitation Agreement and Other Sticky Legal Issues — 161

Common-Law Marriage: a Relic of the Past 162
Palimony: a Figment of the Imagination *162*
The Cohabitation Agreement *163*
What Exactly Is a Cohabitation Agreement? 163
What a Cohabitation Agreement Isn't *164*
Why Do You Need One? *164*
Musts for Cohabs 165
Imagine This Predicament 166
Predicament Number 1 .... *166*
Predicament Number 2 .... *166*
Predicament Number 3 .... *167*
Predicament Number 4 .... *167*
Getting Around Legal Shortcomings 167
Solution to Predicament Number 1 .... *167*
Solution to Predicament Number 2 .... *168*
Solution to Predicament Number 3 .... *168*
Solution to Predicament Number 4 .... *168*
The Truth About Home Buying 168
Practical Measures to Protect Life, Limb, and Pocketbook 169
A Critical List of Nevers 169
The Irony of Another Legal Web 170

14 Drawing Floor Plans — 171

Whose Place? Yours, Mine, or Ours? 172
Learn by Example, Case Number 1 .... *172*
Learn by Example, Case Number 2 .... *173*
Worksheet: Picking an Address *173*
Convening Your Economic Summit 175
Select Your Financial Plan *175*
Worksheet: Developing a Live-In Budget *176*
How Significant Is the Other? 177
Worksheet: Defining Significant Other *178*
When Significant Expectations Aren't Met *179*

Drawing Kids Into the Floor Plan 179
　　　Dealing with the Ex-Spouse 181
　　　Setting the Alarm Clock on Live-In Love 183

15　Finding the Best Building Materials　　　　　　　185

　　　What's in Your Tool Kit? 186
　　　New Nuts and Bolts 186
　　　　Three Imperative Bolts, Three Accompanying Nuts 186
　　　　Test Your Nuts and Bolts 188
　　　A New Way to Look at Love 190
　　　　Making Love Part of Your Concerted Efforts 190
　　　　Your Daily Planner 191
　　　There Is No Substitute for a Healthy Relationship 193

16　Beware of Poor Foundations　　　　　　　　　　195

　　　Too Much Disparity of Style 196
　　　Warm Beds Are Off-Limits 196
　　　Jealousy, Infidelity, and Mistrust 197
　　　　Leave Jealousy on the Doorstep 197
　　　　Infidelity Has a Venomous Bite 197
　　　　Distrust, an Outgrowth of Jealousy and Infidelity 198
　　　　Shelving Your Jealousy 198
　　　　Avoiding Unfaithful Partners 199
　　　Flooding a Partner with Bad Vibes 199
　　　Two Faulty Joints 200
　　　The Danger of Setting Poor Precedents 201
　　　A Case of Poor Precedents 201
　　　　The Backfiring of Poor Precedents 202
　　　　The Final Outcome 202
　　　A Foundation Safety Recheck 202

Part 4: Living Under One Roof　　　　　　　　　　　205

17　A New Lifestyle Vocabulary　　　　　　　　　　　207

　　　Becoming "We" 208
　　　　An Elementary Lesson in "We" 208
　　　　Using "We" in a Sentence 209
　　　Making a Home "Ours" 210
　　　Committing to Practical Maneuvers 210
　　　Coupling: Unveiling a New Duo 211
　　　Growing Into the Word "Couple" 212
　　　　The Expansive Stage 212
　　　　The Contraction and Betrayal Stage 213
　　　　The Resolution Stage 213
　　　　Defining Characteristics of Couples 213
　　　　The Blending Process 214
　　　　Fitting the Pieces Together 214
　　　　Identifying Your Sequences 214
　　　Interdependence: Converging Into One Now and Then 215
　　　　Picturing Interdependence 215
　　　　Rate Your Level of Interdependence 216

18 Living-Together Etiquette — 219

- Etiquette for the Sake of Harmony ...220
- What Is Etiquette? ...220
- Starter Set of Etiquette, Live-In Style ...221
- Etiquette, Room by Room ...222
  - *Etiquette for the Bathroom* ...222
  - *Etiquette for the Dining Room* ...222
  - *Etiquette for the Kitchen* ...223
  - *Etiquette for the Living Room* ...223
  - *Etiquette for the Laundry Room* ...224
  - *Etiquette for the Bedroom* ...224
- Etiquette for a Sound Relationship ...225
- Unsettled Issues of Etiquette ...225
- Family Matters ...226
  - *Sticky Introductions* ...226
- Uncharted Territory ...227
- Adding Your Own Rules of Etiquette ...228

19 Smart Moves — 231

- Simple Do's ...232
- Simple Don'ts ...232
- Four Essential New Moves ...233
  - *Time, Space, and Solitude* ...233
  - *Pick Your Fights* ...234
  - *Befriend Your Partner's Pals and Family Members* ...235
  - *Your Home: A Comfortable Gathering Place* ...236
- Spoilers in the Fine Art of Living Together ...236
  - *Bah Humbug* ...237
  - *Nobody Likes a Whiner* ...237
  - *Uncontained, Runaway Stress* ...237
- Reasonable Expectations ...238
- Precarious Live-In Expectations ...239
  - *An Exercise in Expectations* ...239

20 Keeping Love's Embers Warm — 241

- Beginners Guide to Love Talk ...241
- The Power of Love Messages ...243
- Sending Messages of Love ...243
  - *Men, Women, and Love Messages* ...244
- Time for Creative Thinking ...245
- Romantic Overtures ...245
  - *Romantic Suggestions* ...245
  - *Roxy's Bag of Tricks* ...246
  - *Create Your Own Overtures* ...246
- What to Do About Dormant Emotions ...247
  - *How to Wake Up Dormant Emotions* ...247
  - *Creative Thinking to Combat Dormant Emotions* ...248
- Responsive Love Acts ...248
  - *Increasing Your Understanding of Responsive Love Acts* ...248
  - *Planning Ahead for Love* ...249

21 Sex, Sex, Sex — 251

- The Challenge of Couples' Sex 252
- Gender and Sex: Let's Get the Record Straight 253
  - Varying Sexual Tastes and Practices 253
  - A Distinctly Different Outlook 254
  - Turn-Ons Male/Female Style 254
  - Women's Turn-Ons 255
  - Men's Turn-Ons 255
- Sex Facts You Should Be Familiar With 255
- Common Complaints, Simple Answers 256
- Tips to Alleviate Boredom 257
  - Category Number 1: Change Sexual Maneuvers 257
  - Category Number 2: Sexy Surprises 257
  - Category Number 3: New Tactile Sensations 259
  - Becoming More Orgasmic 259
- Sexual Communication 260
- Your Sexual Rule Book 261

Part 5: If the Roof Caves In — 263

22 Sensing Trouble in Hearth and Home — 265

- Measuring Live-In Happiness 266
- Obvious Troublemakers 268
- Searching for the Roots of Trouble 269
  - Where Does Your Commitment Stand? 269
  - What's Your Take on Love? 270
  - How Bonded Are You as a Couple? 271
  - How Firm Is Your Friendship? 272
- Too Much or Too Little Synergy 273
  - An Example of a Couple's Practical Synergy 274
  - Runaway Synergy 274
  - An Exercise to Evaluate Synergy 274
- Signs of Troubles 275
- Absolute Relationship Breakers 275
- What's Best for You? 276

23 Household Survival Tactics and Patching Materials — 277

- Objectivity Is the Critical Factor 278
  - Three-Part Objectivity 278
  - When Emotions Take Charge 278
  - Detecting Your Lover's Lies 279
- In Which Bed Does Your Problem Lie? 279
  - Bed Number 1: Personality-Based Problems 279
  - Bed Number 2: Situational-Based Problems 280
- How Couples Change 281
- Calling a House Meeting 281
  - The Do's and Don'ts of Expressing Your Frustrations 282
- Three Quick Steps to Improving Home Atmosphere 284
- Designing Checks and Balances 284

24 Getting Out the "For Sale" Sign — 287

- The Dynamics of Breaking Up Your Live-In Relationship 288
  - *A Mental Model of Breaking Up* 288
  - *Getting the Partner Involved* 289
- Stop Wasting Time! 290
- Telling Time 290
  - *Time as a Friend* 291
  - *Time as an Enemy* 291
  - *Three Images of Wasted Moments* 292
- Astrological Corroboration: Yes or No? 294
- Are You Stuck in the Muck? 295

25 Avoiding Moving-Day Disaster — 297

- Moving Out Isn't Going to Be Easy 298
  - *Watch Out!* 298
- Planning Your Departure 299
  - *A Twelve-Step Separation Plan* 299
  - *Moving-Day Rules* 302
- Do's and Don'ts for After the Fact 303
- A Victim's Departure 304
- When Kids Are Involved 305
- Facing Raw Emotions 306
  - *Handling Your Grief* 306
  - *A First-Rate Recovery Tip* 307
  - *Close the Door* 307

Part 5: Moving Toward the Altar — 309

26 Marriage Material—His, Hers, Theirs — 311

- Is Your Live-In Marriage Material? 312
- Laboratory Predictors of Marital Success 313
- Compare Your Marital Risk Factors 313
  - *Risk Factors for Individuals and Couples* 313
  - *Nonnegotiable Risk Factors* 314
- Upgrading Your Live-In Mindset 314
  - *Mental Upgrades* 314
  - *Reducing Your State of Autonomy* 315
- Going for an Educated Mindset 316
  - *The Value of PMC—Premarital Counseling* 317
  - *PMC Isn't Anything to Fear* 317
  - *What PMC Can Reveal About Your Relationship* 317
  - *Satisfied PMC Newlyweds* 318
  - *A Selection of PMC Opportunities* 319
  - *Finding a PMC Program Near You* 319

27 The Transition from Live-In to Marriage — 321

- WARNING LABEL: Mandatory Reading 322
- Ripe and Ready Junctures 322
  - *Identifying Pivotal Moments* 323
  - *Seizing the Moment* 323

    Crossing Over the Line 325
        Distinguishing a Live-In Union from Matrimony *325*
        What You Can Look Forward To *326*
    Revising Expectations 326
        An Imbalance of Power and Lopsided Expectations *327*
        Realistic Expectations and Healthy Precedents *328*
    Making a Fresh Start 329
    Buying Marriage Protection 329
    Your Personal Transition Worksheet 330

28 Newlyweds and Marriage Management   333

    Newlyweds vs. Live-Ins 333
        Advice for Newlyweds *334*
    Before You Take Your Vows 335
        Should You Have a Prenup? *335*
        Averting Financial Disaster *336*
    The Marital Roller Coaster 337
        Added Risks for Second-Time Newlyweds *338*
    Marriage Prerequisites 338
    An Active Role 339
    What Makes Marriage Work? 340
    Use Secret Strategies 341
    Marriage Truths 342

Appendixes

A Men Who Abuse Women   345

B Stress Busters   347

C Premarital and Relationship Courses   349

D Glossary   351

    Index   355

Foreword

Few things are more essential to our well-being than loving and being loved. While we still value marriage and family as the legitimate course for our deepest and most intimate love relationships, people of all ages are embracing cohabitation. When I was dating in the early 1960s, I knew only one unmarried couple intrepid enough to openly live together and risk society's sanction. Today, half of those marrying for the first time have lived and made love together prior to tying the knot, and no one seems to mind!

But living together creates its own risks. What are the real effects of living together without marriage? Does cohabitation bind us closer or lessen our commitment to making the relationship work? Are couples who live together happier, sexier, or richer than those who marry? Do we risk a higher probability of such unwanted consequences as sexual infidelity, deceit, and abuse than we would in marriage?

This book helps the reader identify each partner's motivation for moving in together. It reminds the unwary of the many ways that living together is different from married life and how these differences can lead to serious challenges around finances, family, fidelity, and self-esteem. Reading this book by yourself will give insight and guidance; reading this book with your partner can help you—as a couple—to surface, understand, and discuss issues that could make or break the success of your live-in relationship.

The Complete Idiot's Guide to Living Together provides a rich mix of highly readable facts, information, and stories that reflect what we now know about cohabitation—its upsides and downsides, its critics and its advocates. This book culls from interviews, research, and relationship experts' best advice on making the live-in relationship work, with all its unanticipated pitfalls and unclear role relationships. Using a generous mix of poignant quotes from interviews with men and women who live together and from research findings, this book offers a road map for living together successfully and overcoming the hidden traps that await the uninformed.

The author has created a virtual how-to manual on what to do and what not to overlook, including checklists of signs and signals that tell a couple whether they are on- or off-course in their relationship and when, if necessary, to bail out. The guidance and observations in *The Complete Idiot's Guide to Living Together* are guaranteed to spark lively discussion about what we value in our relationships and in our lives.

Dr. Dory Hollander

Dr. Dory Hollander is the author of *101 Lies Men Tell Women and Why Women Believe Them* and *The Doom Loop System: A Step by Step Guide to Career Management*. Dr. Hollander has been married without cohabiting, is now cohabiting without marrying, and has two children who have cohabited with their partners for two or more years and are now married to them.

Introduction

Love relationships are tricky. No one can dispute that fact, but few realize that love can easily fizzle when two partners naively begin sharing one home. That makes it all the more imperative that partners independently and jointly engage in prudent, judicious, and wise decisions before moving in together.

Living together is a big step in a relationship that is all too often embarked upon with insufficient thought or awareness. Consequences of cohabiting are rarely considered in the wake of passion and convenience. However, the implications of living together on your romantic relationship, yourself, and your family can be more significant and far-reaching than otherwise assumed.

To head off trouble, alleviate heartache, and give your relationship the best chance at success, you should be well-informed. There is no room for fairytales or daydreams here. Reality is central to your immediate and future happiness.

Your relationship well-being is what propels all of the discussions in this guide. None are motivated by moral or ethical judgments made by the author. My only purpose is to give couples the most promising chance at a loving future. If cohabiting is here to stay, which by all indications seems to be the case, it is time to do it well instead of blundering through it as couples have in the past.

Each chapter requires you to make decisions that will affect you and your partner. What you are given are the tools, information, and insights that you should apply to your unique love relationship. Evaluate each issue carefully before putting two names on the mailbox. When comparing marriage and living together, think in terms of your own personal ultimate goals. When deciding if cohabiting is right for you and your partner, make sure the arrangement equitably suits both of your needs and desires.

Living together can be a successful venture despite the odds of failure if your eyes are wide open, your agendas in sync, your love mature, and your decisions pragmatic. Even then, the road may be bumpy without some serious relationship management. The "how-to's" for success are all-encompassing in this book. Ultimately, however, the real work rests on your shoulders. Armed with information, your relationship workload should be lighter and more fun, and your "other" sufficiently significant.

How This Book Is Organized

The Complete Idiot's Guide to Living Together is divided into six important parts. While each of these parts could stand alone, providing plenty of worthwhile information whether you are already involved in a live-in relationship or thinking about moving in, together they give the comprehensive picture each live-in partner should possess.

The sequence of the 29 chapters offers a logical look at the complete story of live-in love. For optimum use, begin at the beginning. However, if you only have time at the moment for a quick fix, take advantage of the material that best answers your question. But don't forget to go back and read every word before you make the critical decision to move in or out.

Part 1, "Thinking About Living Together," updates you step by step on pertinent information regarding matrimony and living together. The purpose of this part is to help you begin your exploration into whether or not living together serves the future well-being of your individual aspirations and relationship. No book on living together is complete without addressing the state of the matrimonial union (Chapter 1) and an honest appraisal of live-in relationships (Chapter 2). The facts are spelled out and the fictions of living together dispelled in Chapter 3. Special risks unique to both men and women are uncovered in Chapters 4 and 5. Finally, Chapter 6 offers tips on how to make a safe decision, play your relationship cards well, and avoid serious misunderstanding with a potential live-in partner.

Part 2, "Coming Up with a Decision on Live-In Love," assists you in making a decision that will meet your romantic objectives and long-term relationship goals. How to devise a romantic agenda is clearly spelled out in Chapter 7. Evaluating your romantic opportunities in terms of potential gains or losses is meticulously accomplished in Chapter 8. How love fits into the picture and how it influences you or your romantic interest's point of view is under consideration in Chapters 9 and 10. Whether you and your love interest are compatible emotionally and sexually rounds out and completes the discussion in Part 2.

Part 3, "Getting Ready to Move In," will prepare you for the move into your cohabitation love nest. Chapter 12 will help you avoid disaster by outlining the importance of one another's relationship history and revealing imperative topics to be dealt with prior to moving in. Whether or not you should consider a cohabitation agreement is examined in Chapter 13. How to draw up your household floor plans, make necessary relationship repairs, and build a foundation that will serve you and your partner well in the future are covered in Chapters 14 through 16.

Part 4, "Living Under One Roof," moves into the heart of your love nest and offers advice on living under the same roof. You will need to become familiar not only with the new vocabulary words in Chapter 17, but with the etiquette, smart moves, and love secrets in subsequent chapters. Chapter 21 is a sizzler chapter on sex and more sex. If Part 4 doesn't maximize the odds for a cozy, satisfying abode, Part 5 will help you move out and on to greater loves.

Part 5, "If the Roof Caves In," helps you deal with troubles of the home, hearth, and heart. Before you can do this effectively, you must search for the roots of your problems. Chapter 22 will help with this task. Plenty of survival tactics are recommended in Chapter 23 and should be tried before getting out the "For Sale" sign and moving out. However, if all else fails, Chapter 25 will help you slip out with the most ease possible in this delicate situation.

Part 6, "Moving Toward the Altar," deals with where most couples head if they don't split up first—down the aisle. However, because of the extreme differences pointed out between marriage and living together in the first few chapters of this guide, caution should be taken to ensure the best chance of matrimonial success. To accomplish this requires evaluating your live-in's matrimonial material as described in Chapter 26 and making the conscious transition outlined in Chapter 27 as well as revising expectations. However, Part 6 does not conclude until the reader is given critical insight into the marriage game and helpful hints on marriage management.

Extras

Some ideas need to stand out so they don't get missed. Scattered throughout the chapters you will find sidebars to help you manage the mechanics of cohabitation, avoid common problems in living together, understand terminology that applies to couples living together, and interpret various research studies on cohabitation.

Love's Hot Line

Love's Hot Line boxes anticipate your romantic or relationship questions and offer sound, personal advice based on facts. These helpful hints should be taken seriously.

Troubles A'Brewing …

Troubles A'Brewing … is a pot boiling with potential disaster. Read each of these as a serious warning and avoid getting burned by your romantic relationship.

Love Stats

Love Stats provide extra bits of information that could affect the end result of your love relationship. Think seriously and carefully about the statistics that more closely resemble your love or live-in relationship.

Sweet Nothings

Sweet Nothings hold vocabulary words that may not be familiar with in the context of love, marital, and live-in relationships. Clarifying their meaning prevents any misinterpretations.

Acknowledgments

Without the individual men and women who so willingly and openly divulged their innermost joys, disappointments, fears, and desires to me, a complete guide to living together would not have been possible. It is their stories that make the research so poignant and important. I am indebted to them for their time and honesty.

My sincere thanks goes to my agent Jeff Herman for his unwavering guidance and support. I remain grateful to my mentor Bob Shook and newspaper editor T. R. Fitchko for their encouragement on each and every project over the years. As always, much appreciation is directed to Mark and my children for their enthusiasm, helpfulness, and interest.

I would be remiss without thanking Randy Ladenheim-Gil and the other editors involved in this project for working with me and for making this a most enjoyable venture.

Trademarks

All terms mentioned in this book that are known to be or are suspected of being trademarks or service marks have been appropriately capitalized. Alpha Books and Macmillan USA, Inc., cannot attest to the accuracy of this information. Use of a term in this book should not be regarded as affecting the validity of any trademark or service mark.

Part 1
Thinking About Living Together

Love has knocked at your door and wants to move in. Should you or shouldn't you add another name to the mailbox? That depends on what you think live-in love is all about and where you want it to take you.

To make an accurate assessment of whether or not living with your love interest could be right for you, you need to be brought up-to-date on the available options. A complete status report on marriage and cohabiting is the place to begin. Next you need to align your expectations with the facts of cohabitation and grasp the risks or benefits that await cohabiting couples.

Part 1 sets the stage and lays the foundation from which your intimate, personal decision making will take place.

Chapter 1

The State of the Union

> **In This Chapter**
>
> ➤ Is marriage in or out?
> ➤ The sunny side of traditional, committed relationships
> ➤ Creative ways to form family units
> ➤ Are we stuck in a divorce culture?
> ➤ The money-marriage equation

In a nutshell, the natural desire to join together with another person, have sex, bear children, and form family groups eventually led to the modern social institution of marriage. Matrimony, characterized by a public and legal contract, was designed in large measure to solidify the family unit and protect the economic rights of partners and offspring.

The original design has changed continuously over time, especially for women. "We've come a long way, baby" is hardly an overstatement when describing the transformation of women's marital roles. In modern, industrialized societies, women have progressed from being their husband's property to being equal partners in the firm and in some cases the primary wage earner.

The state of matrimony and the structure of the family are forever evolving. In the twentieth century, numerous factors erupted to alter the traditional course of love, marriage, and baby carriage. In their wake, a variety of options for coupling have emerged, and they remain viable choices for individuals today as the twenty-first century begins.

In order to embark on the soundest path for your relationship and your future happiness, you would be wise to understand the implications of the available options. Traditional matrimony is a logical place to start.

A Quickie Look at a Century of Matrimony

In the last century, the selection of a marriage partner underwent dramatic changes. The former emphasis on practical considerations gave way to full-blooded romantic considerations as people searched for a suitable life companion. Although marriages in a few pockets of modern society are still arranged by parents or community elders, that is the exception rather than the rule. The heart triumphs over the head in most situations.

Nonetheless, love did not completely dictate the decision-making process, at least not for women. Surveys and in-depth interviews have demonstrated that while men are more likely to be swayed by romantic love and sexual attraction, women still pay silent attention to a man's potential earning power.

During the latter part of the century, three events became noticeable: Men and women married at a later age; the marriage rate fell to its lowest recorded number; and matrimony found itself head-to-head with a viable competitor.

Live-in love was relatively uncommon in 1972. But by the 1990s, the rise of couples living together outside of marriage was staggering. The number of *cohabiting* couples has increased 500 percent since 1970 and 85 percent within the past decade. A thorough look at the why, when, and who of cohabiting will be the topic of Chapter 2, "The Scoop on Live-In Love." For the moment, it is sufficient to know that significant numbers of men and women are opting for live-in love and are either delaying marriage or turning their backs on it altogether.

Another major change that occurred in the matrimonial arena in the last century was a rapidly rising

Love Stats

Today's wide variety of ages at which people marry and have children is a reflection of a "fluid life cycle." Social scientist L. Hirschhorn coined this phrase in 1977 to emphasize the disappearance of the standard timetable by which most marriages and childbearing occurred.

Sweet Nothings

There is nothing judgmental about the word **cohabiting.** It means to live in the same dwelling with someone you are having a romantic and sexual relationship with although you are not married to one another.

divorce rate. In 1970 one in three marriages split. Shortly thereafter, the divorce rate rose higher yet when two easy outs became available: a prevalent notion that an individual's pursuit of happiness was more important than staying in a less-than-satisfying marriage and the introduction of the no-fault divorce statute. Subsequently, the divorce rate climbed by 30 percent and leveled out at one in two marriages biting the dust.

So what happened during the century to the idealistic notion of finding and marrying a Prince Charming or a Sleeping Beauty and then living happily ever after?

The Strong Winds of Social Change

The blustery winds of social change that have affected the state of matrimony include …

- Changes in gender roles.
- Increased lifespans.
- The economic independence of women.
- An emphasis on self-fulfillment.
- Removal of the stigma surrounding divorce and an increase in the ease of obtaining a divorce.
- A rise in premarital sex, abortion, and birth control usage.
- The relaxation of sexual taboos.

Troubles A'Brewing …

American women fail at marriage in larger numbers than do women in several other countries. According to research conducted with a group of 1,000 women in the early 1990s by *USA Today*, of those women getting a divorce, 12 were from Britain, 11 from Canada, 7 from Germany, and 21 from the United States.

Sexual mores have changed to such a great extent that marriage is no longer a precondition for childbearing. Couples aren't rushing to the altar simply to ensure that their children are born in wedlock. Just two generations ago, most children were born into married unions. Today, nearly a third of all children in the United States are born to unwed mothers.

Two other less-obvious but pertinent north winds that continue to impact the decision of when, or whether, to marry are economics and the eruption of the Postponed Generation.

The "Postponed Generation"

The "postponed generation" (PG) are today's young adults who are five years behind their predecessors in terms of major goals: finishing college, marrying, and achieving financial independence. This last goal is particularly difficult to attain because of the burden of college loans, the high cost of living, and entry-level salaries.

As a result, this generation has frequently put off accepting the responsibilities of a traditional marriage or foregone a committed relationship, or has moved in with—rather than married—a romantic partner.

Reverberations of their pairing or lack of it are reflected in the decline of marriage rates.

The Economics of Becoming Mr. and Mrs.

A number of sociologists agree that entering into marriage is accompanied by specific financial expectations. Until a certain level of economic well-being can be met, men and women are putting off becoming Mr. and Mrs. What is considered an appropriate household style is frequently dictated by social norms that vary by time, the person's social status, and the ability to match the lifestyle of their parents at the time of their marriage.

These expectations aren't excuses that academics have cooked up to fill pages. Ask couples who have been engaged for extended periods and may be living together why they haven't tied the knot yet. Their answer often sounds something like this: "We can't afford to get married. We want to pay off our school loans, save money for a honeymoon, and make a down payment on a house. That should take another year or so."

Yet another financial consideration is also creating a detour to the altar, namely, long-range predictions of a potential partner's earnings. Some sociologists think that these expectations may be more important than "wedding-day incomes." If in fact this is the case, an individual may wait until the prospective husband or wife achieves maturity in his or her respective employment and economic potential becomes certain.

Love's Hot Line

Ladies, before you decide to have a baby without a committed partner, you may want to consider the following statement. Maggie Gallagher, director of a research project for the Institute for American Values, says that children from single-parent homes are more likely to use drugs, drop out of school, commit crimes, and develop health problems.

Love Stats

From the 1970s to the mid-1990s, the jump in figures for never-married individuals in their early thirties went from 6 percent to 20 percent for women, and 9 percent to 30 percent for men.

Marriage in the New Millennium

Forecasting the future is always precarious. Exactly how marriage will play out in the year 2000 and beyond no one can say with absolute certainty. However, researchers like to make projections based on present trends. If we follow their train of thought, here's what you might have to look forward to.

Matrimony's Gloomy Forecast

According to some researchers, trends in the new millennium that could put marriage in jeopardy are …

- The declining marriage rate.
- Signs that the institution of marriage is weakening as indicated by the number of children born to unmarried couples.
- Fewer couples reporting that they are "very happy" in their marriages.
- The lesser degree of satisfaction with life that is expressed by married women as opposed to single women.
- The dropping to an all-time low of the proportion of married women to unmarried.
- The U.S. Census Bureau's report of the double-digit rise in never-married individuals from 21.4 million in 1970 to 44.2 million in 1994.
- A divorce culture in which society supports and idealizes the right to individual freedom.
- A rapid growth in the rate of live-in lovers.

Troubles A'Brewing …

If marriage is your bag, take note of the following projection, based on the current trend of live-in love, that spells trouble for holy matrimony. Janice Shaw Crouse, senior fellow at Beverly LaHaye Institute: A Center for Studies in Women's Issues, says that in 1960 there was 1 live-in couple per 90 married ones. She expects that to increase in the year 2010 to 1 live-in couple for every 7 married couples.

A Sunny Forecast for Matrimony

There are, however, rays of light shining through the gloomy marriage forecast. Here are a few to consider.

Ray of Sunshine Number 1

The impact of cohabitation on marriage rates is undeniable, but it by no means signals an extinction of the institution. For instance, Sweden is one of the countries in which cohabitation and sexual freedom have had a long-term and well-accepted presence. Nevertheless, this presence has not dispelled the importance of marriage.

Part 1 ➤ *Thinking About Living Together*

Surveys in Sweden show that 80 percent of those who live together are married and that the family unit is most commonly formed through marriage.

Ray of Sunshine Number 2

Time and again, research has shown that most men and women desire the state of matrimony. Patrick C. McKenry, professor of family relations and human development at Ohio State University, gets right to the heart of the numbers. He says that people still value a committed relationship and 90 percent of them will marry.

Ray of Sunshine Number 3

A Washington-based research group says that the baby boomers have accounted for many of the changes in family and marriage trends over the last 10 years. Now that the boomers are aging, it is predicted that things will settle down and that the American family will get stronger.

Ray of Sunshine Number 4

The Population Reference Bureau reported that the number of households composed of married partners and children has been on the rise since the early 1990s. The upswing shows the reversal of a decline that has lasted for 20 years.

Ray of Sunshine Number 5

Although many teenagers reveal that they have little faith in finding a lifetime mate, more are saying that a good marriage and family are important, notes Rutgers University sociologist Dr. David Popenoe.

Love Stats

Guess which couples are the most happily married? If you said those who have never had children, you're right on target, according to the findings of the American Sociological Association. The least happy are those with teenagers in their households.

Ray of Sunshine Number 6

The interpretation of divorce statistics does indeed show that the number of divorced couples has quadrupled in the last decade from 4.3 million to 17.4 million. However,

Arlene Sluter, author of a Census Bureau report, says that the increase does not reflect the *current* divorce rate. The divorce rate started showing signs of stabilizing in the 1980s, and in recent years there has been a very slight decline in the rate.

Ray of Sunshine Number 7
Some trends reverse themselves. Author William Strauss found that the twentieth century was not the first one in which couples waited until they were older to marry. Actually, the median age for bridegrooms was higher in 1890 than in 1956. The median age did not start rising again until 1962, with the advent of legal abortion, sexual experimentation, and modern feminism.

Ray of Sunshine Number 8
Men who are married reportedly have a better sense of mental and physical well-being and live longer than unmarried men.

Ray of Sunshine Number 9
Experts say that a marriage—even a bad one—provides social support, valued status, and the traditional roles that men prefer.

Ray of Sunshine Number 10
Increasingly, cohabitation is becoming a step taken by individuals before they exchange marriage vows, rather than a step taken as a replacement for matrimony.

Controlling the Winds of Change

In response to the alarmingly high divorce rate and the subsequent threat to well-functioning family groups, a national grass-roots movement has formed to promote marriage. National organizations, state lawmakers, and federal governing bodies view specific social problems, such as crime, drugs, mental illness, school dropout, and teen pregnancy, as the direct result of marital dissolution.

And the problem of divorce is self-perpetuating. Figures released in 1994 and 1995 were alarming:

- ➤ Children from single-parent homes divorce twice as readily as children raised with both biological parents.
- ➤ At least half the kids born in 1994 were destined to spend part of their youth in single-parent homes.

Consequently, divorce has become a serious threat to the institutions of marriage and family.

Champions of Marriage

Those who champion the cause of marriage use heavy artillery to prove their point. For them, marriage is a fundamental social institution that is critical to the well-being of children. Children of divorce have higher dropout rates from school, more premarital pregnancies, and greater emotional problems. In a second round of ammunition, they refer to studies showing that married individuals live longer, have better physical and emotional health, and earn more money than divorced, single, or cohabiting men and women.

Love Stats

Would you believe that married men who are participants in stable relationships are less likely to commit crimes? Well, research has proven this to be true. And some experts link this fact with levels of testosterone, a hormone associated with aggressive, competitive behavior. Men who have stable relationships have lower levels of testosterone. On the other hand, men undergoing a divorce have rising levels.

Diane Sollee, founder of the Coalition for Marriage, Family, and Couples Education, says: "People are so distressed about the state of marriage in America. But we realize that we can teach skills to people to make their marriage strong. What distinguishes marriages that go the distance from those that end in divorce isn't whether couples disagree, but certain behaviors between them." (For a discussion on positive marriage behaviors, see Chapter 28, "Newlyweds and Marriage Management.")

Educating for Marriage

Sollee's organization isn't the only group that feels this way. National and local premarital counseling projects are popping up all over the place. A church-based group called Marriage Savers is trying to organize marital mentoring programs and develop community marital policies. The leader, Mike McManus, is optimistic that a large mobilization of forces could significantly slash the divorce rate in the twenty-first century.

More married men could also mean more males in church. A 1998 study found that marriage is a socializing force for men. Those who marry not only spend more time working but attend church more often and frequent bars less.

Chapter 1 ➤ *The State of the Union*

Troubles A'Brewing ...

Senior researcher Janice Shaw Crouse believes that the rise of live-in relationships and the decline of marriage-based coupling will contribute to the erosion of the traditional family. Consequently, she says, our children will face more hardships and diminished possibilities. For instance, cohabiting couples are less stable economically, break up more readily, and produce less-loving parenting—all of which negatively impact children.

Legislating in Favor of Marriage

Divorce is costing billions of dollars in health care, child services, and unpaid child-support, in addition to the costs that arise from the social problems already mentioned. No wonder state governments are getting into the act of recommending, and even requiring, premarital counseling.

The state of Michigan has proposed laws to delay licenses for couples who have not taken a marriage class. Alaska and Kansas have considered reducing fees for those who have taken such a class.

Among state legislators, there is also a movement to overturn no-fault divorce laws in an effort to reduce marital dissolution and subsequent costs. These laws were originally intended to speed up divorce without either party having to prove cause for marital separation.

Love Stats

According to a variety of sources, "irreconcilable differences" is cited as the reason for nearly two thirds of all divorces. Diane Sollee, founder of the Coalition for Marriage, Family, and Couples Education, calls it "irreconcilable disappointments." These splits do not involve serious conflict or spousal abuse. Rather, couples say they have simply grown apart.

11

During 1996 and 1997, Pennsylvania lawmakers succeeded in taking the no-fault divorce clause out of the state's statutes.

Marriage Covenants Enter the Picture

In 1997 Louisiana was the first state to enact a "covenant marriage" bill. The purpose of the bill is to make divorce more difficult.

Here's how this law works in Louisiana: Marrying couples can choose (a) a standard marriage that will enable them to separate under the no-fault divorce law, if and when they wish to; or (b) a covenant marriage, which is more difficult to enter into and get out of. Marriage counseling is a precondition of the latter, as is a lengthy legal separation period if the couple applies for a divorce in which one person is not proven to be at fault.

With more and more states getting into the act and the federal government taking notice of the costs of divorce, we can rightfully surmise that the problems of marriage and family will not be overlooked. Nor will marriage and divorce remain static.

The Feds to the Rescue

Capitol Hill Republicans went on record as supporting marriage, wrote a *Washington Times* reporter in 1998. "Marriage is the foundation of a successful society," the lawmakers said. To ensure its success, they have raised their hands in favor of a tax code that rewards marriage with large financial grants for teaching sexual abstinence to kids.

Times Are Changing

The crosswinds of change have undoubtedly produced some effects that are here to stay. In fact, it is safe to say that the traditional marriage and family life we once knew will never be the same. That isn't necessarily a bad thing. In fact, some social scientists feel that emerging family structures have accommodated the altered state of matrimony exceedingly well.

What's out?

Love Stats

Five percent of all kids under the age of 18 live in their grandparents' homes. Of those, 47 percent have their mothers living there as well.

➤ **The traditional definition of family** as defined by the 1986 U.S. Census Bureau: two or more persons related by birth, marriage, or adoption and living together.

➤ **Stay-at-home moms.** Economic factors make it impossible for many women to devote themselves to full-time mothering. A survey of 1,500 mothers found that one third would prefer to stay at home.

12

What's in?

- ▶ **Working moms.** In the United States, at least 63 percent of women with preschool-age children and 77 percent of moms with school-age kids are either employed or seeking a job.
- ▶ **A new definition of family.** Professor McKenry, and others in the field of family relations, define a family as "Two or more people who share a common residence, economy, and affection." He says this definition is here to stay. The stipulations that families must have partners of the opposite sex, must raise children, and must be related through either law or blood are gone forever.
- ▶ **Diversity.** No longer is there one and only one concept of how individuals should couple, raise their children, or create a family.

Sweet Nothings

In the formal sense, **diversity** means "variety." As the buzzword of the new millennium, diversity signifies a positive state and an acceptance of individual differences.

The New Family

No one family pattern dominates today, says sociologist Judith Stacey, author of *In the Name of the Family*. Cohabiting couples, relationships formed by young adults living away from home, non-heterosexual unions, close female friends, single adults with children, and empty nesters who form new family links all fit McKenry's definition.

According to experts, nourishing the individual to meet challenges is what family values are all about. The bond among family members, whether the setting is traditional or not, promotes an atmosphere in which members can readily exchange love, share hopes, address fears, solve problems, and relax together, says Andrew J. Cherlin, author of *Public and Private Families* and professor of public policy at Johns Hopkins University.

Changes in the family unit have been followed and recognized even by major American greeting card companies. "Life used to be homogenous, in little boxes. Now these boxes are blending and merging," said Clar Evans of Hallmark Cards.

Love Stats

Patrick C. McKenry, professor of family relations and human development at Ohio State University, says that divorced single-parent families are not "broken families" as the divorce backlash rhetoric suggests. They are just different and can be as successful as two-parent households, given similar economic circumstances.

Hallmark's fact-finding mission, called "The Chosen Family," verified sociologists' evidence of mature, committed, and supportive family-like relationships among people not related by blood or marriage.

A New Greeting Card Family

Two women, Laura and Lynn, together since 1979, have worked hard to construct their family. The first step, Laura says, was to move to the East Coast where Lynn was artificially inseminated. Laura feels that she and Lynn didn't become a complete family until their son, Billy, was born. Laura legally adopted both Billy and a daughter, Sue, born to Lynn.

Laura, a federal consultant for affordable housing, says:

> "I never thought it was possible for me to have children. This family is my life."

What matters in a family, Professor McKenry asserts, is that children feel a part of a group where they are loved unconditionally. A good barometer of how well a family is doing depends on the answer to this question: "Do your children have a good sense of self-esteem?"

Laura replies:

> "They absolutely do. The children are renowned for their self-esteem. This past year Billy went from a rather protected school environment to a public middle school with 700 children, where he knew no one. Before the end of the semester, he was elected to the student council and seen as a leader.
>
> "Billy is more aware than Sue that we don't fit the TV or literary definition of family. Billy knows that one definition of family is not enough and accepts the whole range of diversity—multigenerational, biracial, families like ours, all kinds of families."

Seven-year-old Sue sums it all up:

> "It's really great having two moms. When one is busy, there is always another there to take care of you."

This chapter has looked at the posture of marriage and the family in order to create an important backdrop to the main investigation of this book: the inside and outside of live-in love. Where live-in love fits and how well it succeeds in fulfilling the changing needs of your relationship cannot be thoroughly determined without this landscape. Throughout the remainder of this book, you may find it helpful to keep in mind the closing points mentioned next.

Chapter 1 ➤ *The State of the Union*

> **The Least You Need to Know**
>
> ➤ Marriage is not becoming extinct. Although weakened, it still remains a viable and desirable option for most individuals.
>
> ➤ As a major social force in American society, live-in love is a relatively new phenomenon.
>
> ➤ Cohabitation is a form of coupling that is gaining popularity. As it gains acceptance, it is becoming integrated into relationship patterns.
>
> ➤ Cohabitation does not appear to be a substitute for marriage.
>
> ➤ Marriage and family structures are making accommodations to changes in social forces and values.

Chapter 2

The Scoop on Live-In Love

> **In This Chapter**
> - How live-in love won the popularity contest
> - Who is moving in
> - The most common reasons for becoming a live-in
> - The odds for happy endings
> - How cohabiting impacts family and children

One of the most significant trends in America today is that of moving in together as sexual partners before marriage—and putting two different last names on the mailbox. This trend came about as a complete surprise, experts say.

In this chapter, I'll uncover the whys and wherefores of this new phenomenon. But that is only the beginning. The overview of live-in love provided here will be followed by more in-depth coverage in subsequent chapters. How this experiment in coupling is working and who is moving in will enable you to begin your personal exploration into whether it's time to move in, move out, or move on.

A Bit More History

In just four decades, live-in love in the United States has shed the stigma of being illegal, immoral, and improper. Without any sort of social uproar, the incidence of cohabitation before marriage has changed from a very few instances in the early 1900s to include nearly 50 percent of all couples who plan to marry eventually. (However, fewer than one in two couples actually carry through and marry.) Although some individuals think that *living together* is equivalent to *common-law unions*, a practice that has been around for a while, these are actually two very distinct living arrangements. Proof awaits.

> ### Sweet Nothings
>
> Experts David Popenoe and Barbara Dafoe Whitehead, a team of researchers on the National Marriage Project, provide the following definition: "**Living together**—or unmarried cohabitation—is the status of couples who are sexual partners, not married to each other, and sharing a household." Partners are not considered husband and wife despite a lengthy duration of the union. Nor is their relationship covered by marital law. Any legal arrangement must be made individually and is considered a contractual agreement.
>
> Participants in a **common-law union** must live together for a specified number of years, as determined by each state, before their status is considered equivalent to husband and wife under state law. The union is then recognized and covered by the same laws as those governing matrimony in states that make provisions for common-law marriages.

At first, living together was associated with nontraditional, leftist social activists; in other words, women who were considered foolish enough to give it all away to men who were simply using them. More recently, cohabiting has been viewed as a rather progressive, preferential arrangement that encourages monogamous sex arrangements before marriage.

Acceptance of the practice is so widespread in the United States that social scientists say nonmarital cohabitation is becoming an integral part of courtship and marriage.

At the dawn of the twenty-first century, living together is the most common route that American couples take before entering into family life.

The Climate for Change

Certain factors account for the dramatic change in coupling styles. Without a climate conducive to live-in love, partners might hide behind closed doors or might scrub the option altogether. The presence of a liberal sexual ethic, delayed marriages, women in the work force, and the high rate of divorce have helped open the door for live-in love.

Sex Without Marriage

Good-bye to the 1940s and 1950s, when sex was equated with marriage. Hello to the era of contraception, premarital sex, sexual liberation, unmarried moms, and abortion.

Delayed Marriages

The fact that women and men are delaying tying the knot has necessitated individual adjustments to normal urges. In the 1970s, most men at 23 carried their 20-year-old brides over the threshold. Today the median age of couples who walk through the door—on equal footing—is 25 for women and nearly 27 for men, with a good many brides and grooms on the upper side of these numbers.

Unconcerned about keeping their sexual activity secret during this extended period of being single, men and women ask themselves, "Why not live together?"

Working Women

Women are on their own financial track these days. A good paycheck in hand has diminished some of the economic gains formerly looked for in marriage. During the 1990s, 50 percent of women between 25 and 39 had a live-in partner. She can have her guy and her paycheck too. Studies show that this circumstance is more easily accomplished in a live-in arrangement than in marriage.

Prevalence of Divorce

The high rate of divorce has taught us all that marital relationships initially filled with love and entered into with the best of intentions can fall apart. This outcome has engendered cynicism toward marriage on the part of some youthful lovers who are embarking on a *first-union relationship,* and on other divorced individuals who are seeking new coupling opportunities.

Consequently, couples from both ends of the spectrum have expressed fear at the prospect of exchanging vows and opt to cohabit instead.

> **Sweet Nothings**
>
> A new term in the vocabulary of love is **first-union relationship.** This term refers specifically to the first living-together arrangement that a couple has, whether it is cohabitation or marriage.

Serving Live-In Love

Hearty portions of live-in love increasingly appear on relationship menus. Here are the figures on the number of couples who have tried this slice of American pie:

- In 1960 the number of live-in couples was less than a half million.
- Between 1965 and 1974, less than 11 percent of couples had a live-in relationship before they married.
- By the 1980s, one partner in 44 percent of newly married couples had previously participated in a live-in relationship.
- As of 1997, four million lovers reported trying the pie of cohabitation.

Love Stats

As early as the 1970s, college kids considered cohabitation socially acceptable. When students were asked what they thought about living together before marriage, they indicated that they questioned the worth of legal matrimony and thought that living together was a good way to size up the future of a relationship. However, research carried out by the National Marriage Project, a nonpartisan and nonsectarian initiative, reveals that living together does not prepare couples for matrimony or prevent future divorce. Consequently, professionals associated with the project recommend that couples not live together before marriage as the practice is harmful, not helpful, to the future of the relationship's well-being.

From Hollywood to Hoboken, Guess Who's Moving In

Goldie Hawn, Farrah Fawcett, Cindy Crawford, Christopher Reeves, and Richard Gere have all done it. Here's the profile on the more common, noncelebrity types who form the majority of live-ins.

Personal Profile

According to a variety of detailed studies, look for live-in folks to be ...

- Men whose employment records show erratic patterns or periods of nonwork.
- Individuals who need time for themselves away from partners.

- Men and women who value personal independence.
- Couples whose combined income is less than married couples of comparable age and status.
- Younger women who earn more than their male partners.
- Individuals who are often from broken homes.
- People who are not churchgoers.
- Men and women who are finishing educational programs.
- Young adults who are living farther away from parents.
- Individuals who are at critical stages in building their careers.

> **Love's Hot Line**
>
> If you are one of the 30 to 40 percent of college coeds who plan to move in with someone of the opposite sex, look for a lover who shares your educational goals. Otherwise you might be spending more time making love than good grades.

> **Love Stats**
>
> According to the stats for 1995, here's how the percentages of live-ins were divided up among various religious groups: 8.2 percent were Mormons, approximately 24 percent were Protestant, 23 percent Catholics, 33 percent Jewish, and 45 percent no religious affiliation.

Impersonal Stats

Another way of identifying live-ins is by age. Using Census Bureau data collected in the 1990s, the following table shows the proportion of each age group that had a live-in relationship.

Age Group	15–19	20–24	25–29	30–34	35–39	40–44
Percentage	4.1%	11.2%	9.8%	7.5%	5.2%	4.4%

International Appetites for Live-In Love

Americans aren't the only portion of the world's population to find cohabiting appealing. Scandinavians have been cohabiting longer than individuals on this side of the Atlantic, and with more frequency than many Europeans.

Although British live-ins have doubled since 1979, Scandinavian couples number the most. In 1996 nearly 69 percent of couples under 35 years of age cohabited in northern Norway. Swedish numbers top the Norwegian ones, though. Sweden has even institutionalized live-in love by giving participants specific protections under the law.

> **Love Stats**
>
> On October 13, 1999, the French parliament gave legal status to unmarried heterosexual and homosexual couples. This means that live-in partners have the same rights as married individuals under the law in such matters as inheritance and welfare.

Why Joe and Jane Are Moving In

Forming an arrangement to live together undoubtedly has both perceived and real advantages. I will focus here primarily on the advantages that live-ins hope to obtain and will deal with the reality of them in Chapter 3, "The Facts and Fictions of Living Together."

Each individual brings a unique set of circumstances to a relationship and devises his or her own reasons for moving in with the lover. Nonetheless, it is not difficult to find a consensus among live-ins as to why they chose to share a household. According to nearly 100 cohabiting couples, many of whom I personally interviewed and kept track of, the most popular categories of live-in lovers are: marriage seekers, mutual users, romantic roomies, serious pals and lovers, and true believers.

Marriage Seekers

Women, in particular, have marriage on their minds. And moving in is not interpreted by marriage seekers as a substitute for the real thing, the golden ring; nor does moving in diminish interest in, or desire for, the state of matrimony, found demographer Larry Bumpass.

The vast majority of women want to formally tie the knot at some time or other. Consequently, many women use cohabiting as a way to persuade hesitant, foot-dragging men to walk the aisle.

Priscilla did not deny it:

> "Marriage was my goal. Mark had just gotten a divorce. I thought it was good strategy to move out of town and away from his ex. I followed him to Boston and moved in. If I didn't, I was afraid I would lose him and that we wouldn't get married."

Twenty-somethings Clark and Elizabeth moved in together but not until she extracted the promise of matrimony. Elizabeth explains:

> "Clark asked me to move in. I refused. I told him once we were engaged I would. I thought that would push him into marrying me sooner. We lived together for six months before we got married."

Mutual Users

Mutual users have different goals from marriage seekers. These Joes and Janes are looking for company, convenient and plentiful sex, someone to nurture or be nurtured by, the advantages of sharing household costs without the entanglements of matrimony, or any combination of these. Frequently they move in with someone with whom they have not had a long-term relationship.

> "It was a fling with Ted," Ellen said. "Living together was so we could enjoy each other. I was extremely physically attracted to him."

> "It probably started out as a sexual relationship," admitted 27-year-old Richard, who has lived with 26-year-old Patsy for four years. "But the whole thing was mutually beneficial and made economic sense."

> "I didn't know too many people in Cleveland. I was 23. I met Polly, who was a few years older than me, and we started to date. I never liked coming home to an empty house, and with Polly there I had a companion. Marriage was not on my mind."

> "My buddies and I are looking for mothers, women who take care of us," this honest 30-year-old admitted without shame.

What these couples got was a temporary mutual use—sex, companionship, and a shared abode.

> **Troubles A'Brewing ...**
>
> Don't be misled about cohabitation. According to Whitehead and Dafoe, authors of the National Marriage Project report titled "The State of Our Unions," most people do not perceive cohabitation as an alternative to marriage. The exceptions are found in specific portions of the population, primarily less-advantaged Caucasian women, Afro-Americans, and Puerto Ricans.

Romantic Roomies

Romantic images, a greater degree of emotional involvement, and many of the same benefits sought by the mutual users are what entice couples to become romantic roomies. Despite the presence of a romantic attachment, one or both partners are uncertain about where the relationship will lead and have no serious intentions.

Here's what 26-year-old Val says:

> "We did play house for a while. It was fun, and I liked it for about a year. He kind of charmed his way into my house. He wanted to live with me to prove he could be a good mate, but it turned out he was more emotionally invested in the relationship than I was. He wanted to get married. I didn't. I was really enjoying the relationship and buying time. I knew things wouldn't work forever."

Garth, 48 years old, reports:

> "After my divorce, I wanted a woman whose eyes got real big when she saw me. And that is exactly what Sybil, 15 years my junior, did. I tried to explain to her that this was a temporary relationship even though we had tremendous passion for each other and had fun living together. She fit into my life neatly."

Serious Pals and Lovers

Serious pals and lovers are in the market for a long-term love relationship and think they have found it with each other. Before these folks move in, they get to know each other well. They demonstrate respect for their partner and the partnership, allow their love relationship to develop step by step, and voice serious intentions about the direction of the romance.

Jordan and Amy met on a blind date when they were in their early twenties. They hit it off really well from the get-go. They dated for three months before sleeping with each other. Jordan said it was different from any other sexual experience he had had.

Let's listen to Jordan:

> "Amy was the first woman I wanted to spend the night with. After that first time, I didn't sleep with anyone else. We started talking about living together after five months, but Amy did not move in with me for two years. When she did move in, we had set a secret wedding date for nine months later.
>
> "I did not want to rush things. I had to allow the relationship to grow naturally. I couldn't force it, and I wouldn't allow someone to move in unless I was really serious. I wanted to make sure that Amy was the right woman for me. I had to struggle with the idea that no one is perfect. I would go through periods of doubt when I would step back and reflect on what I really wanted. I needed time to digest what was happening to me. It was important

Troubles A'Brewing ...

Women beware. Professor Marin Clarkberg of Cornell University noted that, if the studies are correct, you are doing more housework than your live-in boyfriends, but less housework than married women.

to feel that I was being cautious. My brother had just gotten divorced, and I did not want to end up the same way.

"I was perfectly honest with Amy. I let her know how I was feeling, but she knew me better than I knew myself. When she did move in, I had every intention of marrying her. We stuck by the wedding date she had set, but I wouldn't have minded waiting another year or two. Living together and getting married was a big transition for me, but I was prepared to make the concessions I thought I should."

Jordan's words reflect the seriousness of his feelings and the respect he had for Amy and their relationship. Living together was hardly a frivolous fling for him.

True Believers

True believers are those who feel that live-in love expresses a complete and permanent relationship without marrying. The partners want a serious love relationship and have absolutely no interest in marriage. True believers are hard to find, particularly among young couples. Just when you think you may have found one, Jane gets pregnant and she and Joe get hitched. The men and women who abide by the definition of true believers the longest are previously married individuals who already have children or who express no interest in becoming a parent.

Here is Roberta's viewpoint:

"I never was, nor am I now, looking to get married. I did not see myself becoming a wife or a mother. There is nothing that marriage could do to make what Alan and I have any better a relationship. Alan and I choose to be together every day. It is my basic personality. I am a gypsy. For four years I lived in a hotel with all of my belongings under the bed. Security is not something I am looking for."

Alan, a father of two children from a previous marriage, had this to say about Roberta.

"She is 100 percent self-sufficient. She knows exactly what direction she is going in. For her that is security. To try and penetrate that would be to take away her security."

At 34 Julie says she was not looking for someone to take care of her. She was divorced, had children, and was financially secure and fiercely independent.

"Barry and I developed a very special relationship dating over a two-year period. He knew me better than anyone ever had. But that wasn't all; he was romantic, caring, and generous, and he had a great sense of humor and zest for life that kept my daughters and me up.

"I had no problem with living with a man outside of marriage. I had been introduced to nontraditional lifestyles from a young age. My father's business gave us the opportunity to spend extended periods of time in Sweden, where living together was commonplace, and I had lived with my husband before we married.

"You shouldn't be set just on marriage. Second marriages come with a lot of baggage. You need to know how that affects life together. There were too many complications for me to marry Barry even though he wanted to. If we were married, I would put more demands on him. I would probably be more possessive of his time and even expect him to spend more of his money on me. I might not be so understanding of his generosity to his ex-wife and all the thousands of extra dollars he spends on his children."

Not only does Julie feel more free, a quality she values, but she does not have to compromise the security of her sizeable financial assets, which would become accessible to Barry if they married. Julie adds:

"Fortunately Barry was willing to continue our live-in relationship without being married."

Julie has not wavered from her belief in living together over the course of the past 12 years. The last time I checked with her, everything was as wonderful as it had always been.

Do Live-In Lovers Find Satisfaction?

Yes and no. It all depends on what the participants wanted.

The following information is not intended to shake a finger at live-in love or to say it never works. On the contrary, these findings are presented so that those who decide to move in can adjust their expectations or can more carefully plan how to make live-in love work for them. Exactly how to accomplish that task awaits you later on as you make your way through this guide. For now, read carefully these rather surprising results:

➤ If couples wanted a long-term relationship, did they most often get it? The answer is no.

On the average, live-in relationships are short and end before two years. Considering that 75 percent of all infatuations fizzle out, this result isn't all that unexpected.

➤ If couples wanted a relationship that ended in matrimony, did they get it? The answer is no.

Chapter 2 ➤ *The Scoop on Live-In Love*

Fewer than one in two couples pair off in a lasting marriage relationship. And of those live-ins who had kids together, the most recent data show that only 44 percent married. This figure is down from the previously recorded 57 percent.

➤ If the partners wanted a sure-fire test of their marital compatibility, did they get it? The answer is no.

Couples who live together before marrying one another were divorced at a higher rate than those who did not cohabit. The reason will be revealed in Chapter 3 when we look at the differences between marital and live-in unions.

➤ If the participants wanted a satisfying relationship, did they get it? The answer is, possibly.

The degree of satisfaction here is telling. Those who cohabit appear to find significantly less happiness with the relationship than do married couples, according to a survey of 18,000 adults.

➤ If the couples wanted to improve their standard of living, did they accomplish that? The answer is, sometimes.

Two incomes are not always better than one if there is significant disparity between the two partners' paychecks.

Love's Hot Line

Interested parties: Enter through the portal of live-in love carefully. Learn how to map out your best chances for a successful, fulfilling, and happy live-in relationship before you take the plunge. For starters, keep reading!

The point is that the outcome and expectations of live-in love don't always meet; success or failure is judged on individual goals and desires.

How Live-In Love Impacts Family and Kids

If contemporary marriages are under scrutiny when it comes to effects on family and children, then live-in relationships also should be examined for their influence on family and children.

The number of children in these households is indeed significant. In 1997, 36 percent of live-in couples had a child of 18 in the home. Some estimates say that half of all children will live in a cohabited home before reaching the age of 16.

Although many women who cohabit and become pregnant do not end up with a marriage license, I have interviewed countless others who say that if and when they decide to have a child, they will end the live-in segment of their union and marry. At the present time, my observations lead me to believe that this type of decision is primarily based on the woman's socio-economic status.

27

If we apply the definition of family, as given in Chapter 1, "The State of the Union," these groups of individuals can certainly function as stable, supportive family units. Whether or not they do is debatable in most cases, however.

Trouble for Kids with a Capital "T"

The largest group of children with a cohabiting parent live with their natural mom and their mother's boyfriend, who is not their biological father. Research has shown that these children are at much greater risk for being abused because of the presence of an unrelated male in the household.

Furthermore, studies show that kids who live with mom and her partner exhibit more behavioral problems and perform lower academically than children from homes that are intact. Cohabiting couples with kids will split at a higher rate than married couples with children. This, too, can be a seriously disruptive and problematic change for a child.

When Joe Doesn't Want to Parent

Some men readily jump into family life, yet others remain primarily just lovers. If you want a family man but he only wants to be your lover, you will empathize with Liz and her tale of woe.

Liz, a relatively comfortable divorced suburbanite, met Hank and fell madly in love with him.

> "I thought I was a practical person until I became obsessed with Hank."

After eight years of a rocky relationship with him, she finally convinced him to move into her home, where she would have him all to herself. Although a live-in relationship is what she had been striving for, Liz admitted:

> "Having Hank live with me and my two children has been a real strain at times. It is hard to be on your best behavior while you are taking care of the kids, the house, and your business and trying to be a lover carrying on a romance. I hesitate to ask Hank to run carpools or help with dinner, but I do ask him to go to the cleaners for me. I was out to dinner with Hank, my children, and other family members a few nights ago. I noticed and admired at another table a mother, father, and kids that looked so happy. I had to laugh to myself thinking how that image compared with my own and the tension I felt at our table because of Hank."

Liz's statement reflects her disappointment in Hank's unwillingness to create a family atmosphere. What she may be sacrificing for love is the well-being of her children.

Chapter 2 ➤ *The Scoop on Live-In Love*

A Forecast for Live-In Love

The number of couples forming live-in relationships has grown so large that cohabiting is now considered normative behavior. A report on the social health of marriage determined that more than half of teenage America felt that living with someone before marriage was a good test to see whether or not they got along. If that's the case, a whole new crop of live-in lovers is on the way.

Perhaps these young people can learn from the experiences of others that there is more to living together than meets the eye and that happiness is possible but not guaranteed.

The Least You Need to Know

➤ Living together is here to stay.

➤ Live-in couples often have not yet mastered the means to achieve a satisfactory relationship or to meet their primary goals.

➤ Living together is not always founded on the desire for a long-term relationship, nor does everyone share the same live-in agenda.

➤ Serious pals and lovers make the best cohabiting partners.

➤ Live-in relationships can adversely affect the children of cohabiting individuals.

29

Chapter 3

The Facts and Fictions of Living Together

> **In This Chapter**
> - The in's and out's of commitment
> - Defining live-in love
> - Dispelling common misbeliefs about live-in love
> - Comparing partnerships among married couples and live-ins
> - When cohabiting is a prelude to marriage
> - How significant is a "significant other"?

In this chapter, I'll bring you up-to-date on the very latest news about cohabiting with a lover. During the 1990s, studies by social scientists about cohabiting arrived on the scene in abundance. The studies not only revealed what is true and false about living together but also provided valuable information for would-be live-ins.

Understanding the basis for commitment and the possible hazards that await a naïve live-in couple will help you begin to determine your own odds for success. This information will become pertinent when you fill out the scorecards given in Part 2, "Coming Up with a Decision on Live-In Love." Subsequently you may either form a better relationship or look for a new one.

Truth or Consequences, a Self-Test

In case you think you already know all the answers, try the following quiz. Each question is significant and could affect your future well-being. If you don't find an explanation for an answer in this chapter, you will find it in one of the next three chapters that complete Part 1, "Thinking About Living Together."

Part 1 ▸ *Thinking About Living Together*

True	False	
❏	❏	1. Having a live-in love relationship increases most women's level of self-esteem.
❏	❏	2. Commitment to your live-in partner is equal to the commitment found between spouses.
❏	❏	3. Live-in lovers have better sex than married couples.
❏	❏	4. Married couples are less monogamous than cohabiting partners.
❏	❏	5. Living together is the same as being married.
❏	❏	6. Men and women nearly always choose to cohabit with someone whom they think will be marriage material.
❏	❏	7. Dissolving a live-in relationship is relatively easy.
❏	❏	8. Marriage relationships require more time than live-in love.
❏	❏	9. Cohabiting couples qualify as common-law partners.
❏	❏	10. "Significant others" are accepted and treated with the same respect as spouses.
❏	❏	11. On the average, couples who cohabit are less committed to the institution of marriage even if they express the desire to marry.
❏	❏	12. Serial live-ins (individuals who have a string of partners) have a higher rate of divorce if and when they do marry.
❏	❏	13. Live-in lovers who are engaged before they move in together have the greatest chance of romantic and marital success.
❏	❏	14. Married couples are more likely than live-ins to sweep touchy relationship issues under the rug.
❏	❏	15. Men never get a raw deal in live-in love.
❏	❏	16. Live-in couples frequently slip-slide into marriage.
❏	❏	17. Many couples who think they should live-in to test their relationships actually have a lower-quality relationship than couples who marry without first cohabiting.
❏	❏	18. When experts who study cohabitation express concern about it or disapproval, they are being influenced by their moral or religious beliefs.
❏	❏	19. Whether or not a cohabiting couple moves on to marriage is largely dependent on their financial status.
❏	❏	20. Cohabiting between two independent, equitable partners may pose a higher risk for a poor relationship outcome.

Answers

1 to 7—False; 8—True; 9, 10—False; 11 to 13—True; 14, 15—False; 16, 17—True; 18—False; 19, 20—False.

Unless you got a perfect score—without guessing at the answers—and responded with knowledge and logic, you still have a lot to learn.

Commitment with a Capital "C"

When people try to pinpoint the one big difference between living together and being married, the word "commitment" often pops up as the answer. In this section, we'll look at what the word actually means when it comes to the dynamics of a love relationship.

Webster's is always a fun and easy way to begin an exploration of any word. According to the dictionary, the most common meaning of the noun *commitment* is "act of committing"; or "a pledge; something undertaken." The meaning of the verb *to commit* is "to entrust to another's care"; or "to bind oneself; pledge."

Most people would agree that these definitions are fairly straightforward. However, researchers who study the issue of commitment find that defining it is much more complicated. Their versions take a lot more words. Let's look at some of them.

> **Love's Hot Line**
>
> It is folly to think that lasting love *is* simply a matter of the heart. Thought, understanding, and finesse are needed to head off factors that send love down a bumpy path. The best relationships have an informed captain at the helm. Each partnership requires someone to steer the love boat. Women, according to my research, usually get the job.

Joint Investments

Sharing values and lifestyles (1) encourages positive matches among individuals, and (2) promotes making *joint investments* that add glue to a relationship. According to experts, this glue is more accurately called "commitment." Joint investments in children, leisure time, social lives, and financial well-being act as cohesive forces that enhance commitment in relationships.

For example, couples that buy a house together, play together, make decisions together, participate in a social life together, make love together, and together support each other are making joint investments that strengthen the bond between them.

Without all this togetherness, you aren't spelling commitment.

Trading Assets, Making Concessions

Here's a second take on commitment. Trading assets and joint investments aren't mutually exclusive ideas, but neither are they the same thing. I see them as complementary, as two aspects of the glue that holds a couple together.

Another group of experts has a different slant on how commitment works. According to this group, relationships that are succeeding show evidence of …

- An exchange of services.
- A trading of services.
- The making of concessions.

Notice that these three processes show an investment both in the other partner and in the relationship. The bargaining that enables these processes to take place fosters the critical practices of communication, agreement, and gift-giving. In turn, these practices create staying power and relationship satisfaction while also fueling the growth of commitment.

But that's not all. Couples who specialize in certain tasks inherent in household relationships appear to make critical, mutual concessions more readily.

Those couples who do not accept a division of labor are not good bargainers and are generally competitors. They vie for more power and are unable to make agreements or concessions that would otherwise benefit the growth of commitment, staying power, and relationship satisfaction.

A Tale of Commitment

Let's take Sally and Fred. Fred was offered a promotion that would necessitate relocating. Sally was happy with her present work, the kid's school, and the proximity to extended family members. Nonetheless, they had made the decision years ago that Fred's career would take precedence over Sally's part-time work until the children went to college. Her income would be saved for the children's education, and they would live off his. They agreed to fewer frills in order to be more financially secure.

Sally was okay with all of this. She wasn't in competition with Fred, and their plan took pressure off her to work full-time when the kids were young. However, before agreeing to move, she wanted to check out the school and the future market for her own career. If those things checked out satisfactorily, then she agreed that Fred should accept the promotion.

Fred realized that Sally was making difficult concessions by moving, setting up a new home, and waiting to go back to work until she got the kids settled in school. In order to show Sally how much he appreciated her support and cooperation, he drove weekend carpools for the kids and played golf with her instead

> **Love's Hot Line**
>
> A university study showed that most individuals who cohabit describe themselves as "never married" rather than as "married." Do you know anyone who calls his or her live-in partner a spouse? Probably not. Therefore, don't fool yourself into thinking that cohabiting equals marriage unless you and your housemate agree that it does.

of the guys on Sunday morning. After several months in the new city, he said he would like to splurge and buy tickets for the whole family to visit her folks.

A relationship like Sally and Fred's has all the ingredients for fostering commitment: joint investments, mutual concessions, exchange of services, and specialization of roles and labor.

Marriage, Living Together, and Commitment

Now that you are equipped with some definitions of commitment, you are ready to explore the role that commitment plays in both marriage and living together. A study in the 1999 *American Sociological Review* by Julie Brines and Karen Jupner stated plainly that married and live-in couples treat differently the factors that promote commitment. Empirical measurements of the way both types of couples work, handle money, spend leisure time, divide household labor, and conduct social and family relationships support this thesis.

So, which of the two couples engages in behavior that promotes the growth of commitment within their relationships?

The married ones, these experts say. And here's why:

1. Married couples monitor one another's behavior and formulate expectations that encourage the development of specialties and the essential division of labor.
2. They share more resources, making them less vulnerable as a couple and more vulnerable as individuals.
3. Married couples are more likely to be committed to social institutions, such as organized religion, that support the growth of cohesive and solid family relationships.
4. They are more likely to be engaged in raising children. Child rearing fosters a division of labor and joint investments.

Each of these examples adds to the cohesiveness and joint participation that encourages the continued commitment of married couples or live-ins.

The Great Debate

"Living together is just like being married." You've heard it; I've heard it. "Marriage is only a piece of paper." But you won't be able to convince those who have looked at both marriage and cohabiting that the two are the same.

Sociologists Julie Brines and Kara Joyner say the differences are more involved than you think. Brines and Joyner suggest that for a relationship to continue there must be a way to accommodate both interests of the parties. They think that the marriage contract helps do that.

Part 1 ➤ *Thinking About Living Together*

Love Stats

A study reviewed by authors in the 1995 *American Sociological Review* by Professors Arland Thornton, William Ayinn, and Jay Teachman revealed that cohabiting couples get more financial assistance from parents than do married couples. The financial help received by live-ins could be due to a lack of maturity and to finances that are more precarious than those of married couples. However, the problem is that this dependency may negatively affect the formation of a cohesive partnership.

Sweet Nothings

Logrolling is the act of mutually trading off concessions or assets between partners. For instance, a mutual tradeoff might be giving up a weekend to visit his parents if he agrees to attend a business function she prefers he join her at.

Here's how. A legal covenant like a marriage agreement implies security, certainty, and an expectation of permanence. Even if the marriage relationship does end, the labor of the spouses and their joint investments are protected by law.

Living together without a legally binding document, such as a marriage license, implies uncertainty, Brines and Joyner say. This, in turn, discourages joint investments or concession making and impedes the formation of a strong, committed relationship. *Logrolling,* or making trade-offs, becomes too risky for live-ins without the security of a defined future, Brines and Joyner claim.

The researchers emphasize their point by citing data proving that live-in unions split more often than married ones. And that cohabitors who marry split at a higher rate than couples who did not cohabit.

Differences Between Marriage and Living Together

The literature on live-ins and spouses describes several differences between marriage and living together, and these are given in the following list. After the list, you'll find another list giving the similarities.

1. A big difference between live-ins and spouses is the way they view stability within their relationship. "Stability is a function of economic equality in cohabiting relationships, and a function of specialization in marriage," Brines and Joyner say.

Cohabiting relationships in which the woman's income exceeds, rather than equals, her partner's are more likely to end. On the other hand, husbands report satisfaction when their wives are more successful.

2. Cohabiting couples are less socially integrated than married ones. In other words, the degree of joint social participation with friends, family, or the community is greater for marrieds; and their mutual social circles are larger than they are for cohabiting couples.

3. Married people are more likely to believe in traditional gender roles than cohabitors. This belief encompasses the specialization of labor that is so essential to the formation of commitment.

4. Live-ins are less willing to share their financial resources. This reluctance does not promote the joint investments vital to the continuation of the relationship.

5. Because of the time and effort needed to successfully maintain a marriage relationship, a married relationship is considered more constraining than a live-in one.

6. Marriage and cohabiting differ in that the cohabiting couple with children living in the home are more likely to break up than married couples with kids in the home.

We cannot point to one distinct difference that tells the whole story between marriage and cohabitation. There are, as seen from this list, a number of significant factors.

Similarities Between Marriage and Cohabitation

Despite the vast differences, there are similarities between cohabiting partners and married ones that are worth taking note of. This is what they have in common:

➤ A co-residential living arrangement
➤ An intimate relationship

Troubles A'Brewing ...

Watch out. Your live-in partner statistically has a three times greater chance of suffering depression than a spousal partner. Whether these odds are due to the uncertainty of the relationship or are a function of the personality types who opt to cohabit, the chance of depression is there.

Love's Hot Line

If you accept the fact, supported by current data, that married men experience an increase in average wages and workdays, then your live-in male lover may not be meeting his full earning potential.

Part 1 ➤ Thinking About Living Together

> ➤ The co-mingling of at least some financial resources
> ➤ The diversion of time away from the relationship and the attention to other things

This list of similarities is minimal in content when compared to the extent of differences.

Does Living Together Have to Look Like Marriage?

Of course not. But then let's be frank about living together. Living together is not all that similar to the state of matrimony. The implication that is of critical importance to us as we move forward in subsequent chapters is: How can you increase the odds of relationship satisfaction and add glue to partnership?

If It Isn't Marriage, What Is It?

If living together isn't the same as marriage, then what should we call it? Descriptions to consider include: substitute, alternative, intermediate step, prelude to marriage, delaying tactic, and transition phase. Let's look at what living together entails.

> **Love's Hot Line**
>
> In my investigation of love and marriage, I have come up with a Golden Rule that I believe makes the difference between successful or unsuccessful matrimony. The Golden Rule of a happy marriage is: Learn to please and appease, and do it often! The rule could just as easily be applied to live-in partners.

Living Together Is Not ...

The consensus of opinion in the United States is that living together is not yet considered a substitute for marriage. Most people still value and desire the state of matrimony rather than living together. Still, we all know those couples who would never replace a cohabiting relationship with marriage. Although cohabiting is not a substitute for marriage, you could play with words and say that cohabiting is their *alternative to marrying*.

Generally the couples who consider cohabiting as an alternative to marriage are older, divorced or widowed individuals who have passed the childbearing stage and are extremely independent. In many cases, they have a cohabitation agreement that contractually spells out specific financial arrangements. The contract may cover ownership of property, the division of goods and finances in the event the couple ends the relationship, and any inheritance rights they wish to extend to their live-in partner.

Chapter 3 ➤ *The Facts and Fictions of Living Together*

Living Together Is ...

For younger couples who use living together as a way to delay the onset of marriage, cohabitation could be called a *delaying tactic.*

Numerous studies and interviews suggest that young cohabiting couples will hold off marrying until they achieve what they believe is an appropriate level of economic well-being for marriage. This interpretation makes sense when you consider those couples who live together and share expenses yet say they are waiting to tie the knot until they pay off debt, buy a house, or can afford an extravagant honeymoon.

Sixty percent of couples who form a live-in relationship as a first-time union do go on to marry. Therefore, some demographers and social scientists concede that cohabiting fits the description of a *prelude to marriage.* Because cohabiting neatly fits in-between these couples' courtships and marriages, by definition it could therefore also be called an *intermediate step to matrimony.*

Living together can provide a *time for transition* among those engaged, committed live-ins on their way to matrimony. Beth tells us why living together proved to be an important transition phase for her and Jamie.

At age 23, Beth met 24-year-old Jamie in a romantic setting on the west coast of Florida. Her vacation romance bloomed into a long-distance love affair. Within 10 months, the native of Michigan was engaged to the handsome Florida resident. Jamie wanted Beth to relocate to the seaside, move in, and put an end to living in separate cities. Beth agreed, but only after an on-the-knee proposal and a ring on her finger.

Actually it was Beth's mom who encouraged her to live with Jamie during their engagement. Beth marvels that her mother always seems to know best. Beth explains that she had a lot to get used to before she tied the knot and made a permanent commitment:

> "I moved down and moved in. I started working for Jamie's family, so I spent all of my time with him and his parents. I was way too dependent on Jamie as my friend, lover, family, and fiancé. I had moved totally into his world.

> "After six months when all the playing house stuff was over, it got rocky between us. I went to Scotland with my mom for two weeks, and then on Jamie's birthday we had a major blowout. I gave him his ring back, walked to a pay phone, and called my mom's friend. My best friend in Michigan sent her husband down to drive me home with all my stuff. I was in Michigan for one week. Jamie called every day."

Despite the shortness of the time she lived with Jamie, Beth realized she had lost some of her self-confidence and knew things would have to be different. She was not going to be Jamie's maid, and they would have to stop fighting one another to gain the upper hand. Beth goes on:

> "It was time Jamie stopped thinking he was a bachelor living with a chicky-baby."

She insisted on using the next 10 months before their wedding to make necessary changes in their lives that would better ensure a happy ending. Fortunately Jamie's response proved his true love. He tried harder at home to be neat and made more of an effort to help her feel comfortable in his territory.

Buying a house together, moving into it, and finding her own job seemed imperative to Beth. The accomplishment of these goals enabled her to bring friends into their relationship, and the house gave them something to work on together. Beth adds:

> "I told Jamie Sundays were our day to do things in the house we needed to. Jamie respects me more now that I have a life. I know he understands my boundaries and what I won't put up with. We discuss plans together and show respect and common courtesy for one another. If we had gotten married when I first moved down, I would have felt trapped. Living together provided an important transition for me."

Love's Hot Line

Ladies, the concept of freedom is a major issue for men considering cohabitation and/or marriage. It isn't something they like to give up. Handle the issue with finesse. Don't battle loudly for control or insist on putting on the reins. Slowly and quietly teach them how much or how little freedom fits into good relationships. It is important that both partners in a relationship, whether spouses or live-ins, maintain some arena in which they function totally independently of one another. However, there is enough information in this chapter to prove that commitment in good relationships precludes excessive separation in leisure or household activities. Men who value independent leisure, according to Professor Morin Clarkberg, do not avoid unions but prefer less-committed relationships that require more sharing of leisure time.

Dispelling Fictions

Common misconceptions about living together are spread by word of mouth. It is time to acknowledge these fictions and dispel them.

Fiction: The sex is better among live-ins.

Fact: Researchers at the University of California at Los Angeles found that cohabiting partners report less sexual satisfaction. It has been suggested that the uncertainty of live-in relationships contributes to sexual anxiety.

Fiction: Living together promotes sexual fidelity.

Fact: Studies reported in the late 1980s and the 1990s demonstrate that married couples disapprove of infidelity more readily than cohabitors. An interesting aside is that women who had a live-in relationship and eventually married are more likely to have a secondary sex partner after saying "I do."

Fiction: Living together is a good compatibility test for marriage.

Fact: The risk of divorce among those who cohabit is nearly twice as great as for married couples who did not cohabit. This landmark discovery was made by Larry L. Bumpass and James A. Sweet. One reason for their surprising data is that cohabiting brings together vastly different individuals on separate tracks.

> **Sweet Nothings**
>
> **Monogamy** means having one sexual partner. These days you will also encounter the term **serial monogamy,** which means a succession of monogamous sexual relationships.

How Significant Is a "Significant Other"?

It's nice to have a title that is widely known and accepted, but exactly how significant is a "significant other"?

That's a good question. How significant varies by degree from one couple to another. If John or Meagan both wish to be viewed as a couple by family, friends, and business associates, it is up to them to make that point indisputably clear. A problem occurs when one partner treats the other less significantly than he or she wishes.

> **Love Stats**
>
> Several researchers describe cohabiting as a distinct institutional form of relationship that is defined by a "looser bond" than matrimony. Those who cohabit act more in accordance with behavior subscribed to by singles."

Insignificant Others

After dating for two years, Lena, 30 and divorced, moved in with Martin, older and the part-time custodian of his teenage daughter. Lena had been living with him less than a year when a family wedding became a major issue.

41

Lena explains:

> "The parents of the bride had visited us. I welcomed them in Max's home and helped wine and dine them. I could hardly believe it when they invited Max and his daughter but not me to the wedding.
>
> "Max's attitude was, 'What do you want me to do? It's not my affair.' Well I guess I wanted him to pick up the goddamn telephone and say, 'Why didn't you invite Lena? I'm not coming unless she does.'
>
> "I guess I saw us as a couple. Evidently he and his family didn't. That weekend I stayed home and took care of his house and his dog. I thought the next weekend he would take me away alone to make up. But instead he gave in to his daughter's demands that he chaperone her and her friends on a weekend trip. He invited me, but I declined. I moved out shortly after that."

A Checklist for a Significant Other

At the very least, a significant other should be …

- ✔ Accepted as an equal social partner.
- ✔ Shown consideration and respect by his or her partner.
- ✔ Championed and supported by his or her partner.
- ✔ Treated as a priority by his or her partner.
- ✔ Viewed as a unified couple by his or her live-in partner.

Troubles A'Brewing …

Unless the minimum attitude requirements for a significant other are fulfilled, a live-in relationship spells trouble for at least one of the participants. He or she is sure to experience a weakened self-concept and diminished self-esteem.

Put the facts and fictions of living together in your back pocket. You will need to take them out later. They will be helpful in determining whether your love interest is a good live-in risk and whether your expectations are reasonable.

Chapter 3 ➤ *The Facts and Fictions of Living Together*

> **The Least You Need to Know**
>
> ➤ Commitment is essential to forming a cohesive, lasting relationship. It isn't expressed by words alone; it must be accompanied by deeds.
>
> ➤ Married and live-in partners exhibit different degrees of commitment.
>
> ➤ On the whole, living together is not like being married.
>
> ➤ Living together acts as a transition stage into matrimony for many young couples today.
>
> ➤ Live-in partners should make sure they are significant partners with a capital "S."

Chapter 4

Special Risks for Women

In This Chapter

- ➤ Identifying women most at risk to love's darker side
- ➤ Learning how men interact with vulnerable women
- ➤ Self-testing your risk factor
- ➤ Uncovering common concerns of women
- ➤ Stepping out of harm's way

Life is full of risks. Relationships are part of the package. They are joint explorations fueled by natural desires and passions. Because the outcome of relationships can be uncertain, they pose particular risks to participants. However, certain men and women are more vulnerable and more likely to get hurt than others, particularly by live-in love.

The purpose of this chapter is to help identify those women, pinpoint the factors that get them into trouble, and place them on more solid ground.

Women at a Disadvantage

Certain women put themselves at a distinct disadvantage because of the way they think. Consequently they become embroiled in shaky episodes of live-in love.

Part 1 ➤ *Thinking About Living Together*

Love Stats

A 1997 study found that women who cohabit were more irritable, anxious, and unhappy than other women.

Generally these women ...

➤ Trust their lovers too much.
➤ Aren't nearly skeptical enough.
➤ Lack tools to wisely evaluate relationships.
➤ Show signs of romantic desperation.

It might be helpful for women at risk to start practicing an axiom offered by psychologist and author David J. Lieberman, Ph.D.: Approach each new relationship with *cautious* optimism.

Self-Testing Your Risk Factor

Don't be afraid to take this test. Finding out that you are a woman at risk doesn't mean you have to wear this badge for a lifetime. What the test should do is awaken you to the potential for trouble and encourage you to be alert when making critical romantic decisions.

True	False	
❑	❑	I have little experience in love relationships.
❑	❑	I have only a basic understanding of how a healthy relationship works.
❑	❑	I don't know what constitutes wise or unwise motives for moving in.
❑	❑	I have recently undergone a significant change in my personal life.
❑	❑	I am fearful of not finding love and being alone forever.
❑	❑	I have a tendency to see things through rose-colored glasses.
❑	❑	I am an overly nurturing and giving person.
❑	❑	I am a follower, not a leader.
❑	❑	I don't value myself highly.
❑	❑	I lack personal goals.
❑	❑	I feel like my biological clock is running out of time.
❑	❑	I want and need someone to take care of me.

Add up your true and false answers. Now and then we all have a down day. If so, retest yourself in a day or two. The presence of more than two checkmarks in the True column puts you dangerously close to romantic risk.

Desperation, an Element of Probable Risk

You aren't alone if you are desperate for love. The problem is, desperation fosters unsound decision making, makes you vulnerable, and repels men.

We have already found that most women are in the market for marriage. How they see and project themselves in that marketplace is a very important factor. Women who test positive on the risk test, have low self-esteem, or buy into a male shortage are more likely to exhibit signs and behavior that make them act weak and appear desperate.

Chances are that men's radar will eventually pick up these signals. Men then become either suspicious of a woman's motives or leery of her sincerity. They say to themselves, "This is a woman who will latch onto anything in pants. She's fearful that she may never meet a decent man and won't have the opportunity to marry."

The point is, desperation is hard to hide and lessens a woman's attractiveness. Consequently it weakens her position in the marriage market.

Now for the kicker—Alan Booth and David Johnson's article in the *Journal of Family Issues* states that women in weak "marriage-market positions" will be more likely to cohabit than individuals in a strong market position. But more than that, they found that these live-in relationships are more unstable and less satisfactory than others. No wonder.

> **Troubles A'Brewing ...**
>
> Ladies watch out. According to psychology professor Keith Davis, Ph.D., in areas where there are more men than women, males have less incentive to date only one woman or to make a commitment. A city where this is true is Washington, D.C.

> **Love Stats**
>
> According to my interviews with single men, they believe that women over 30 are desperate for a man—any man. "I haven't met a woman without an agenda," reported one eligible bachelor. The mere perception of this belief places women at a disadvantage."

Low Self-Esteem, an Undeniable Risk

Low *self-esteem* plays dirty tricks on all of us.

➤ It causes us to shy away from certain situations or get out of other ones.

➤ It sets up men and women for disappointment and failure.

➤ It prevents individuals from making changes that affect their well-being.

Feminist leader and author Gloria Steinem wrote that a lack of self-esteem increases neediness and vulnerability in romantic relationships and encourages images of illusionary, magic rescues.

No wonder women who have low self-esteem are less equipped to deal with inequities in love relationships, including marriage and living together. When a woman doesn't value herself, she doesn't think her lover will either. She lives in a world of fantasy. In order to maintain affection and interest, a woman who does not see herself as worthy defers more often to her partner's preferences than to her own, even at the expense of her own well-being. She is satisfied with mere crumbs of approval. These are not indications of a healthy relationship or of individual happiness.

A woman shouldering this outlook is definitely headed for trouble.

> **Sweet Nothings**
>
> Everyone needs to be reminded often of the definition of **self-esteem.** It means to have respect, love, and appreciation for yourself, as well as pride, belief, and confidence in yourself.

Madge, Not an Exemplary Example

Madge knew that she had a case of low self-esteem.

> "One of my college professors told me he had never seen anyone who had so little self-confidence. I attribute that to the unending criticism of my father."

What she didn't understand was how low self-esteem could get her into trouble when dealing with the opposite sex.

Her problems started out innocently enough. Just after college, waiting to begin her job as a high-school math teacher, Madge met Nelson at the hospital where they both worked the night shift. He was married with a baby on the way and owed back child support to a daughter born out of wedlock.

> "I wouldn't have had an affair and gotten into a relationship like that if I had had a better self-image," she protested.

In hindsight, Madge understands how her low self-esteem allowed her to be talked into an unwise love affair.

How's Your Self-Esteem?

To assess your level of self-esteem, ask yourself whether you think you are ...

- ➤ Competent.
- ➤ Lovable.
- ➤ Deserving of love, admiration, respect, and happiness.

If you didn't answer yes to all three points, you probably don't have a healthy level of self-esteem, says psychoanalyst Nathaniel Branden.

When thinking of moving in with someone you love, there is no substitute for adequate self-esteem. If it is too low, you won't be able to hold your own, and you could drop to unbearable levels if your live-in venture fails.

> **Love Stats**
>
> A report released by the National Institute of Health said that women who cohabit suffer from depression at least three times the rate of other women.

Reported Risks

Like any relationship, a live-in relationship can be a risky business. I would be remiss if I didn't tell you about the potential problems that many women have reported finding with live-in love. These constitute risk for all women.

According to these women, living together has the potential to ...

- ➤ Lower your self-esteem.
- ➤ Cloud your judgement.
- ➤ Cause you to lose control over your own destiny.
- ➤ Influence you to unwisely hand over financial assets.
- ➤ Cause you to put your needs second to your lover's.
- ➤ Make you too dependent.

It is imperative that women keep this in mind when deciding whether or not to move in with a lover.

> **Troubles A'Brewing ...**
>
> Seventy percent of the women I interviewed expressed a diminished level of self-esteem after the breakup of a live-in relationship.

Risky Scenarios

Many of the women who have had an unsuccessful and unhappy go at live-in love say that the one thing they hope for is that other women will learn by their experiences. Their stories, which you will hear in the following sections, are not unique episodes. Rather they illustrate the same plot repeated over and over by different women but with slightly altered details.

What emerged from listening to so many women were five typical risk scenarios. These situations occurred more often than others. In each of the five scenarios, the woman did not take a divorced man at his word, she engaged in love on the rebound, she accidentally walked into harm's way, she exchanged love for debt, and she put her dreams on hold.

The real-life stories of these women are more than tales offered for voyeuristic entertainment. Pay attention to the details of the risky business, but, even more important, consider how these situations could have been avoided.

The House with No Windows

At 25, Bridget started dating Stan and bought her own home. Stan spent hours helping her fix it up. The problem was that Bridget allowed Stan to cover up the windows of her inner house, and she lost sight of what was outside. Here's her story:

> "It seemed natural to have Stan move in with me. I loved him and thought we were headed for marriage. Then I received the job offer of a lifetime, but it meant I would have to live out of state. I thought I could take the job and that Stan, a teacher employed for nine months out of the year, could come up for the summer. That way we wouldn't have to be away from each other as much."

Stan refused to consider Bridget's plan, and told Bridget if she moved it was over.

> "I didn't want to give Stan up. It was a hard decision. If we hadn't been living together, I would have taken the job, but I didn't feel like I was in a very secure position to fight for my side. If we were married, I would have felt I had more leverage and could have fought harder and more safely for my point of view.
>
> "Things went downhill after that. I felt like I was at a standstill for a whole year. It would have been more tolerable if at least my relationship with him was moving forward. He didn't want to become engaged. He said we might be doing it for the wrong reasons.

> **Love's Hot Line**
>
> No matter how astute or aggressive a woman may be in the workplace, if she doesn't use those same skills to manage her live-in relationship and keep sight of her personal goals, she may not be able to find a way out of the house.

"I knew I had to make some changes, but I wanted to go in a direction that Stan would approve of. I decided to apply to graduate school."

With Bridget's credentials, she was accepted to a top Ivy League school and was offered a free ride. Again, Stan wouldn't move. He wanted to stay in the Midwest where they were living. It wasn't until Bridget found a more satisfying job that she started to feel more like herself. She realized that the atmosphere in her home was stifling her. She felt trapped and stepped back to look at her relationship objectively.

"I was putting Stan's agenda ahead of mine. I realized he was the one who wasn't compromising and was forcing me to make all of the concessions. All of a sudden, all of my options were available to me again."

Bridget allowed her heart to take over for her head. Images of romantic rescues prevented her from asking herself what road she and Stan were headed down and made her lose sight of who she was. The investment she had made in becoming a live-in lover prevented her from taking action earlier that would have benefited her career and self-image.

The Case of the House with the Locked Door

Gregory, a family man if ever there was one, was faced with a wife who wanted a divorce after 20 years of marriage. He was shocked, devastated, and excruciatingly pained when his world fell apart. When he found himself dating a woman who was heading him toward church bells again, he told her, "I am through with marriage." The woman politely bid Gregory adieu.

Next he became involved with Roz. Six months after they had been dating, she moved in, quietly angling toward matrimony.

Gregory insists he has been up-front with Roz about marriage.

"I told her from the beginning that she shouldn't come on to me about marriage. She doesn't totally believe me and feels once I get over the pain of my divorce, I'll change my mind. She thinks the reason I haven't told her I love her is that it is difficult for me to say. But I don't love her. I do believe there is a right person out there for me, and some day I could find her. There is a chance that I could commit to her for the rest of my life."

Love's Hot Line

Women often have a problem listening to what men say, especially when men use the divorce story as the reason they plan never to remarry. If a guy is telling you that he doesn't want to get married, chances are that even if he does eventually marry, he won't be marrying you. Moving in, tying up your options, and setting your sights on this John opens the door to risky business.

Part 1 ➤ *Thinking About Living Together*

Before Roz opened the door, she should have listened to what Gregory was saying. He was trying to tell the truth. Unless she wanted simply a live-in lover, she let in the wrong guy.

The House with the Trapdoor

In her mid-20s, Hannah made a tremendous financial investment in her relationship with Ronnie. When she moved in, the arrangement was suppose to be temporary. But before long, they were talking about love and a lifetime for two. That's when Hannah decided she needed to help Ronnie get his life on sound financial footing and to help reduce his $40,000 worth of accumulated debt.

Three years later the debt had dwindled to $20,000 under her scrutiny and contributions. Nonetheless, Ronnie argued he didn't want Hannah responsible for the remaining $20,000, so he couldn't possibly marry her. Still, that didn't stop him from asking her to transfer with him to a new city and sign a lease that he couldn't get without her name on the dotted line.

Twice during the last few years, I've checked in with Hannah's friend. The first time she reported that they were still together but not married. The second time she said that Hannah had split but was having a tough time extricating herself financially from Ronnie. It seems she had also cosigned for his new car.

> **Love Stats**
>
> After a breakup, the average length of time that women in their twenties wait to enter a new relationship is 11½ months. Men of the same age wait nearly 15 months to begin anew.

Hannah made several mistakes. She allowed herself to fall in love with Ronnie; then she tried to barter her love for his debt. She made the dangerous assumption that she had the power to get him ready to assume the responsibilities of matrimony, even though Ronnie gave no signs of agreeing with her plan.

The Rebound Duplex

With the demise of her 11-year marriage, April was shattered and lonely. She was frightened by life alone in a large Detroit suburban house with two children.

> "I knew my husband was having an affair. I kept asking myself if it was my fault and what I had done wrong."

Six months later she met Trent while visiting her parents in Cleveland.

> "It wasn't hard to fall for him. I had been neglected sexually and emotionally. He paid a lot of attention to me and made me feel good. Later when my divorce was final, I got a ton of money and moved to Cleveland. I bought a duplex. I lived on one side, and Trent lived on the other rent-free.

Chapter 4 ➤ Special Risks for Women

> **Troubles A'Brewing ...**
>
> According to a Washington State University study, the risk of abuse and becoming victims of domestic violence is twice as high for women who cohabit. Department of Justice statistics show that women are assaulted significantly more often by live-in partners than by spouses. Women are in jeopardy during a period of separation and should seek extra precautions when leaving an abusive partner. Authors Neil Jacobson, Ph.D., and John Gottman, Ph.D., recommend in their book *When Men Batter Women* that women create a safety plan. This includes locating shelters, finding emotional support, making legal contacts, packing a survival kit, and having an escape plan. A 1997 mortality report from the Florida Governor's Task Force on Domestic and Sexual Violence underscored the importance of precautionary measures: "Sixty-five percent of intimate homicide victims physically separated from the perpetrator prior to their death."

"After a year and a half I thought he should move in with me so I could rent out the other half. It made more sense. It cured my loneliness and gave me a new sense of security.

"I trusted Trent completely. I wanted to marry him but never said anything about it. I guess I was afraid he might leave me, and I wasn't ready for that. Now I see I had him move in to get over my husband. It was paramount in my mind to prove that I could make it work.

"We lived together for about two years and traveled a lot until things went sour and he lost interest. We went through all of my settlement, hundreds of thousands of dollars. I feel like I bought him off. He still owes me $30,000."

April made the fatal error of becoming involved before she was ready and asking Trent to move in on the rebound. She should have gotten rid of her baggage, cured her ills, repaired her confidence, made a plan, and consulted a qualified financial advisor before playing house with Trent. Good relationships don't expose partners to a lot of risk, and they take place between healthy, healed individuals.

The Dangerous House on Main Street

Kathy was raised in a protected upper-middle-class home. Despite the protest of anxious parents, she had her first live-in relationship at age 20. By the time she turned 26, Craig was her third.

"It was one of those relationships that belong on Oprah. He was so charming and attractive. I thought, 'Wow! I can't believe this incredible-looking guy likes me.' I would have gone to any lengths at the time to make sure we were together. I thought having him move in with me put me more in control. By supporting him, I could manipulate him into needing me and staying.

"Craig worked on my self-esteem and would say things that made me feel so bad. He said I was crazy. I began to question my own self-worth and sanity. He controlled me by manipulating the way I thought about myself. Craig knew that I needed and wanted sex and attention. Consequently he was loving and comforting to me when I got very angry with him and he thought I might throw him out. Generally, however, he withheld sex entirely from me and made me feel that no one else would want me.

"The whole thing got really ugly. I still can't believe I allowed this to happen. It was a very violent relationship with yelling, screaming, and hitting. When I think of it, I think, 'Oh God, I can't believe it was me.' He pushed me down one night, bruising me all over and knocking out several teeth. I had to be taken to the hospital. When he threatened to kill me, I called my parents. I had to get a restraining order to protect myself.

"I remember sitting in the prosecutor's office when the clerk told me I was the sixth or seventh woman who had filed a domestic violence complaint against Craig. I was kidding myself about the whole relationship. It has taken several years to build back my self-esteem."

Kathy's first mistake was not checking this guy out. You have to be careful whom you let into your house. Her second mistake was putting herself in such a vulnerable position that she became captive in her own home. Her third was not throwing him out the minute he began to emotionally abuse her.

> **Love's Hot Line**
>
> If you are a victim of abuse, call the National Domestic Violence Hot Line at 1-800-799-7233 day or night!

One Last Warning

After being bombarded in this chapter by all the risks that women must look out for, let me add that certain men are just as much in the line of fire. What both of you have to do is determine "where" or "if" you fit into this chapter and the next. Then if the opportunity for live-in love arises, you will be better equipped to deal with it and all of its benefits and weaknesses.

> **The Least You Need to Know**
>
> ➤ Don't be dissuaded from love because it is full of risk. Instead, approach it wisely.
>
> ➤ Women with poor self-esteem place themselves in harm's way.
>
> ➤ Cohabitation should not be full of one-sided sacrifices.
>
> ➤ Live-in lovers should never assume their partner's debt.
>
> ➤ Women who cohabit are more likely to experience domestic violence. No one is immune to this fact.

Chapter 5

Unique Concerns for Men

> **In This Chapter**
> ➤ Men who don't do well with live-in love
> ➤ Women who spell trouble
> ➤ The influence of sex on men's decision-making process
> ➤ Horror stories for vivid contemplation
> ➤ Risk evaluation

Men, now it is your turn at the plate. Certain men don't seem to fare as well as others in live-in relationships. Naturally you won't hear these guys bragging about having their hearts broken or their pockets picked. In most cases they are in denial, full of guilt and protective of their macho image. However, they haven't learned a thing, and neither will you if we all continue to allow these men to blame their woes on their female partners. The women probably didn't deliberately set out to wreak havoc on their lives, although in some cases it wasn't hard to do. Like the women in the preceding chapter, some men have specific attitudes and personality traits that make them easy targets for Cupid's twisted bow.

This chapter will help you decide whether you are one of those in the line of fire and tell you how to avoid being wounded. Experience in romantic relationships, even previous live-in unions, does not mean you won't be struck again. It's all in the attitude, boys.

Separating the Boys from the Men

It isn't difficult to come up with a list of qualities that identify the men who have the least success with cohabiting. They tend to be ...

- Nice guys.
- Poor judges of women.
- Lonely.
- Impulsive.
- Gullible.
- Nurturers and caretakers.
- Uncomfortable with confrontation.
- Ruled by a male ego.
- Easily manipulated by women and sex.
- Overcome by passionate infatuations.

> **Troubles A'Brewing ...**
>
> Guys, you are more vulnerable than you think. As never-married single men, you are more likely to suffer from emotional or physical ailments than never-married single women.

You don't have to lay claim to all of these conditions to be at risk; that would be a fatal package. Any combination of them is enough to put you on the wounded list.

Additional Warnings

There are special circumstances that make men, any man, vulnerable at one time or another. You could be the most sensible, logical, well-grounded guy around, but watch out! Remember, we aren't talking about how men conduct themselves in the workplace. This is romance we're addressing. If you fit any of the following descriptions, now isn't the time to decide to move in with someone. Wait until your life is back on track, your head is on straight, and your feet are firmly planted on solid ground. Don't put two names on the mailbox when ...

- You are in love or lust.
- You are just re-entering single life.
- You have just ended a live-in union.
- You are on the rebound.
- You can't seem to live alone.
- You are suffering a money pinch.

Each of these conditions clouds your judgment.

Men Who Are Successful Live-Ins

After several years of interviewing, watching, and waiting, here is what I have come up with. One particular group of men appear to be better equipped to avoid and handle the possible pitfalls of living together. They have satisfying live-in love relationships, get what they want, and have no regrets. Their bio looks like this. They tend to …

- Be older and mature.
- Be a good judge of women.
- Have an understanding of the seriousness of their relationship.
- Decide for themselves and not be easily talked into anything.
- Be solid, careful thinkers.
- Have a clear idea of what they want out of the relationship.
- Know how to pick a woman who can abide by their rules.
- Be emotionally and financially secure.
- Be self-sufficient.
- Dislike playing romantic games, including house.

> **Love's Hot Line**
>
> Women do better than men after the divorce is final. According to experts, women spend a great deal of time before the divorce preparing a plan for life after marriage, and they have already dealt with critical issues when they sign the papers.

These guys have their heads on their shoulders and are equipped to make sound romantic judgments.

For Divorced Men Only

If your divorce happened less than two and a half years ago, listen carefully. After separating from your wife, experts say you need a period of two and a half years to regain a sense of order in your life. Moving in with someone while your mind and life are still discombobulated is a high-risk deal.

Part of the reason the average guy needs two and a half years to get his life together is that he never developed a postmarriage plan before the divorce took place. Furthermore, he is reluctant to seek professional help or the comfort of friends afterward. Instead, studies show he feels both embarrassed and guilty, preferring to suffer silently. He may isolate himself or work compulsively to avoid dealing with his emotional baggage. As a result, he is three times more likely to develop a clinical depression than his ex-wife. The problem is that he is also likely to date indiscriminately and frenetically and resort to drugs or alcohol. That combination is explosive. Under those influences, it wouldn't be difficult for a woman to make her way into his homestead.

Part 1 ➤ *Thinking About Living Together*

Sex on the Mind

Freud discovered that nothing disrupts the rational thought process like the male instinctual sex drive. The need to fulfill sexual desire and seek sexual pleasure influences nearly everything a male does, Freud said. Although some contemporary experts have tried to dispute his findings, the consensus of opinion remains firm that men have a stronger sex drive than women. The simplest things turn men on. Deborah Blum, author and University of Wisconsin professor, wrote in her book *Sex on the Brain* that "In humans, the male system sometimes seems so jittery with sexual readiness that just about anything—high-heeled shoes, a smile, a friendly conversation—will produce a sexual response."

Not only are men aroused more easily than women, Blum says, but on the average men think about sex more often and pursue orgasms with greater single-mindedness. As evidence, she points to data that show that men masturbate with greater frequency than women do and that, on the average, the thought of sex crosses a guy's mind at least several times a day; women take a week to match that.

There isn't anything wrong with sexual appetite, guys. Where you get into trouble is when you allow it to cloud your judgement and confuse lust with love. Sex is like a switch. It can turn on, or turn off, the lights of a romantic relationship. When the voltage reaches top level, watch out. You wouldn't be the first guy to put out the welcome mat, hand over a key, and make room in your closet based on a purely sexual relationship. The problem occurs when the voltage diminishes and the lights start to flicker, and you have difficulty reclaiming your territory.

Women Who Spell Trouble

She may turn you on. You may even be in love. She may be the most wonderful woman you've ever met.

> **Love Stats**
>
> Deborah Blum, author of *Sex on the Brain*, says that men don't need to have an experienced partner to enjoy sex, because of their ability to readily climax. In fact, whether or not their female partner reaches an orgasm, men climax approximately 80 percent of the time.

> **Love's Hot Line**
>
> Pornography is a $500 million business. Whom is it catering to? The answer is men. Women aren't turned on nearly as often by nude photos as are men, studies prove. According to experts, the industry that gets women's money puts out romantic flicks and novels with enough room for sexual fantasy steeped in love and commitment.

But, if she comes too close to the following description, she very likely spells trouble. Watch out for women who …

- Lack the ability to be independent.
- Are financially insecure.
- Are inexperienced at living on their own.
- Don't like being alone.
- Have a variety of personal problems.
- Lack maturity and personal growth.
- Do not have enough self-esteem.

These women may not mean to break your heart or take advantage of your hospitality. But in the end, you could be had.

> **Love Stats**
>
> According to a national men's health magazine, single men fear being rejected by women. They also fear an inability to live up to their masculine image, and they fear premature ejaculations or performance problems.

Men Who Have Been Had

Take some lessons from men who have gone before you. Most of their sagas clump nicely into distinct categories. Naturally not all live-in mishaps fit precisely into these neat little groupings, but the tales that follow have a great deal of universality about them.

The Runaway Mutual User

For Kevin, what started out as a mutual user (see Chapter 2, "The Scoop on Live-In Love"), with himself seemingly in the driver's seat, evolved into a relationship in which he lost control over his own destiny. At age 24, Kevin, the quintessential non-confrontational pleasing middle child, met 23-year-old Rosemary at work. She had been in town only a few months and had no prospects for permanent housing and even less money.

As Kevin relates:

> "What attracted me to her originally was sex. At the beginning there was an eagerness to do whatever I suggested. Consequently, Rosemary stayed over 90 percent of the time. I don't think I ever consented to her moving in. It just happened. I really didn't want it from the get-go, but I felt kind of responsible for her. Her parents felt more comfortable having her live with me than alone."

Kevin will concede that, although things just kind of happened, there were some benefits in the deal for him. He was tired of the singles game and enjoyed the companionship, not to mention the sex. The fact that Rosemary put in money for food and incidentals helped him out on the financial front, too. He had been struggling to pay off college loans and make mortgage payments on his house.

Actually, the first year together was pretty good, Kevin said. He was seriously considering a date for a wedding ceremony until he realized that, though he loved Rosemary as a person and cared about her well-being, his love wasn't the kind needed for a wife with whom he would spend the rest of his life. As soon as he realized his mistake, Rosemary's other faults became glaringly visible.

> "She was bitchy and too dependent. Sex had become practically nonexistent. I should have left right away, but I wasn't ready for it to be over either. I was weak and didn't tell her how I was feeling. She started calling me a liar and throwing it up to me because we weren't getting married. I couldn't find a way to end the relationship. She went to school to become a paralegal, and I footed all of the household bills. I just couldn't boot her out of my house. I wanted her to save as much money as she could until she could be independent. She didn't graduate on time because of her mother's illness. A year later she was still there. I couldn't get on with my life."

Kevin was thinking about selling his house just to get her out. What he did instead was wait month after month for something to happen. Nearly 12 months later, she exited his house and his life.

Jumping Over the Threshold

Lucas is one of those guys who has to have a woman around at all times. He impulsively forms relationships and loves showering women with gifts. "I'm a pushover," he admits. And since his divorce, he's been pushed over at least three times. This will tell the story of his second failed live-in union.

Lucas was on the rebound when a friendship with Nancy, who lived out of town, turned to love. She was a single, pregnant woman he had known for years. And no, he said, he was not the father of her baby, although he did go through the Lamaze course and the delivery with her. Their passionate affair started after the birth of Nancy's baby girl. She wrote letters convincing Lucas of her love and said that living in separate cities inhibited the growth of their relationship. Nancy and baby came to live in Lucas's new, luxurious home, and he became a surrogate, doting dad.

"Without a doubt it was stupid," Lucas said. After a hectic workweek that included a lot of travel, Lucas would spend Friday nights feeding, bathing, and putting Nancy's daughter to bed. Nancy, young and

> **Sweet Nothings**
>
> Ever hear of the term **cuddle-buddies?** Singles use it to describe a friendly, minutely romantic heterosexual relationship that includes petting and snuggling all night without sex.

vivacious, was ready to swing after her week at work and taking care of the baby. Lucas stayed home, and Nancy usually hit the singles scene. After two years when Nancy said it was best they split, Lucas was a little angry.

> "I put two years into this and thought we would settle down. I didn't want to be at home when she moved out. It was very hard."

Nancy is a master manipulator who played her tune well on Lucas. Feeling guilty that he had encouraged her to move so far from her home to be with him, Lucas offered a generous send-off. He helped pay Nancy's credit cards, provided deposits for furniture, and gave her all the baby furniture he had bought.

> **Troubles A'Brewing ...**
>
> Studies by Ruben and Raquel Gur on human emotion found that men do not notice those changes in women's facial expressions that are subtle, only those that are extremely exaggerated. No wonder, then, that so many men report surprise and dismay when their live-in partners appear to decide to leave suddenly. These guys probably don't notice and can't read the signs. Women may get a better score on reading facial expressions but can be just as surprised by a partner's request to break up. Self-deception is a key factor in ignoring a love interest's overt or covert message, noted David D. Lieberman, Ph.D., and author of *Never Be Lied to Again*. Women, according to men who have tried to break up with them, don't want to see the writing on the wall.

The Knight in Shining Armor

In the long-ago tales of King Arthur and his knights, damsels in distress were always being rescued by chivalrous knights. But in the story that follows, it's the guy in shining armor who needs rescuing. The conflict begins as soon as a woman entrusts herself into a man's keeping and he feels emotionally gratified at becoming her keeper.

Helen was just coming out of a bad relationship when she reacquainted herself with Sam, an old friend from her undergrad days. After a dismal love affair with the wrong kind of man, she decided she was going to look for the right kind—someone who would protect her, provide and share an ample salary, and offer intellectual companionship. Attraction, sex, and passion were put in second place. Sam gallantly and willingly came to her rescue and surrendered his sword at her feet.

Helen says:

> "I was scared to be independent. I was sort of coming out of my parents' nest and out of school at the same time. It was scary having to think of taking care of myself. Going into a safe relationship where there wasn't a whole lot of emotional investment—plus the benefits of a beautiful apartment in an expensive large city—seemed perfect. He was supposedly in love with me when I accepted his invitation to move in. I made a conscious choice to make Sam my partner and hoped to learn to love him."

Sam and Helen had been living together for two years. As Helen's career flourished, she began to recognize some of her own inner strengths and also to realize how dependent she was on Sam. However, she was too tied to his umbilical cord to consider moving out.

> "In a lot of ways he was my mentor, but he was smothering. He wanted someone to love him so completely."

Sam's job took him to a new locale for a year, and it was decided Helen would stay put in their apartment for just a short while. Sam may have been her knight in shining armor, but he wasn't a total fool. He sensed she had begun an affair, told her to pack her bags, and demanded she join him at once. He was too good a marriage prospect to let get away, Helen decided. They married, but a year later when she wasn't under his watchful eye, Helen began another affair. This time it was with Tim, who eventually became her new hubby and happily remains so 21 years later.

> "Sam was extremely bitter. He had absolutely no idea what had gone wrong and probably doesn't to this day. I was never really honest with him about why I went into the relationship in the first place."

Dumped at Bedside

Cindy and Hal were in college when their romance bloomed and progressed from nightly sleepovers to more-convenient living in. The incentives to live together were those typically expressed by coeds. Such live-in relationships are based on superficial commitment and pragmatic benefits, such as sexual convenience, sharing finances, and companionship.

However, Hal mistakenly took the act of living together as a sign of true love. He thought that he and Cindy would eventually marry. But that day was not to come. Hal graduated, spent long hours working, and thought that Cindy was busy studying at the library.

Hal says:

> "Cindy was a very good and serious student. I never questioned her if there was anyone else until I found a man's watch in the apartment and a friend of hers

told me she was tired of seeing me get messed around. Cindy had been sleeping with another guy for two months, and I failed to see all of the signs I now know were there. I think I subconsciously knew something was going on, but I ignored it. There was a lot of security and safety in having this relationship. I think we should have formed a better foundation for our relationship before even thinking of moving in together. I would do it over differently today."

Hal shared his story in the hope that another guy wouldn't be fooled by another Cindy.

> **Love's Hot Line**
>
> Men, attached or otherwise, feel that the ultimate form of betrayal is sexual indiscretion. It is viewed as a form of rejection and cuts to the core of the male ego.

Men as Serial Live-Ins

Okay, Hal who got dumped at bedside says he would handle live-in love a little more cautiously these days. Would other guys? Some would and some wouldn't. The concrete and undeniable evidence is that men are more likely to form serial live-in relationships than women. These men seem to be propelled into new live-in arrangements by old needs and by new convictions that they are wiser this time around. When love ends, they aren't so sure.

Selecting a new live-in and establishing a sizeable list of successive relationships is habit forming. In the long run, these men ignore the problems and instead stack up chapters of unhappy endings. Their relationship perspective is flawed, creating risk for them and their female live-in partners.

Learning to Evaluate Risk

If you are a man at risk who is considering a live-in lover, try the following "Stop, Look, and Listen" exercise. It may keep you out of trouble.

1. Step back and take an honest look at your relationship.
2. Ask yourself what each of you would be getting out of the arrangement.
3. Define her motives. Ask pertinent, pointed questions if you have to.
4. Read between the lines. She may not spell it out for you.

> **Troubles A'Brewing ...**
>
> Serial live-in lovers aren't likely to commit to marriage. They have already established a preference for a less-committed relationship, and that attitude isn't likely to change.

5. Ask yourself, "Am I in a situation where I stand a good chance of being had?"
6. If it still isn't abundantly clear in which direction you should go, be sure to err on the side of caution.

Caution signs: This chapter is intended to forewarn men about the possible risks of living together. Without testing for and acknowledging what trouble may lie ahead, men are overlooking valid signs to tread cautiously.

> **The Least You Need to Know**
>
> ➤ Some men are better equipped than others to handle the perils of live-in love. The prudent man finds out which camp he belongs to.
>
> ➤ Passion is not a good substitute for sound thinking in matters of live-in love.
>
> ➤ Women who lack self-esteem and have obvious personal issues are likely to mean trouble.
>
> ➤ If you are a serial live-in lover, you should carefully examine the basis for your relationships.

Chapter 6

Playing It Safe

In This Chapter

➤ Assessing whether your love interest is marriage material or cohabiting material

➤ Taking the serendipity out of choosing a mate

➤ Learning whether living together screens out poor marriage risks

➤ Avoiding games you don't want to play

➤ Exploring how misunderstandings arise

Approximately 35 percent of the men and women born in the 1960s lived with someone before they reached the ripe old age of 25. With cohabiting so firmly entrenched in the dating cycle these days, you can hazard a pretty safe guess that this percentage will rise for individuals born in subsequent decades. At the very least, it will be a passing thought for nearly every couple, and a real consideration for countless others.

But let's back up just one minute. The person whom you actually pick as a partner is, in fact, influenced by what you want out of a relationship, says Johns Hopkins University researchers Robert Schoen and Robin M. Weinick.

Unfortunately, when you do your picking, it isn't always a conscious decision, or even one based on solid information. This chapter will help you understand the selection process and will introduce a number of safety measures to lessen the chance of a checkmate.

Part 1 ➤ *Thinking About Living Together*

Playing for Marriage

The majority of today's cohabitors think that they are on their way to matrimony—or they want to be. Here are the results of several studies about this issue:

➤ Three out of four people living together plan to marry their cohabiting partner.

➤ Fifty percent of couples in their 20s and 30s will live with their partner before marriage.

➤ Seventy-six percent of those canvassed in one study said they planned to marry their live-in partner; fewer than that followed through, however.

Consequently, there is a big future riding on the person you move-in with.

> **Troubles A'Brewing ...**
>
> A family and marriage expert at the University of Washington says couples who cohabit do so because they already think their relationship won't really work. Their attitude therefore becomes a self-fulfilling prophecy.

Theoretically Speaking

Theoretically, some experts say, cohabitation allows a couple to assess long-term compatibility, and it also contributes to the success of subsequent marriage with that partner. By living in a marriagelike setting, a couple has the perfect opportunity to evaluate and observe one another. Doing so should reveal pertinent information about habits, attributes, or less-desirable personality traits, and should also provide time for adaptation, these experts espouse. In fact, they argue that living together screens out nonmatrimonial couples.

Inaccurate or underreporting of the number of cohabiting couples, particularly short-term cohabitors, makes it difficult to conclusively deny this thesis. Nonetheless, there is plenty of data with enlightened chunks of reality to keep this matter from being a total guessing game.

Realistically Speaking

According to Marin Clarkberg, a Cornell University sociologist who has extensively researched live-in unions, there is little in the composite of studies to support the view that cohabitation is any more effective than traditional courtship methods in helping young couples evaluate their compatibility for marriage and reduce the risk of divorce.

Instead, Clarkberg asserts that the results suggest cohabitation may be a "slippery slope" to matrimony for men and women who might otherwise never have wed. Certainly the fact that there is a higher divorce rate among those who cohabit shakes loose the theoretical argument.

Avoiding the Slippery Slope

Caroline, at age 22, slid right into marriage while sitting at her mother's kitchen table during a Thanksgiving weekend. Like many young people her age, the decision to live together was not thoroughly planned nor was it motivated by thoughts of forming a permanent, lifetime relationship. Nonetheless, when discussion of her sister's wedding led to the suggestion of making it a double wedding, Caroline initially thought the idea was a good one. Spontaneously, she agreed to it.

Shortly thereafter she had some serious doubts:

> "It would have been easy to back out if we weren't living together. We thought we loved each other but never seriously gave marriage the kind of consideration we should have. My ex-husband never got down on his knees and said, 'Marry me. I love you more than life.'

> "Once the wedding invitations were out, I decided he was crazy and realized he had a serious drinking problem. I actually ran away. I was afraid of him. I didn't want to go through with the marriage, but I had my wedding gown and the invitations were already out. I couldn't call everyone on the guest list and tell them only my sister would be getting married. So I just thought, I'll get divorced later if I have to."

That's exactly what Caroline did one year after her nuptials.

> **Love Stats**
>
> David Popenoe and Barbara Dafoe Whitehead, authors of a report for the National Marriage Project, say, "There is no evidence that if you decide to cohabit before marriage you will have a stronger marriage than those who don't live together."

Playing with Finesse

If you are in the market for a lifetime matrimonial partner, studies show that you are most likely going to look for someone like yourself in terms of age, religion, race, and kinship ties. Additionally, many women will be on the lookout for men who have more education than they themselves do.

If you are picking a live-in partner, these characteristics will not be as important. Instead, you will be more interested in finding someone with the same level of education and job achievement.

That's the easy part. You know what you want—a marriage partner or a live-in. But is there a way to determine what your love interest wants?

If in doubt, check the following lists. Individuals who tend toward marriage versus those who tend only toward cohabitation exhibit very different characteristics. The distinguishing characteristics that may encourage a man or a woman to choose one lifestyle over the other—at least for the moment—are provided for you.

Cohabitor or Marriage Partner?

Take time to figure out if you or your partner look more like a cohabitor or a marriage candidate. Compare and contrast the information that follows.

Male Cohabitors ...

- Place greater emphasis on leisure time.
- Have a liberal view of sex.
- Enjoy a nontraditional lifestyle.
- Lack interest in kinship bonding with family.
- May still be in school.
- Are serial live-ins.
- Worry about divorce.

Male Marriage Partners ...

- Are looking for a marriage partner.
- Are settled financially.
- Have completed their education.
- Have steady work.
- Are financially independent.
- Place great importance on marriage.
- Come from a family in which the parents never divorced.

> **Love's Hot Line**
>
> Ladies, be wary of men who are totally focused on accumulating a lot of money. They are likely to delay forming any kind of union. Men, if you are looking for a marriage partner, be wary of women who are totally focused on accumulating money. Such a goal inhibits the formation of a marriage relationship, though not a live-in union.

Female Cohabitors ...

- Place great importance on career success.
- Highly value career and money.
- Are not seeking a matrimonial lifestyle.
- Show no interest in kinship bonding with family.
- May still be in school.
- Are serial live-ins.
- Have a family history of divorce.
- Think divorce is a real possibility.

Female Marriage Partners ...

➤ Enjoy close kinship ties to parents.
➤ Are connected to church and community.
➤ Attach greater importance to marriage.
➤ Feel ready to begin a family.
➤ Have traditional values.
➤ Have less-liberal sexual views.
➤ Are looking for a permanent partner.

Which Cohabitors Become Marriage Partners and Why

Sociologist Marin Clarkberg makes an important point: Live-in unions are dynamic and evolving, not static as earlier research suggested. Consequently, in order to gain insight into which cohabiting couples marry and why, Clarkberg says that live-in relationships should be thought of as a process.

Young cohabiting couples may not be thinking long-range. Rather they are more focused on what is happening to them at the moment, Clarkberg suggests. Graduate school and stopgap jobs delay their consideration of a permanent mate. Given their present circumstances, living together is more attractive than marriage. Thus, they elect to cohabit, the Cornell professor says.

Because live-in unions are not static, Clarkberg proposes factors that account for their conversion or transition into matrimony.

Factors That Promote Conversion to Marriage

If you know what you are looking for, you may be able to spot opportunities for moving your partner from live-in to spouse.

Three factors that encourage the conversion of a cohabiting relationship into a married one are ...

➤ Improvement in economic well-being.
➤ A belief that family life is "very important."
➤ A family history of having lived with both biological parents through high school.

Love Stats

Clarkberg believes that Catholics are more likely to convert their live-in unions to marriage. On the other hand, minorities with lower-than-average marriage rates tend not to do so.

A Factor That May Inhibit Conversion to Marriage

Penn State researchers Dr. Alan Booth and Susan L. Brown found that cohabiting couples with absolutely no intention of marrying have a history of failed unions. Furthermore, these couples argue more frequently and do not have an equitable division of labor.

Games You Don't Want to Play

If matrimony is your choice, there are several games that you should avoid at all costs. These games are played by live-ins. They produce impassable stalemates, lull partners into complacency, and turn lovers into adversaries.

Don't be fooled by the notion that "time is on your side." Studies show that the longer a couple lives together, the more entrenched the type of commitment associated with cohabiting, not marriage, becomes. Check out Chapter 3, "The Facts and Fictions of Living Together," for the difference in commitment styles.

If you find yourself a player in one of the following three games, there is a distinct possibility your relationship will never be converted into marriage.

The Cat and Mouse Chase

Neither Liz nor Hank is divorced from their respective spouses. Nevertheless, they have been living together for years. After Liz found out that her husband was gay, she started having an affair with Hank and admittedly became obsessed with him. It took five years to get him under her roof. Hank, afraid of marriage, has never been in a hurry to get a divorce; neither has Liz's husband. She is the perfect cover for his closet game, and he is a generous financial contributor to her household. "I suppose it could go on forever this way," acknowledges Liz.

Liz is happy enough but is not completely satisfied with, or fulfilled by, the in-house proximity to Hank. However, she isn't about to chance losing him by chasing Hank in the direction of her ultimate goal—marriage. Whether the chase speeds up over time is questionable. Whether Hank lets himself get caught is, in my opinion, pretty doubtful.

The last time I checked, they were still playing cat and mouse.

> **Love's Hot Line**
>
> Couples who engage in a live-in stalemate typically avoid confronting important issues, try to keep life quietly under control, and forego personal satisfaction. Think about it, or you may wake up one morning surprised and disillusioned.

Sweeping Issues Under the Rug

"I hope by the time I'm 80 I am finally remarried," Janice said. At the time she was in her 40s, had been living with Bradley for three years, and had dated him a decade before that. They had taken up residence in a home they purchased together and planned to share as Mr. and Mrs. Janice did remarry six years later. But it wasn't Bradley who walked down the aisle with her.

Both Janice and Bradley were proficient at sweeping things under the rug, ignoring important but troublesome issues; and this practice prevented them from exchanging vows. They had differing views on religion, family, and lifestyle. Bradley was a quintessential liberal, an intellectual with nonmaterialistic leanings. Janice enjoyed country club living, her traditional friends, and intellectual stimulation. To bridge the gap while living together, Janice attended religious services, social functions, and family gatherings alone.

Janice relates:

> "Living together allowed me not to face some of the problems in our relationship. If we were married, I would have expected Bradley to participate more in the relationship and be more of a couple.
>
> "We had a discussion about a week ago about being a couple and presenting yourself that way to the world. He had no idea what I meant and said it was the most superficial thing he had ever heard of. Attitudes like that make me disappointed in him. He senses that, and we both end up angry. Then there are days that I am glad I'm here, and it seems like everything will be fine. I know it sounds like an impossible situation, but I hate to admit that."

Eventually she did. Five years later, Janice lifted the rug and swept out the old dirt. When she did, she and Bradley sold the house and parted ways. It wasn't long after their parting that Janice met someone who shared the things she valued. They fell in love and married quickly.

Love Stats

Research shows that couples having the greatest propensity to cohabit for 18 months or longer are more likely to be low-income couples. The reverse is also true. Cohabiting couples having the greatest propensity to separate are high-income, traditional breadwinner/homemaker types. Of course, there are exceptions to every generalization.

Substituting Complacency for Answers

Bill and Donna have been together for 10 years now. I met them more than six years ago. She first moved into his home when she needed a place to stay. Because Bill was an older man and family friend, hanging out for a while at his place seemed safe. But Bill was very attractive to Donna, and they began a more intimate relationship. Donna, 27 at the time, very much wanted to have children and looked forward to marriage.

Bill, on the other hand, had some very specific issues. He wasn't sure he wanted children or marriage. In fact, he wasn't sure whether he was enough in love with Donna to make a commitment like marriage.

Donna, knowing all of this, said that what Bill needed was some professional help to get a better handle on what relationships were all about. Bill agreed to the plan, but he noted that loving someone so passionately that you would do anything for them isn't something you can learn. Things like that just happen.

Here's how he described Donna:

> "She has a sort of innocence about her. She is angelic. I love that part of her, but it doesn't excite me sexually. She isn't my ideal of a sexual woman. If she were a better sex partner, I think our relationship would be better. But I also believe there is chemistry between two people that needs to be there. I don't know if this is a relationship that I want for a lifetime."

So far it seems neither Bill nor Donna has found the answers they are looking for. However, each seems willing to allow time to provide the answers—unless someone catches Bill's eye first or Donna fears she can't beat her biological clock.

> **Troubles A'Brewing ...**
>
> Researchers for the nonpartisan, nonsectarian National Marriage Project said, "Contrary to popular wisdom, you do not learn to have better relationships from multiple failed cohabiting relationships. In fact, multiple live-in unions are a strong predictor for future failed relationships."

Misunderstandings: Innocent and Intentional

Many romantic plays have a plot based on simple misunderstandings between the characters. Alan L. Sillars from the University of Montana describes these misunderstandings as "the result of innocent assumptions, a lack of information, or a failure to communicate explicitly." Such miscommunications are akin to mix-ups in real life over when and where to meet for dinner or who is supposed to call to confirm the plans.

Misunderstandings in relationships are much more complex. Sillars notes that they are likely to be disagreements over the course of action to take and are compounded by each participant's inaccurate assumption of the other's thoughts, desires, and intentions.

> **Sweet Nothings**
>
> **Misunderstanding** is the lack of congruence, harmony, and agreement between one person's **metaperspective** (his or her estimate of the partner's perspective) and the other person's **direct perspective** (what the other person actually thinks). A woman may think that a man does not find her sexually appealing because he does nothing to promote intimacy when they are alone on a trip. However, the male partner is thinking that he wants to engage her in sex once the timing is more appropriate for him and he can focus solely on her. That may entail finishing pressing business matters first. The scenario could go the other way too. In either case, someone walks away feeling rejected. This demonstrates how easily a misunderstanding can occur when information is processed from one point of view.

How Misunderstandings Develop

If you get a grip on how misunderstandings develop, you will be better equipped to prevent them from creating problems in your relationship. Sillars, along with other experts, points to the factors listed next. Misunderstandings are likely to occur when ...

- ➤ There is a lack of shared communication.
- ➤ There is inadequate mutual knowledge.
- ➤ Tangled motivations cause individuals to process or ignore information.
- ➤ Information is ambiguous.
- ➤ One partner is dishonest.
- ➤ Trepidation prevents an individual from asking pertinent questions.
- ➤ A partner hides his/her real side.
- ➤ One person translates information incorrectly.

Now that you know how misunderstandings are hatched, you can more consciously try to avoid senseless ones.

How to Prevent Romantic Misunderstandings

To keep any of the preceding factors from creeping into your exchange with your love interest ...

- ➤ Don't jump to conclusions.
- ➤ Ask plenty of questions.
- ➤ Make sure you detect agreement between words and action.
- ➤ Do plenty of talking.
- ➤ Clarify doubt.
- ➤ Try to see things from the other's point of view.
- ➤ Be honest with your love interest and yourself.

These simple suggestions will promote understanding and work toward building a harmonious relationship.

Detecting the Lying Game

Learning how to detect lies can keep you from tumbling into a risky situation. You will always be ahead of the game if you can accurately tell whether you are getting truth or lies.

> **Love's Hot Line**
>
> Ladies, when you meet a new love interest, you need the information provided by author Dory Hollander, Ph.D., in her book *101 Lies Men Tell Women* (HarperCollins, 1995). According to her research, although both men and women lie to each other, men's lies produce more devastating consequences.
>
> For a more complete description on how to pick up on lies, also consult David J. Lieberman's *Never Be Lied to Again* (St. Martin's Press, 1998). In the meantime, listen carefully to the spoken word and pay attention to the messenger.

In his book *Never Be Lied to Again,* David J. Lieberman, Ph.D., provides numerous ways to detect lies. For starters, someone telling a lie ...

Chapter 6 — Playing It Safe

- Does not make eye contact.
- May get caught in contradictions.
- Has a false, fixed smile.
- Becomes defensive if questioned.
- Will not touch you during the process.
- Uses forced, mumbled speech.

All of the above are glaring signs of insincerity to the partner with eyes wide open.

Safest Calls

In certain situations, living together poses the least amount of risk to both participants. This fact came through loud and clear after I had conducted countless interviews with live-ins. Normally the safest calls include:

1. Moving in after becoming engaged and setting a firm wedding date or
2. Carefully electing to live long-term with someone as a postmarriage arrangement when financial considerations make marriage imprudent.

What Makes These Folks Special?

The best of live-in lovers have distinguishing characteristics that separate them from the rest of cohabiting couples. These individuals join their households after they develop …

- A relationship that has been nurtured over time.
- A love relationship that is based on trust and friendship.
- A mutual readiness to participate in an intimate, exclusive relationship.
- Respect for their partner and their relationship.
- A serious, marriagelike commitment to each other and their relationship.

These aren't magical ingredients, but they sure are essential if the object of your game is successful cohabiting.

> **Love's Hot Line**
>
> For the best premarital game plan, make sure your live-in period is short. You don't want to let any of those single ways take hold. They will conflict with married life later.

77

Part 1 ➤ *Thinking About Living Together*

The Best of Live-In Love

Here is the story of two young lovers, Jeffrey and Elizabeth.

Elizabeth was 25 when she started dating 22–year-old Jeffrey. Once they fell in love, Elizabeth knew she would have to give Jeffrey time to grow up before they got married. He was pressing hard during their three-year courtship for the two of them to live together, but Elizabeth said:

"No way. Not until we are engaged and have a wedding date."

Retelling the story of their relationship three years into his marriage, Jeffrey admits:

"Even though I wasn't ready to get married yet, I got engaged. I wanted to because I loved making Elizabeth happy. I wasn't quite ready to give up my freedom though."

Elizabeth, too, had trepidation about moving in. She knew her family disapproved. Still, she was firmly convinced that she and Jeffrey had something special and lasting. She truly thought that living together would help him grow up a little faster.

Jeffrey adds:

"The funny thing is, I am really a homebody and realized that shortly after Elizabeth moved in. We treated each other with respect and consideration."

Elizabeth and Jeffrey have been happily married for nearly 10 years now. Life couldn't possibly be better! The fact is, Elizabeth was a smart young woman, employed good judgement, had carefully assessed her relationship, and knew her guy.

To help you arrive at the same good decision making, be sure to read Part 2, "Coming Up with a Decision on Live-In Love," and Part 3, "Getting Ready to Move In." The chapters in these parts are designed to lead you meticulously through the decision-making process and give you the necessary tools to size up your relationship.

Chapter 6 ➤ *Playing It Safe*

> **The Least You Need to Know**
>
> ➤ If you move in, you could find yourself standing in front of the judge, mouthing "I do."
>
> ➤ Living together does not prepare you for marriage.
>
> ➤ Caution, thought, and observation are required before you fall in love and move in with Joe or Jane.
>
> ➤ Couples who progress from living together to marriage believe that family life is "very important."
>
> ➤ Some misunderstandings can be averted.
>
> ➤ Younger live-ins who have definite marriage plans also have the safest game plan.

Part 2

Coming Up with a Decision on Live-In Love

Should you move in? Should you ask your lover to move in? Should you say, "No thank you," "Never," "Not now, maybe later"? Part 2 will lead you step by step through this decision-making process and pose important ideas for your consideration. To ensure that you make the best possible decision for your love relationship, your present happiness, and your future satisfaction, don't rush through this part.

Coming up with your romantic motives and agenda, as well as those of your lover's, is the first step. Once you feel confident that you and your love interest know what you are hinging your expectations upon, you can more accurately size up what you might actually get out of cohabiting.

In order to complete the process and arrive at a comfortable decision, you must have a clear understanding of love, the impact that love has on a relationship, and the way in which love affects the outcome of moving in. Of course, you can't leave your knowledge of love on the doorstep but must use it to test whether love is what you and your would-be live-in share.

If love is present, it enhances the probability of partnership potential. However, without checking for the ingredients of core and sexual compatibility, which determine your ability to resolve your differences and communicate openly, you may be going through a revolving door.

Chapter 7

Devising Romantic Motives and Lovers' Agendas

In This Chapter

➤ Discovering the ins and outs of romantic decision-making

➤ Learning how to decide whether or not to move in

➤ Identifying your romantic motives

➤ Creating a realistic agenda for love

➤ Uncovering a lover's secret agenda

Love may be blind, but that doesn't mean it's okay to make a critical, romantic decision while blindfolded—unless you like surprise endings, that is. And don't argue that once under the passionate spell of love, decision-making is entirely out of the picture. Psychologist R. J. Sternberg would take issue with your assumption that love and sound decision-making don't go together. In his triangular theory of love, one of the three major components is the *decision/commitment component*. This component involves making two very important decisions. First, you must decide in the short-term that you actually love someone. Second, you must decide whether or not to make a long-term commitment to that love relationship.

These decisions are tricky. The mind and the body each pull for a say. Both need to be heard, but not to the exclusion of the other. If the chemical underpinnings of attraction form the basis for your love relationship, motives, and agenda, you're probably headed for trouble. If you rely solely on rational thinking to determine the pros and cons of a potential love interest, you are missing the most delectable parts.

Consequently, once attraction is in place, it is time to bring in the forces of rational evaluation. Sound decision-making could mean the difference between success or failure in a love relationship. This chapter will walk you through the decision-making process, take a critical look at your relationship motives, and finally assist you in outlining your romantic agenda. These are the first of many steps you should take before moving in or, if already there, staying or moving out.

Learning to Make Good Decisions

> **Love Stats**
>
> Studies show that individuals regret, in equal measure, both inaction and action. What tips the scale and makes the action choice even more regrettable is when inaction would have produced the same poor result.

When was the last time you took a trip only to find out that you didn't really like the vacation spot you had chosen? Have you ever bought a car and then realized it couldn't accommodate all of your gear? Do you know anyone who accepted a job who was later frustrated by his or her responsibilities?

What went wrong here? You or your pal did not make a good decision picking a place to vacation, a car to drive, or a job to take.

The purpose of decision-making is to determine a course of behavior in which you will be satisfied with the outcome. That's the only real measure of whether you have made a good decision.

Chances are if your decision does not prove harmful and if it satisfies a purpose, solves a problem, and comes with no regrets, you've done a decent job of employing good decision-making techniques.

Good Decision-Making Techniques

Techniques that head you in the direction of satisfactory decisions are based on the rational thought process. Follow this design for optimal success:

1. Gather sufficient information. If you need more facts, read, ask questions, and observe.
2. Select the pertinent information from what you have gathered.
3. Try to visualize the problem from different points of view.
4. Go for the best available option.

Don't be lazy and use only one of the four techniques. They are a package deal.

A Handy Tool, "Reversibility Thinking"

Reversibility thinking is something that should develop around age 11, writes Joan Borysenko, Ph.D., author of *A Woman's Book of Life*. As a handy mental tool, reversibility thinking allows an individual to see things from different points of view and then return to the original starting point.

This tool is particularly beneficial when making a decision that involves another individual, since we don't all think alike. That's an understatement when it comes to men and women—as plenty of research has proved. Gender does make a difference, so does age. If you can see an issue from your friend's, mother's, boss's, or child's point of view, add that view to your information pool and select the pertinent data. If you engage this process, you will increase your chances for a good decision.

> **Love's Hot Line**
>
> When communicating with the opposite sex, it is imperative to understand how gender can influence styles of communication. Sociolinguist Deborah Tannen presented this idea in her ground-breaking book *You Just Don't Understand* (Random House, 1991). If you need assistance in this area, see what Tannen has to say.

Applying Good Decision-Making to Love Relationships

Trying to make a good decision when you're in a love relationship is tough. Emotions enter into the picture big time, and right or wrong they influence your decisions.

Evidence shows that certain emotions, such as pleasure and fear, can benefit your decision-making. For instance, they could steer you away from perceived danger and toward imagined safety. Tests of human behavior also reveal that the decision-making process is influenced by sadness or anxiety. That's why it is best to avoid making important decisions when experiencing swings of emotion. But we all know that refraining from making big decisions is hard to do, because romantic involvements are full of emotional ups and downs.

The challenge, therefore, is to keep a lid on emotions that cloud your judgement when you are trying to make prudent decisions in the face of love.

Decision-Making for Two

According to some experts, decision-making between two individuals who are not romantically linked looks like this:

> Giving Information + Receiving Information = Communication That Determines the Decision

Decision-making between two individuals who *are* romantically linked looks like this:

Giving Information + Receiving Information = Implies a Power Struggle That Is Resolved by the Decision to Exchange Something for Something

Implications of Romantic Partnership Decisions

Decision-making in a romantic partnership is continual and deals with important issues such as boundaries, limitations, and codes of behavior. In case you don't get it, these issues are the concrete ones of daily life: how money is spent, who cooks, whether you go to his or her family's house for dinner, whether you take a vacation alone, whether a couch has to be mutually agreed upon, who gets a night out alone, what kind of sex you engage in, if you live together, when you might marry, and whether you take on the responsibility of kids.

Sociologists argue that, in the past, this process was simpler and less fraught with a power struggle because gender roles were more specific and more well-defined. To arrive at a decision these days requires more time for bargaining.

Deciding on Romantic Motives

So far you have learned how to make a decision, you understand the implications of joint decision-making, and you are aware that there is a "decision/commitment component" to love. You are now ready to proceed with the subject of romantic motives.

Motives are inner drives or impulses that cause you to act in a certain way. Human motivations that underline many of our actions include the need to find social approval, satisfy sexual desire, have companionship, and share love.

If you are honest and do some real soul-searching, you should be able to come up with a list of your past, present, and future romantic motives. Once you have written these motives down in black-and-white, you

> **Troubles A'Brewing ...**
>
> If we agree that cohabiting relationships are less defined by conventional gender roles than marriage relationships, we easily conclude that decision-making among live-in couples is potentially more difficult. Watch out for major power struggles that might arise.

> **Love Stats**
>
> Psychology professor Sharon S. Brehm wrote that the desire for loyal, passionate love is motivated by more than the desire to procreate or maintain efficient pair-bonding. "... the function of passionate love is that this intense combination of imagination and emotion serves to motivate human beings to construct" and create a better world.

can begin to assess whether your current list represents good decision-making and whether it will help you hook up with a desirable love interest.

Listing Your Romantic Motives

To help you jump into this exercise on romantic motives, sample motives appear in the three columns. Remember, your own motives should reflect those inner drives and impulses that prompt your actions in a romantic situation or in a love relationship.

Previous Motives	Current Motives	Future Motives
Desire for a sex partner	Need for a meal ticket	Want to marry
1.		
2.		
3.		
4.		
5.		

Troubles A'Brewing ...

In the opinion of some theorists, a difficulty or an inability in achieving a goal makes the goal more attractive. If this opinion is true, it spells trouble for the lover who is in pursuit of an unobtainable love interest.

What Constitutes a Good or a Bad Romantic Motive?

If your romantic motives meet all of the requirements in the following list, chances are you're on the side of all that is good. Check the appropriate items that you agree with.

My motives:

- ❏ Serve my intermediate or ultimate needs and goals.
- ❏ Benefit me but not at the expense of my love interest.
- ❏ Have a clear-cut purpose.
- ❏ Send my intended message.
- ❏ Are not ambiguous.
- ❏ Are honest not deceitful.
- ❏ Reflect the best of who I am.
- ❏ Prompt action that will benefit my love relationship.
- ❏ Are born out of my strengths and not my weaknesses.
- ❏ Are genuine and sincere.

Once you have established your motives, you are ready to create your Love Agenda.

The Art of Agenda Making

Agendas are "lists of things to get done" in an orderly, logical, businesslike sequence. In a romantic relationship, they can be quite useful. They curb part of the blind, directionless emotion and plug in a valuable rational thought process that puts order into the development of a love relationship.

In other words, agendas are …

- ➤ Pragmatic roadmaps.
- ➤ Realistic timetables.
- ➤ Paths for finding and cultivating romance.

Managing Love's Growth

Taken right out of the annals of *Association Management* are three steps to follow in creating your agenda. All we've done is substitute love for business.

1. How you proceed should be determined in a way that leads to the "desired" outcome with "obvious" progress along the way.

> **Love's Hot Line**
>
> I won't deny that some are luckier in love than others. And, yes, a certain portion of luck is beyond human control. However, good decision-making, stepping into sound, reality-based love relationships, and putting your best foot forward all reduce the element of luck.

2. Your policies and procedures should ensure "effective" progress and should develop interest and "willing participation" in others.
3. Your actions should be such that they "entice" the opposing party into your camp.

When you take out the business connotation and add in the romantic element, you get the prime atmosphere for *relationship negotiation*.

The Best Romantic Agendas from Start to Finish

Everyone must create his or her own agenda. The one that follows is a good example of orderly planning. Going from step A to B to C, and so forth, requires astute, sound decision-making that only you can supply.

> **Sweet Nothings**
>
> The act of **relationship negotiation** means to arrange mutually satisfying terms of a transaction or contract by using verbal communication. Think of it as doing business and trading terms.

Agenda for Finding a Lovemate	
January	Get my act together and my self-esteem in peak form. (Motive: to attract someone of the opposite sex)
February	Attend parties and new events with friends. (Motive: to meet someone new and get myself out there)
February 15	Call Susie and have her set me up with her cousin. (Motive: to find someone interesting. If her cousin isn't the one, he/she may have friends that are interesting.)
March	Invite love potential for dinner at home. (Motive: to have a cozy place to spend the evening and get to know each other)
Late March	Suggest that each of us plan a surprise afternoon or evening. (Motive: to see whether this potential love interest has paid attention to what I might like to do and is creative, or whether this person is just plain boring)
June	Invite love interest to a family function. (Motive: to take the opportunity to evaluate where the relationship might be headed and find out if we have similar agendas)
July	Spend time alone with yourself to think. (Motive: to determine whether this relationship has a chance at the future I desire. If not, decide on my course of action.)
August	Go on a romantic picnic. (Motive: to set the stage for a serious conversation to see if we are on the same track)

continues

continued

Agenda for Finding a Lovemate	
October	Suggest a spring break for two. (Motive: to see if thinking is still long-range)
December 31	Stay sober on New Year's Eve. (Motive: to take advantage of the perfect time to get a commitment for the new year)

Agenda Tips

Remember that the preceding agenda is an "ideal" agenda, not necessarily a real agenda.

When you make your own agenda, be particularly realistic about your time line. You can't rush your agenda along if you have a long-term goal in mind. Furthermore, never try to complete an agenda that isn't working. You must be able to alter, scrap, or restart your agenda depending on how things go.

However, the title of your agenda should not be altered. Otherwise you will be too easily sidetracked from your original purpose. In the case of romantic involvements, you might label your agenda as a romantic agenda for dating around, an agenda for finding the perfect companion, or an agenda for finding a lifetime mate.

What is absolutely essential is that if you become interested in someone, the two of you share the same agenda.

Uncovering Your Partner's Agenda

Uncovering a love interest's motives or agenda may be more difficult for women than it is for men. However, if you are a woman, this difficulty doesn't excuse you from trying to detect whether there is something hiding in the shadows when he asks you to move in. The following are reasons why women find it harder to discern a hidden agenda:

1. Men lie more than women. I'm not saying that women don't lie. Dory Hollander, Ph.D., author of *101 Lies Men Tell Women,* says there is an epidemic of lying in America these days. One out of every five people tells at least one lie a day. However, Hollander, who has worked with *many* men who lie to women, says, "Some men even boasted about their ability to fool the women in their lives, or their uncanny, espionage-like ability to keep their intentions secret."

2. Men seem to think they already have a handle on a woman's agenda—marriage. They lie to keep from getting trapped into it.

3. Women trust too easily, says Hollander. She believes that trust isn't an automatic between men and women; trust has to be earned. If skepticism is considered out

of place in a new romantic relationship, Hollander says you are setting yourself up for disappointment.

4. We all commit lies by default or by the omission of pertinent information.

To avoid being accused of male-bashing here, let me turn the tables and tell you about a woman who was guilty of lies of omission. Sally had been relatively happily married. But after her rich husband fell for his nurse, everything changed. Once the divorce was final, Sally started a relationship with a really nice guy who gave her a ring. Even though they both talked of love and she knew that he considered the ring an engagement ring, she was careful never to tell her beau she would marry him. In fact, the real truth was that she had absolutely no intention of ever becoming his wife. She was enjoying his company, benefiting by his affection, and going along for the ride.

> **Troubles A'Brewing ...**
>
> Experts on the subject of male honesty say it's time women develop a greater awareness that men lie. Evidently their studies show that men are intentionally sending out more incorrect information to women than most men are willing to acknowledge.

Is Moving In on Your Agenda?

Should you move in, move out, or move on? This question doesn't have a quick yes or no answer, nor should you want to come up with an answer just yet.

Try to be patient. You are moving toward that decision faster than you realize. Your thinking still needs a little more organizing, and perhaps your motives and agenda need a bit more refining. You probably won't be ready to make a good decision by the end of this chapter. There is much information yet to gather. Try to wait until the last word in this book. Only then will you have all the information you need to use the good decision-making tools outlined for you in the beginning of the chapter.

> **Love's Hot Line**
>
> Guys, it is happening more and more. You are being used for sex, companionship, healing, and support. Don't let your ego get in the way of this important revelation!

Nonetheless, you *are* ready to begin creating your own personal workbook to live-in love. When the question arises, "Should cohabiting be on my agenda?" all you will have to do is open this book for an answer. Begin filling in the blank spaces when you feel comfortable that you have the right answers.

91

Part 2 ➤ *Coming Up with a Decision on Live-In Love*

Love's Hot Line

Until you are certain about the motives and agendas on both sides of the fence, avoid moving in, no matter what. Drop the issue completely if the two of you do not agree about what moving in means. Poor motives for moving in are unrequited love, love on the rebound, loneliness, fear of finding a partner, horniness, desperation, or the need to nurture. Look for better reasons, and don't move in until you find some.

My Personal Workbook to Live-In Love
by (fill in your name) _____

Section 1: My Predisposition to Live-In Love

Fill in the blanks.

1. Live-in love to me is a good way to get to know someone intimately _____, a satisfactory way to have a monogamous, short-term relationship _____, a substitute for marriage, _____ a prelude to marriage _____. (Check the appropriate answers.)

2. Live-in love fits my ultimate goal which is to _____
   _____.
   (Provide at least one sentence.)

3. I plan to live with someone before we marry. _____ (Answer yes or no.)

Section 2: Given My Present Relationship

1. Do I have sufficient information to make a decision? _____ (Answer yes, no, or maybe.)

2. My motives for moving in are ... (Give several.) _____
   _____
   _____
   _____
   _____

3. I should scratch from my list the following motives: _____,
   _____, _____ and add these motives:
   _____, _____, _____.

Chapter 7 ➤ *Devising Romantic Motives and Lovers' Agendas*

4. My personal agenda looks like this: (Outline your agenda chronologically.)
   _____
   _____
   _____
   _____
   _____

5. Here is what I have to gain if I move in: (List several things.)
   _____
   _____
   _____
   _____
   _____

6. Here is what I have to lose if I move in: (List several things.)
   _____
   _____
   _____
   _____
   _____

7. Why living together is mutually advantageous: (Come up with two reasons.)
   _____
   _____

Section 3: What I Still Need to Know
   1. Do we share the same long-term relationship goals? _____ (Yes/No)
   2. Are we equally committed to the relationship? _____ (Yes/No)
   3. Do I know this person well enough to move in with him or her? _____ (Yes/No)
   4. I still need to learn the following about my love interest: (List at least four things.)
      _____
      _____
      _____
      _____

Section 4: Precautions I Have Taken
   1. I have pretested our compatibility _____, the odds for success _____, preempted any foreseeable disasters _____, sized up our relationship _____, made realistic living arrangements _____, created a solid foundation _____, and formed realistic expectations _____. (Place a check mark after each completed suggestion.)

continues

continued

2. We have resolved important relationship issues _____. (Yes or no.)
3. The preparations I have made to protect myself should the arrangement not work out are … (Clearly specify.)

_____

_____

_____

Section 5: What We Still Need to Do
(Answer all questions yes or no.)

1. Create living arrangements that are satisfactory to both of us. _____
2. Develop a live-in etiquette. _____
3. Spell out what "significant other" means to us. _____
4. Make our expectations clear. _____
5. Develop good communication tools. _____
6. Promise to advise the other party if our agendas change. _____
7. Devise a plan should we separate. _____
8. Other: _____

Section 6: My Latest Agenda
(Take each step and complete it thoroughly.)

1. Determine my ultimate goal.
2. Develop a timetable.
3. Determine motives and appropriate actions.
4. Evaluate my motives in accordance with what constitutes good and bad motives.
5. Go into action.

This chapter gave you a lot of information about decision making and showed you how to begin evaluating your decision to move in. Chapter 8, "Sizing Up Potential Gains or Losses," will add more information and show you how to determine your potential gains or losses should you decide on live-in love.

Chapter 7 ➤ *Devising Romantic Motives and Lovers' Agendas*

> **The Least You Need to Know**
>
> ➤ Good decision-making requires sufficient information and objective thinking.
>
> ➤ Inherent within the decision-making process for romantic couples is a power struggle.
>
> ➤ Romantic motives and agendas should be carefully planned to maximize their effectiveness.
>
> ➤ The right or wrong motives and subsequent action can turn your love interest on or off.
>
> ➤ It is worth taking your time to carefully consider whether moving in will help or hurt your long-term chances of love and happiness.

Chapter 8

Sizing Up Potential Gains or Losses

In This Chapter

➤ Learning to measure your live-in opportunity

➤ Qualifiers of bona fide, blue-ribbon opportunities

➤ Getting a glimpse of opportune moments

➤ Revealing the dark side of opportunity

➤ Tools for rethinking "golden opportunities"

Reading about the experiences of others who have moved in together gives you insight into live-in love. From others' experiences, you can learn about the potential gains and losses of this living arrangement. The general population statistics have provided the overall odds of success, but there is no substitute for figuring out your own personal scoreboard. So get out your pencils and be prepared to go to work.

You don't have to be a statistician or a fortune teller to come up with a pretty accurate glance at your future. What you do have to be is honest, open-minded, inquisitive, and astute in determining whether or not moving in provides a window of opportunity.

Creating a Menu of Opportunity

In certain circumstances, living together provides the only path of opportunity to achieve your goals. However, this choice by no means diminishes the seriousness of

> **Love's Hot Line**
>
> Hippocrates may not have been addressing lovers when he wrote, "Life is short, the art long, opportunity fleeting, experience treacherous, judgement difficult," but how appropriately wise his words are for the occasion.

the information already provided in earlier chapters. Before you decide that living together presents a bona fide opportunity for you, complete this chapter and review it if necessary.

According to my conversations with live-ins and my review of other studies, the following are genuine opportunities—if the circumstances prove to be just right:

1. Living together is the only road to matrimony.
2. Living together is an alternative to marriage.
3. Living together is a transition into marriage.

What is your selection? Choose either 1, 2, or 3.

Your selection _____

Selection other than one from the list _____

Note: If your choice is not one from the list, it may not be an appropriate opportunity.

Opportunity Qualifiers

How do you know whether the opportunity knocking at your door is the real thing? See how your opportunity stacks up against these points.

- **Does the proposed opportunity fit your purpose well?** For example, you might ask yourself whether moving in enhances the prospect for a long-term, committed relationship, if that's what you want. Be specific, however, and back up your answer.

- **Is this opportunity well-timed?** For example, you might ask yourself if living together fits your time frame or if this opportunity would prevent you from taking advantage of something else that is pressing on your agenda. Again, back up your answer.

- **Will taking advantage of this opportunity further your goal?** For example, you are in love with a man or a woman who refuses to tie the knot unless you live together first, and marriage is the title of your agenda. Would moving in put you closer to getting hitched? Again, back up your answer, please.

- **Are the circumstances favorable?** For example, you may want to ask yourself whether you are at the stage in your relationship that warrants making this commitment, whether moving in is a sign of your strengths or weaknesses (or any other considerations that seem appropriate). Once you answer, provide some sound reasoning to back up your answer.

➤ **Does the opportunity reflect commitment?** If moving in is a casual sort of arrangement, it may not qualify as a bona fide opportunity. A test of something more enduring is whether or not it holds any promise or pledge for future action. That, says psychologist Ann L. Weber of the University of North Carolina, is what commitment means.

Are You Astute Enough to Evaluate an Opportunity?

Alicia thought she was worldly wise when it came to men. After all, by age 30 she had already experienced marriage, divorce, and a long-term affair. Nonetheless, she overestimated her ability to evaluate bona fide opportunities and to handle her love relationship with Torrance, a wealthy man recently widowed.

After five months of dating, he asked her to move in. She agreed, if they became engaged. Their engagement was an informal sort of private agreement. He had some family business to clean up first, he said, and made it clear he was not interested in kids and there was to be no interfering with his business.

When they finally did marry, he insisted it be kept secret for at least a month. When the cat was out of the bag, her life was hell. His grown kids refused to talk to Alicia. She lamented:

> "I thought we would be a happy family and that I would be given the opportunity to enjoy their babies, since I would never have my own."

As if that weren't bad enough, Torrance turned into a very negative guy—not the prince she imagined. As for Alicia, her duties were to cook, clean, work, keep him sexually satisfied, and show up at the country club to socialize with his pals 30 years her senior. She got the raw end of the divorce, too!

An Exercise in Opportunity

Write down your opportunity and measure it against the following qualifiers:

Your opportunity _____

Does it fit your purpose? (Yes/No) How? _____

Is it well-timed? (Yes/No) Why? _____

> **Troubles A'Brewing ...**
>
> Psychologist Ann L. Weber of the University of North Carolina wrote in her paper on coping with nonmarital breakups, "We are social creatures; we need each other, our presence, the possibility of closeness. Relationships confer unique benefits on individuals, the promise of which can outweigh the liabilities of even risky liaisons."

Part 2 ➤ *Coming Up with a Decision on Live-In Love*

Will it further your goal? (Yes/No) Explain. _____
_____

Are circumstances favorable? (Yes/No) Why? _____

Are there signs of a commitment? (Yes/No) What are they? _____
_____

If the preceding exercise provides a preponderance of evidence against qualifying as a bona fide opportunity, you may have to reconsider your decision. My recommendation is, don't delay!

Opportune Moments

Just so there is no confusion over what genuine opportunities look like, here are two for you to consider.

> **Love's Hot Line**
>
> Heed the words of philosopher Francis Bacon: "A wise man will make more opportunities than he finds." And forget the saying "Opportunity knocks but once in a lifetime."

Liza and Tim's Opportune Moment

Liza in her early 30s and Tim in his late 30s had each been married. When they met, the attraction was fast, furious, and intense on both an emotional and a physical level. Liza, a very logical gal, was convinced by the nature of their avowed love relationship that it would last and had no doubt whatsoever that eventually they would marry. However, she recognized that Tim needed time to work through the aftermath of his divorce, and she wanted to make sure her boys could accept Tim.

Tim had no problem with the notion of remarriage. What he wanted to make sure of was that she was the right woman, that he could maintain a sound, working relationship with his children, and that he could create a family unit with Liza and her children.

Liza admitted ...

> "It was emotionally dangerous turning myself and the kids over to Tim. But I knew that he was a man of great integrity who took his responsibilities seriously. I also didn't want to take the chance of losing what we had. It was too valuable. I knew that our relationship was more important to him than almost anything. He always put my kids first and even signed them up for a prepaid college program. I also knew I would be strong enough to get out and take care of myself. By the time I moved in, I wasn't walking around blindly in love."

Liza took the opportunity Tim provided, but not at the expense of her better judgment or values as many opportunists do.

Kathy and Tom's Opportune Moment

Kathy consciously and pragmatically planned to use moving in with Tom as a compatibility test for marriage. Both had already been there and done that before. Besides, she had been divorced for five years and was ready to remarry. Although she was in love with Tom, she knew that living with him probably wouldn't be easy. However, she was willing to accept him, faults and all, if living together did not prove too troublesome.

> **Sweet Nothings**
>
> An **opportunist** according to *Webster's* is "one who endeavors to turn circumstances to his advantage." The problem is that opportunists may seize the opportunity without regard to basic values or subsequent consequences.

Tom did not try to fool her. He told her:

"I am not a good guy to be married to."

Kathy says:

"I knew I would have to be realistic. Living with him was difficult. Had we not gone through much of this before we got married, I would have been devastated and our marriage most likely would have failed. Sharing a home with Tom did not increase my influence over Tom the way I thought it would. I could not change the fact that he was headstrong and would accept things one way—his.

"It is true that if I were writing a love story, I wouldn't write it this way. I was looking for companionship, love, and financial security. I would be lying if I didn't say that was important. I had struggled going to school and getting a job. Working was fine, but it looked better when it was a secondary source of revenue."

After living with Tom, Kathy said:

"There were definitely pros and cons about marrying Tom, but I looked at the total package. Some of the things that were missing were not that significant to me. I was really into maintaining my own independence, so the fact that he wanted to spend a lot of time on his own was not a problem.

"When Tom said to me one day, 'Let's get married in a month,' I was prepared to say yes. I had come to terms with myself about the kind of marriage I was getting into. There was absolutely no doubt that things would have to be done his way. He made me promise that I could live with that. The only thing I made him promise was that he would be faithful. That was the one thing I could not

Part 2 ➤ *Coming Up with a Decision on Live-In Love*

tolerate. We agreed on financial arrangements and negotiated a solid picture of a future for both of us.

"I got just about what I bargained for and agreed I could live with," Kathy said, after nearly 20 years of marriage.

Kathy borders on the side of opportunism. She took a less than ideal live-in and marriage package and turned them around to fit her most pressing need and desire—a permanent partner.

The Underside of Opportunity

Love relationships can be hard to handle when you get something entirely different from what you bargained for. Breaking up, though, is even harder; it's tough on everyone. In my book *The Complete Idiot's Guide to Handling a Breakup* (Alpha Books, 1999), I emphasized that breaking up is no one's fault. It is never easy. Someone is always going to feel bad and look bad. When you add in the element of live-in unions, there is an extra measure of grief, pain, stress, rejection, and embarrassment, as well as a chorus of "I told you so."

> **Love Stats**
>
> A study of 500 individuals by human nature scientist Dr. Dorothy Tennov found that love was a strong activator of pleasure, perhaps even the strongest feeling humans experience. At the same time, a lover fluctuates between fear and torment caused by the uncertainty of reciprocated love. No wonder nearly all of the participants in her study believed "passionate love" was a "bittersweet experience."

Getting Out of a Live-In Relationship

The dark side of a live-in relationship is getting out of it. Here are a few reasons why breaking up can become awfully bleak:

> **Sweet Nothings**
>
> **Unrequited love** is love that is not reciprocated by a would-be lover. This very often engenders feelings of rejection, devastating pain, and exaggerated anger.

➤ Getting out of a live-in relationship can be difficult. In fact, a man who had experienced cohabiting and marriage told me that getting out of his live-in union was harder than getting his divorce. He wasn't the first person to say this.

➤ Breaking up can play havoc on children's emotional and physical well-being, even if the participants go their separate ways amicably.

➤ When you move in with someone, your actions are full of love, hope, and optimism. When you move out, *unrequited love* unleashes anger and causes pain.

> It is too easy to slip-slide into a marriage that should have never taken place.

> Dismantling a household and separating finances can be a major war or nightmare.

Dissolving a live-in relationship presents an explosive cluster of elements. Recognizing this can help defuse the potential for anger.

When Moving Out Turns Ugly and Spiteful

Sandra and Henry's tale tops the list of bad breakups. Wait until you get to the end to see if you can up this one.

After three years of living together in relative peace, harmony, and love, Sandra, in her early 20s, decided Henry, in his early 30s, was never going to get married.

Concluding a major fight, he gave Sandra two weeks to get out of his house and demanded that she leave behind even such inexpensive items as a potpourri burner he had given her. Sandra left with her clothes and a minimum of household items. She felt that she was entitled to much more and that she should have been compensated for the wallpaper and curtains she purchased for the house.

When Henry was out of town several weeks later, Sandra rented a truck and her friends helped her remove items from the house that she considered rightfully hers. Henry didn't see it that way. He had always been generous about buying her personal gifts and thought she walked out with plenty as it was. He became so furious over the missing grandfather clock that he filed criminal charges against her.

However, Sandra was not going to let him get away with this legal charade for nothing. Nearly two years later, she wrote his boss, reported some business shenanigans of Henry's, and got him fired from a six-figure job.

By the way, Sandra's original assessment was right. Ten years later, Henry still has not married any of his three subsequent live-in lovers.

Testing for Potential Losses

Rather than rely on disaster relief, calculate the potential for losses before you move in. Try this test. Put an "X" in the column that best reflects your answer.

Love's Hot Line

To gamble is to play a game by placing a bet. Gambling implies the chance of losing by poorly playing or reading the odds. Losing in this way is to squander or waste resources.

Part 2 ➤ *Coming Up with a Decision on Live-In Love*

Yes	No	Partially	
❏	❏	❏	I feel comfortable and confident with my decision to move in.
❏	❏	❏	I will be able to deal with the likely emotions if this arrangement fails.
❏	❏	❏	I know my partner well enough that I do not anticipate any surprises.
❏	❏	❏	I have consulted others on how to protect myself and my financial interests.
❏	❏	❏	This is definitely a genuine love relationship.
❏	❏	❏	This is an equitable partnership.
❏	❏	❏	There are pluses for both of us in choosing to live together.
❏	❏	❏	Our agendas and motives are compatible.
❏	❏	❏	I have dealt with any and all doubts.
❏	❏	❏	My intended live-in and I are committed partners.
❏	❏	❏	My intended live-in and I are compatible.
❏	❏	❏	We have discussed living together, finances, and household arrangements.
❏	❏	❏	We have compromised equally over issues where there was a difference of opinion.
❏	❏	❏	We share a set of expectations.
❏	❏	❏	We have resolved major differences.
❏	❏	❏	I have shed my rose-colored glasses.
____	____	____	**Total for each column**

Important notice: If you are interested in minimizing your losses, all of your X marks should be in the Yes column. Even one stray line could signal the potential for a loss.

Minimizing Potential Losses

You can eliminate the potential for loss in live-in relationships by taking positive action:

- ➤ Choose your partner wisely.
- ➤ Test your live-in preparedness.
- ➤ Draw up plans for preempting disaster.
- ➤ Methodically rate your partner's potential.
- ➤ Draw up solid floor plans.
- ➤ Compare agendas.
- ➤ Resolve unsettled issues.
- ➤ Prevent *regret*.

The remaining three chapters of Part 2, "Coming Up with a Decision on Live-In Love," and the five chapters in Part 3, "Getting Ready to Move In," will examine the issues in this list and help you take care of them. Stay tuned.

Tools for Rethinking a "Golden Opportunity"

The three problem-solving tools provided in this section are a bonus offering. Try all of them. They will enhance your ability to look at an opportunity more thoroughly and thoughtfully from different angles. A mastery of these tools ought to be reflected in your gains and losses in the face of love.

When in doubt, do one or all of the following:

1. Make an old-fashioned list of pros and cons.
2. Ask an objective but caring observer.
3. Diagram the issue.

There is a handy way to do number 3, called *webbing*. Start with one large circle and add onto it. An example of a webbed love question that explores options and issues is presented for you. There is another web waiting for you to fill in. What you do is start with one question or one topic and keep expanding it so that you are able to see all of the issues, questions, or possibilities that are related to it.

> **Love's Hot Line**
>
> "... the only way to know is to have lived and loved and cursed and floundered and enjoyed and suffered. ... I only regret, in my chilled age, certain occasions and possibilities I didn't embrace."
>
> —Henry James, writer

> **Sweet Nothings**
>
> "Sorrow or remorse over something that has happened, especially over something that one has done or left undone" is **regret**, according to *Webster's*.

Part 2 ➤ *Coming Up with a Decision on Live-In Love*

An example:

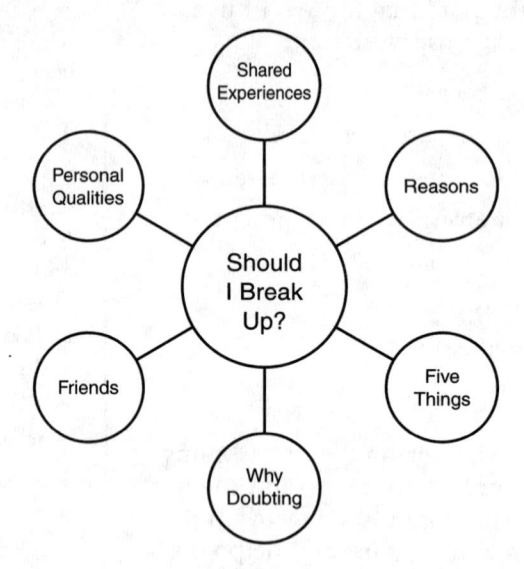

- Shared Experiences
- Reasons
- Five Things
- Why Doubting
- Friends
- Personal Qualities

Center: **Should I Break Up?**

Fill in this one:

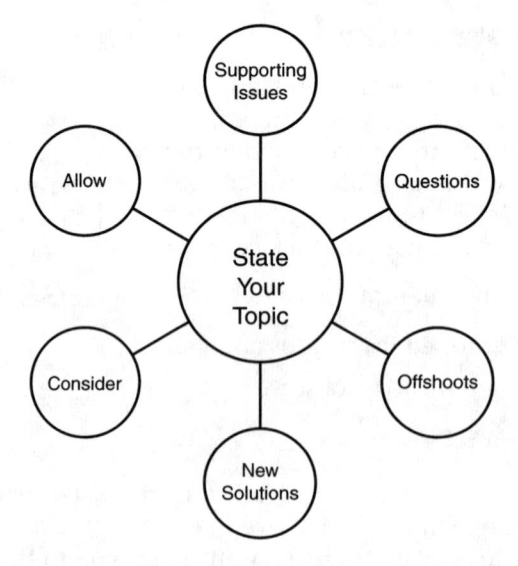

- Supporting Issues
- Questions
- Offshoots
- New Solutions
- Consider
- Allow

Center: **State Your Topic**

106

Chapter 8 ➤ *Sizing Up Potential Gains or Losses*

> **The Least You Need to Know**
>
> ➤ Every love interest does not represent an equally good opportunity.
>
> ➤ A bona fide opportunity reduces the losses incurred by live-in love.
>
> ➤ Real opportunities have real future possibilities for success.
>
> ➤ Getting out of a live-in relationship can be more difficult than breaking up a marital or nonmarital relationship.
>
> ➤ You have the power to lessen the losses and improve the gains from live-in unions.

Chapter 9

The Power of Love

In This Chapter

- ➤ What is this thing called love?
- ➤ How love begins and ends
- ➤ How love influences behavior
- ➤ When Cupid shoots a crooked arrow
- ➤ What are some theories of love?

The power of love has moved mountains, crumbled empires, and bestowed hope on the forsaken. This chapter explains the power of this strongest of human emotions and gives you a useful measure with which to evaluate your relationship. Once you see how powerful love can be, you will understand why its presence might improve a romantic outcome and encourage you to take up the offer of moving in. On the other hand, the absence of love may cause you to decline the invitation.

Your immediate goal, however, is to learn as much as you can about this thing called love.

Love, the Big Motivator

Love is so overpowering and such a strong motivational force that it has caused a king to abdicate his throne and a grieving widower to build one of the Seven Wonders of the World.

Part 2 ➤ *Coming Up with a Decision on Live-In Love*

Edward VIII gave up his right to the British throne in order to marry the American divorcée Wallis Simpson in 1937, and the Taj Mahal in India was built by the grief-stricken Shah-Jahan as a tomb for his 39-year-old wife, Mumtaz, who died during the birth of their fourteenth child.

Love, the powerful motivator of humans, is not restricted to the famous or the past. John Gray, Ph.D., the *Mars and Venus* expert, said, "When a man loves a woman, his primary goal is to make her happy." Now that's a force any woman would like to unleash.

> **Love Stats**
>
> Cupid, a figure in Roman mythology, is considered the counterpart of Eros, the Greek god of love. Originally Cupid was depicted as a young man. Today this son of Venus and Mercury is envisioned as a winged cherub.

Uncovering Cupid's Secrets

Love begins with a basic attraction. Much evidence today ties that attraction to the brain and the release of natural chemical substances in the body. The first stage of attraction is infatuation. It has a high mortality rate. Seventy-five percent of couples who are infatuated with one another do not end up having a lasting relationship.

Those experts who believe in the biological basis of love attribute much of this quick-paced progression to the evolutionary process of reproduction. If a relationship does not become substantial within an 18-month period, the biological and chemical basis for the attachment normally fizzles out.

Nonetheless, a sexual attraction between persons may initiate or ignite the growth of a deeper, enduring, and *companionate love* style over time. This kind of love can be nurtured to the stage in which it encompasses more-mature signs of love such as ...

> **Sweet Nothings**
>
> **Companionate love** is what psychologists term "mature love," which embodies feelings of affection, intimacy, and attachment to individuals with whom our lives are intricately interwoven.

➤ Compassion.
➤ Appreciation.
➤ Concern.
➤ Passion.
➤ Genuine caring for one's partner.

Growing Into Love

For attraction, infatuation, and attachment between two individuals to grow into love, the growth cycle of rapport, self-disclosure, mutual dependence, and intimacy identified by sociologist Ira Reiss must occur repeatedly. The diagram that follows shows the continuous progression of this cycle.

> **Rapport** means the development of a harmonious relationship that provides comfort and pleasure to both participants.

> **Self-disclosure** is the exchange of personal information about oneself.

> **Mutual dependence** is the practice of mutually benefiting one another through an exchange of actions and emotions.

> **Intimacy** is familiarity with each other's private emotional and physical being.

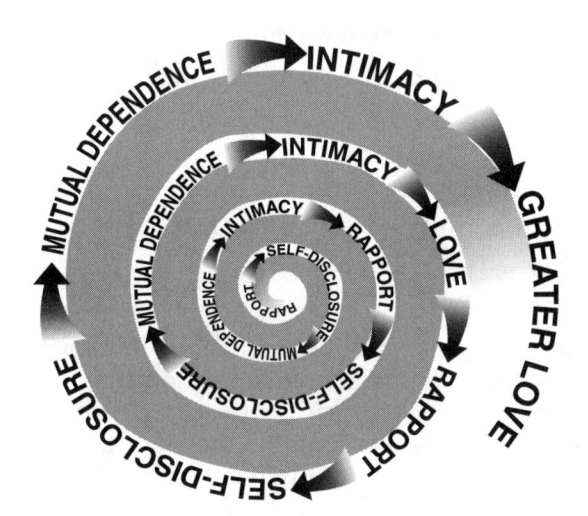

Growth cycle of love.

At last you begin to get some semblance of love. The more you repeat this magic formula, the greater the love. But when you stop, the reverse is true and love dwindles to nothing. Love is a continuous process.

Love's Nutrients

A few of love's nutrients include providing your romantic interest with …

> Friendship.
> Emotional support.
> Ego tending.
> Genuine affection.
> Acceptance.
> Kind words and sweet deeds.

> Sex.
> Caring.
> Kindness.
> Attention.
> Stroking.

Try to provide them all and see what sprouts!

Part 2 ➤ Coming Up with a Decision on Live-In Love

Love's Rewards

Love's rewards can be plentiful. Just to mention a few, love …

- ➤ Satisfies the human need to connect.
- ➤ Puts an end to natural loneliness.
- ➤ Provides companionship.
- ➤ Encourages intimacy through self-disclosure.
- ➤ Nurtures the feeling of being self-enhanced.
- ➤ Supplies comfort.
- ➤ Encourages a partner in problem solving.
- ➤ Gives a richness and fullness to life.
- ➤ Provides a helpmate.

> **Love Stats**
>
> Human beings are one of less than a handful of species who engage in sex for the sheer pleasure of it. Dolphins also fall into that category.

There are plenty of other benefits. You can fill in your own meaningful details.

Love Issues

Issue #1: Love is not a constant. You can't expect to maintain its fevered pitch at all times. Actually, even in the most loving, long-term marital relationships, couples admit they don't feel in love 100 percent of the time. Thirty-eight percent of the women I polled for my survey for *Marriage Secrets* admitted there was a short period of time in which they did not love their husbands. Twenty-five percent of men said the same about their wives.

Issue #2: You don't have to constantly be in a new relationship to experience the intensity of love. On the contrary, it seems to me that people who are serial lovers never give themselves the opportunity to develop a lasting love, one that is built out of rapport, self-disclosure, mutual dependence, and intimacy. Serial lovers either (1) avoid the intimacy, commitment, or responsibility inherent in deeper love; (2) are in love with love and incapable of concentrating their affection on one person for very long; or (3) repeatedly fall in love with the wrong people.

Issue #3: Who is the best candidate for you to fall in love with? If you ask some experts, they will tell you that opposites attract; but then they will reveal that opposites don't make the best love matches. Nurturing a love relationship with someone who is very different from yourself leaves the door open for conflict.

> **Love's Hot Line**
>
> Michael Broder, Ph.D., author of *The Art of Living Single* (William Morrow & Col, 1990), explains that **love-proneness** refers to an individual who falls in love habitually, possibly without realizing that he or she has control over his or her emotions.

112

There is evidence that two people who share greater similarity will find love's road paved more smoothly—unless they are so much alike that life together proves terribly dull. Normally, however, that is not what happens. Between two people who share similar backgrounds, ages, hopes, dreams, desires, goals, and values, they will find enough diversity to allow for growth and experimental activity.

Furthermore, there are comforting, reassuring, and positive aspects about starting a love relationship with an individual similar to oneself, researchers say. For example, becoming interested in someone who is like yourself validates your own perspectives and ideas. Furthermore, it is easier to understand this person and form realistic expectations about him or her.

Cupid's Crooked Arrow

Cupid's arrow doesn't always hit the right target, nor does it land unscarred. When the arrow lands askew, it is best to disregard the attempt at love and start anew. A crooked arrow could induce a fatal attraction or the immature love known as *limerence,* or an obsessive love.

Some experts who have studied love worldwide claim that not all societies share or experience the passionate style of love (being head over heels in love) that is so prevalent in the United States. It was found to be absent in Tahitian and South Pacific societies.

> **Sweet Nothings**
>
> **Limerence** is a state of love defined by psychologist Dorothy Tennov, Ph.D. It places emphasis on fantasy, anxiety, infatuation, and obsession. In severe states, Tennov associated limerence with emotional instability and suffering.

The Fatal Attraction

We aren't talking about the kind of fatal attraction Hollywood movies portray. Instead, University of California researcher Diane H. Felmlee defines a fatal attraction as attraction to elements in a love interest that will, in time, prove fatal to the relationship.

Why these individuals become disenchanted with a love interest is caused by the reversal of qualities originally seen as positive or appealing into something they perceive as negative or unattractive, Felmlee says. For examples, she uses the individual who was attracted to a "funny and fun" partner but who later found that she couldn't stand that person's "constant silliness," and a man who described a woman he fell in love with as "refreshingly innocent" but later concluded she simply lacked maturity.

You have heard this saying before, but now perhaps it appears with new understanding: Familiarity breeds contempt.

Women, Felmlee says, are slightly more likely to experience fatal attractions than men. The reason is that men are more apt to be attracted to the opposite sex because of physical features that do not become negative once they are further revealed. A man who falls for a woman because she is gorgeous is not likely to consider her ugly when she strips down to her bare self. The fact that men use less-specific terminology when describing a love interest and do not evaluate their relationships as intensely as women further contributes to women having a greater likelihood for forming a fatal attraction than men.

Limerence vs. Romantic Love

Individuals who confuse the state of limerence with a more-positive state of love should be careful. The topic has been researched and written about by Dorothy Tennov, author of *Love and Limerence* (second edition, Scarborough House, 1995). When a person is in limerence, the most important desires are a reciprocation of interest, a longing to be in that person's company, and the establishment of exclusivity.

The individual who is in limerence feels uncomfortably anxious, may experience frightening obsessions, feels terribly out of control, and is frequently attracted to someone with whom a love relationship is bound to be painful and to fail.

To some, the state of being limerent is an illness or a biological condition that produces a loss of reason and self-consciousness or a loss of coping skills. Others view limerence more characteristically as an immature love frequently expressed by teens. Adults who use this love style lack mature or adult relationship skills, experts claim. In any case, the fact remains that being in limerence doesn't sound like you got the best arrow Cupid had in his bag.

> **Love's Hot Line**
>
> Ladies, if you've fallen for a guy and want to entice him to love you back, show him that you accept who and what he is, says John Gray. One way to do that, suggests the *Mars/Venus* expert, is to allow him some space.

> **Love Stats**
>
> Previous research indicates that women form more-intimate social ties than men do and receive more social support from relationships. Men are much less likely to find a confidante and make the kind of personal disclosures women do.

The Obsessive Lover

Men and women may both exhibit behavior described as obsessive when it comes to love. *Obsessive lovers* lose control over their own will to stop loving, become consumed and crazed by passion, or are fixated on an individual. They simply cannot let go of the emotion, the person, or the idea of not winning the affection of their love interest.

The true obsessive lover is oftentimes someone who has suffered numerous failed relationships and is generally lonely, socially isolated, narcissistic, and egocentric, say university researchers William R. Cupach and Brian H. Spitzberg.

You will know if and when you are faced with an obsessed estranged lover. According to Cupach and Spitzberg, these men and women may ...

➤ Repeatedly call by phone, either arguing or hanging up.
➤ Harass and watch that person from a distance.
➤ Leave notes on the windshield of the person's car.
➤ Show up at the person's workplace or school.
➤ Make up lies about the relationship.
➤ Refuse to take no for an answer.
➤ Become physically abusive.
➤ Constantly drive by the person's home or place of work.
➤ Talk about the relationship to others.
➤ Make accusations of infidelity.
➤ Seek retribution.

The excuse most often given by these estranged lovers for their obtrusive behavior is the attempt to bring about a reconciliation, Cupach and Spitzberg say. However, if you are the object of these annoying, frightening, and perhaps dangerous attempts, reconciliation is probably the furthest thing from your mind.

Love's Unrealistic Idols

Enough of love's dark side. Let's talk about idols of love and romance. Cleopatra is queen of them all. She is thought to have been so alluring that men could not resist her. Diane Ackerman, author of *The History of Love* (Vintage Books, 1995), wrote that Cleopatra was glamorous, dramatic, nervy, and flamboyant. Ackerman also pulls the plug on Cleopatra and Mark Anthony's tragic and romantic double suicide in the name of love. After much historical digging, Ackerman contends that although the defeated Mark Anthony and Cleopatra may have chosen death because they were unable to endure life without one another, the more likely motive for their suicides was the thought of the public humiliation and torture they would have undergone.

And what about Orpheus, the hero of a Greek myth who is supposed to exemplify man's greatest love for a woman? Ackerman suggests that the story of his heroic journey into the dangerous cave of death to try to retrieve his Eurydice, only to lose her forever, may be more of a statement about

Love Stats

According to some experts, love in such places as ancient Greece and China was described as an attachment of a tender nature between men, not an attachment between the two sexes.

Greek society than an example of great love. Orpheus, it seems, was unable to complete his bargain with the gods, who demanded that he not look back to see whether Eurydice was following him out of the dark cave of death into the lightness of life. "In Greece, a woman was a man's property, so he [Orpheus] would naturally assume that when he stepped into the light his possessions went with him. Perhaps his tragedy was that he didn't think of Eurydice as having a separate destiny," writes Ackerman.

No section on the idols of love would be complete without a mention of Romeo and Juliet. Suffice it to say, Ackerman puts a dagger to this romantic tale as well. Shakespeare, she asserts, was the object of a jilted lover at the time he wrote *Romeo and Juliet*. Therefore, she says, "I think he wished to demonstrate in *Romeo and Juliet* how reckless, labile, and ephemeral the emotion of love is …."

Do not mourn the toppling of these romantic idols of love. Love in the twenty-first century must encompass truth and reality—not myth, fiction, fabrication, or exaggeration—in order to survive the pathos of its participants.

What Is Love at Its Best?

We have beaten around the bush and discussed love from all angles. Now it is time to describe in the most specific way what love in our lifetime represents. Of the experts I have read, I like author and psychotherapist Stanton Peele's description the best. His concrete analysis offers key elements that will allow us to measure whether we are in love and whether we are in love with the right kind of person. In his article "Fools for Love" from *The Psychology of Love* (collection of articles edited by Robert Sternberg and Michael Barnes, Yale University Press, 1988), he says that love is a committed, close, intimate, and sexual relationship, but it is also more:

> "Love is an awakening, expansive experience that makes the person more alive, daring, and exposed."

> "Love … is a helping relationship in which people trust each other to offer and accept criticism without feeling that their basic worth is being undermined."

> "Love means valuing a relationship and a lover because they are successful in the outer world."

> "Not only should love be pleasurable, but it should inspire and benefit from the joy lovers feel toward life."

> "Love is … an enhancing experience, one that improves its participants."

> Love is "a natural outgrowth of one's life and a secure part of oneself."

> Love is "having a belief in that person's value and goodness."

> Love is "a state of heightened awareness and responsibility."

Chapter 9 ➤ *The Power of Love*

We will take these ideas and use them in the next chapter when we address the question "Is it love?"

> **The Least You Need to Know**
> ➤ Love can move mountains.
> ➤ Mature love takes time to grow and can be purposely nurtured.
> ➤ Certain types of love and lovers pose serious, undesirable consequences.
> ➤ Love's flawed idols are no substitute for romantic reality.
> ➤ Love can be put to the test and measured against specific standards.

Chapter 10

Is It Love?

In This Chapter

➤ Identifying love styles

➤ Discovering the most- and least-dependable lovers

➤ Determining your love style

➤ Passing the love test

➤ Asking yourself if love is a necessary bedfellow for living together

Only you can judge whether the feelings you have for someone are love. Even though love seems a subjective emotion, there is much you can do to judge it objectively. Determining the depth of your affection and your partner's is a prudent exercise that will help solve the pressing problem of whether or not to move in.

Take your time with this chapter. No one will see the scores on your love tests. And no one except you will reap the benefits or feel the consequences of your answers.

Identifying Love Styles

The love styles identified by a variety of researchers are neither the gospel nor the last word on the subject. They are merely one more handy tool to help you evaluate the kind of lovers that you and your romantic interest are and whether or not the two of you might be a good or a poor love match.

Part 2 ➤ *Coming Up with a Decision on Live-In Love*

The love style you fit into depends upon …

- ➤ Gender.
- ➤ Stage.
- ➤ Needs.
- ➤ Sense of self.

It is extremely important to keep in mind that you do not have to be stuck in one love style forever. Everything in the preceding list, except gender, can easily change.

Love Style Choices

The following love-style categories are described in "Love Styles," an article written by University of Toronto sociology professor John Alan Lee (*The Psychology of Love,* Yale University Press, 1988). Lee believes these are the most common love styles, though he adds that not everyone can be pigeonholed into only eight styles. These categories are not hard and fast; instead, think of them as degrees of love styles that hold worthwhile hints about your romantic interest's predisposition toward love.

Eros. Erotic lovers are ready for the risks of love and clearly describe the body type that is most attractive to them. When they find that person, even in a photo, they experience great excitement. They eagerly wish to get to know the person quickly, intensely, and sexually. Finding this mate, developing an exclusive relationship, and living with this love interest are very high priorities in their lives.

Ludus. Ludic lovers cannot commit themselves to love and settle down. They are easily attracted to many individuals of the opposite sex, find no difficulty switching from one partner to another, and do not fall in love. In other words, they don't play love for keeps. They are aloof, hesitate to make future plans, and do not spend a great deal of time with a romantic partner. Although sex is an important part of their lives, it does not express any type of commitment.

Storge. Storge lovers are, overall, happy individuals who express this in their love relationships. Friendship, companionship, and family are expected elements of their love relationships. They are not demonstrative about their feelings in public and go about becoming friends before becoming lovers.

Mania. Manic lovers are insecure and lonely in life and love. Although they desire love and express a need to be loved, they fear pain will be associated with it. If they find themselves in love with a type they don't like, they will still try to perpetuate the relationship,

> **Troubles A'Brewing …**
>
> It should be obvious that a ludic lover and a storge lover who start a romance are headed for trials, tribulations, and trouble unless one of them adopts a new approach to love.

becoming very jealous, demanding, and possessive. Rarely will they find sex satisfying.

Pragma. Pragmatic lovers are the practical, plodding lovers who are following an outline for love and life. They seek compatible, thoughtful partners who will fit well into their chosen lifestyle and who demonstrate signs of being sociable, subdued emotionally in public, and sexually compatible. Skill rather than passion may describe sexual compatibility to them.

Storgic Eros. The mix of storgic and eros into one type describes the individual who views love as an essential part of adulthood, as a choice that leads to fulfillment. The storgic eros lovers are not picky about the way a love interest looks necessarily and see most individuals as worthy of being considered potential partners. While loving a partner gives meaning to their lives, sexual intimacy does not have to be part of the bargain. Generous friendship and acts of loving are the mainstay of their relationship behavior.

Ludic Eros. They are lovers who are looking for a fun variety of partners without having special emotions for a particular one. Any of a multitude of partners could be satisfying because love is not related to the essence of that one other human being. Love to them is supposed to be a mutually enjoyable experience but not much else.

Storgic Ludus. These lovers are more sexually oriented and concerned about "affairs" rather than being involved in relationships. They also account for many of the folks engaged in extramarital affairs, Professor Lee adds.

> **Sweet Nothings**
>
> **Agape** is a love style influenced by Christian thinking, but it is the least in evidence in real, romantic relationships. Its followers love in a selfless, altruistic, and giving manner that is based on duty.

Gender and Love Styles

There is sufficient research about the relationship between gender and love styles to warrant your attention. Studies show that men and women fall into separate categories of love styles. Hazard a guess as to who falls into which styles before you read on.

Men are more focused on game playing; women are more attuned to love based on friendship. Several studies of university students revealed that men tend to be erotic and ludic lovers, whereas women are storgic, manic, and pragmatic types.

A Typical Ludic Eros Lover

Here is 31-year-old Randy's outlook:

> "I have to have a girlfriend who is readily available, none of this long-distance stuff. I dated a girl all summer who I had a great time with. In my own way I

121

loved her. She turned me on, but when she went back to grad school in another city it was over. If and when she moves back here for work, I would like to be with her again."

Randy is a player who needs a handy playmate, and he's had several. He likes having a good time, slipping in and out of warm beds, but he isn't ready for any type of strings or commitment. He is a free agent and plans to stay that way. It's a good thing, too, because new and exciting women easily catch his eye.

> **Troubles A'Brewing ...**
>
> Mutual love can trip you up. Don't be lulled into thinking everything is perfect because you and your partner share in love. Mutual love is not a matter of how much you love, Professor Lee says, but of which kinds of lovers have come together. The catch is, love can be mutual and satisfying yet not the kind that lasts.

Finding Out Your Love Type

The following questions will help you determine your love type. The same questions can also be used to evaluate your love interest's type. After you know the love type for both of you, you can figure out what kind of a love match the two of you make.

1. Do you have a mental image of the one and only body type that turns you on? _____

2. Is pursuing someone with this body type a high priority? _____
3. Are your lovers expendable as individuals, whereas pleasurable love and fun are not? _____
4. Are you looking for someone to love who is a friend before becoming a lover? _____

5. Are you jealous and demanding of a love interest whom you like and dislike at various times? _____
6. Do you think there is more to love than sex? _____
7. Do you think that sex can be improved upon if other elements of a loving relationship are present? _____

122

8. Are you a happy and satisfied individual with a good sense of self?

9. Do you tend to feel lonely and insecure a good deal of the time?

10. Do you have a plan for how you will live your life and for what type of partner will fit well into that scheme?

11. Are you more interested in finding a companion who understands you and with whom you have shared interests than you are in finding a sexually attractive partner who turns you on?

12. Are you a no-strings-attached lover who isn't ready for anything more than fun?

13. In starting up a new relationship, is your primary aim sexual gratification?

14. Does sex with a partner signify any type of commitment to the relationship?

Once you have determined your love style and your partner's, seriously consider whether either of you is at the stage where love can be a lasting, committed adventure. You will need this answer before embarking on Part 3, "Getting Ready to Move In." However, don't panic if you can't come up with an answer yet. The next three tests will help you arrive at your destination.

How you view, value, and regard yourself determines the way in which you expect a lover to treat and relate to you. My recommendation is to measure your *self-esteem* and *self-respect* before embarking on a new relationship. Until you compose lofty expectations, stay home.

Reality Checkups for Love

Considering the fact that a study conducted by a popular monthly magazine found 65 percent of respondents believed in the fairy-tale fantasy of love at first sight, more than half of us are in trouble from the outset. Remember, true love has to grow. What these folks believe in is a romantic attraction of huge proportion. What you really need for a long-term relationship is true love and a massive dose of reality.

> **Sweet Nothings**
>
> Self-respect is different from self-esteem, argues Ellen Langer, professor of psychology at Harvard University. Self-respect is liking oneself irrespective of, and not contingent upon, personal success. Self-respect is, she says, liking "ourselves because of who we are and not because of what we can or cannot do."

Part 2 ➤ *Coming Up with a Decision on Live-In Love*

See where you stand. Take the next three tests and think of them as your reality checkup for love. Apply each question to yourself and then to your love interest.

A Checkup for Beginners

Are there signs of being in love? You cannot sufficiently answer this question yes or no unless you submit to a love test. Take time to measure the appropriateness of your response.

Your Performance

Yes	No	
❏	❏	Do you verbally express your love for your romantic interest?
❏	❏	Do you demonstrate care and concern for his/her feelings?
❏	❏	Do you support your love interest's decisions and stand up for him or her?
❏	❏	Do you perform visible deeds of love for your partner?
❏	❏	Do you prefer your love interest's company over others', but not exclusively?
❏	❏	Do you consider your lover a good friend?
❏	❏	Are you concerned over your partner's general level of happiness?
❏	❏	Do you intentionally do things to make your love interest happy?
❏	❏	Can you express yourself sexually with this person?
❏	❏	Do you compliment your partner and make your partner feel good about him- or herself?
❏	❏	Do you behave in a way that will earn the genuine trust of your love interest?

Chapter 10 ➤ *Is It Love?*

Your Love Interest's Performance

Yes	No	
❏	❏	Does your love interest verbally express love for you?
❏	❏	Does he or she demonstrate care and concern for your feelings?
❏	❏	Does he or she support your love decisions and stand up for you?
❏	❏	Does he or she perform visible deeds of love for you?
❏	❏	Does he or she prefer your company over others', but not exclusively?
❏	❏	Does your lover consider you a good friend?
❏	❏	Is your lover concerned about your general level of happiness?
❏	❏	Does he or she intentionally do things to make you happy?
❏	❏	Does your love interest freely express him- or herself sexually with you?
❏	❏	Does this person compliment you and make you feel good about yourself?
❏	❏	Does he or she behave in a way to earn your genuine trust?

Scoring: A perfect chorus of "Yes, Yes, Yes" is what we are looking for. After all, this is the most elementary of love tests.

Love Stats

Ladies, are you aware that American men are the most romantic in the world? According to a Harlequin Enterprises study of over 5,000 men from 19 countries, those from the United States say "I love you" and do something romantic more often even than guys from France.

125

Part 2 ➤ *Coming Up with a Decision on Live-In Love*

A Checkup for Intermediate Lovers

Before you pronounce that your love has progressed to a more meaningful level of connection, rate your performance. Love is no place for guessing games.

Your Performance

Yes	No	
❑	❑	Does this relationship encompass more-advanced levels of love?
❑	❑	Does this love relationship give you the opportunity to grow, experience new things, and feel vitalized?
❑	❑	Do you recognize your partner's imperfections and feel that you can live with your partner and love him or her anyway?
❑	❑	If your partner gives you constructive criticism that will help you grow, can you accept it?
❑	❑	Are you comfortable giving your partner constructive criticism that will help him or her grow?
❑	❑	Is your lover important to you because he or she is a valuable person worthy of love, admiration, and respect?
❑	❑	Does your relationship satisfy you partly because it protects you from pain in the world but mostly because you gain pleasure, excitement, and passion from it?
❑	❑	Does your love relationship elevate you to a new and deeper level of human expression?
❑	❑	Do you feel responsible for furthering your love relationship?
❑	❑	Do you feel a responsibility to treat your partner with respect and care?
❑	❑	Does your love partner bolster, rather than attack or diminish, your self-esteem?

Your Love Interest's Performance

Yes	No	
☐	☐	Does this love relationship give you the opportunity to grow, experience new things, and feel vitalized?
☐	☐	Do you recognize your partner's imperfections and feel that you can live with, and love, him or her anyway?
☐	☐	If your partner gives you constructive criticism that will help you grow, can you accept it?
☐	☐	Are you comfortable giving your partner constructive criticism that helps him or her grow?
☐	☐	Is your lover important to you because he or she is a valuable person worthy of love, admiration, and respect?
☐	☐	Does your relationship satisfy you partly because it protects you from pain in the world but mostly because you gain pleasure, excitement, and passion from it?
☐	☐	Does your love relationship elevate you to a new and deeper level of human expression?
☐	☐	Do you feel a responsibility to treat your partner with respect and care?
☐	☐	Does your love partner bolster, rather than attack or diminish, your self-esteem?

Scoring: The answers for both of you should be overwhelmingly positive. Unless both individuals in the relationship have a high number of yes answers, chances are the two of you won't pass the next test, the one for advanced lovers. Go back and either take the test again—understanding that you don't need to answer yes a hundred percent of the time—or work on the areas where you aren't up to the mark for a positive response. Remember, developing long-term love takes time and tending.

Part 2 ➤ *Coming Up with a Decision on Live-In Love*

A Checkup for Advanced Lovers

To wear this title rightfully, you must pass the following performance test. Love is more than a feeling; it is a combination of actions.

Your Performance

Yes	No	
❑	❑	Does your love meet the criteria of a committed relationship?
❑	❑	Are you ready to make joint investments in the future by buying a home together, planning future trips, or sharing a savings account?
❑	❑	Are you willing to make concessions to accommodate your partner's needs and desires?
❑	❑	Are you ready to be his or her lifetime helpmate?
❑	❑	Do you want to make life easier for this person?
❑	❑	Are you able to put your partner's needs ahead of your own now and then?
❑	❑	Are you willing to share and trade tasks for the good of your relationship?
❑	❑	Do you monitor your lover's behavior to make sure that it is in accordance with a good relationship?
❑	❑	Do you share financial resources without a problem?
❑	❑	Do you want to create a relationship that complements you as individuals and as a pair?
❑	❑	Do you see the two of you as a family?
❑	❑	Do you give your lover gifts?
❑	❑	Do you choose to be with this person despite the availability of other options?

According to author and love expert John Gray, a woman—from deep within herself—"longs to relax, let go, and surrender to someone she trusts to care for and support her." If a man doesn't understand this or can't comply, he is denying a woman what she truly wants and needs out of a relationship.

Your Love Interest's Performance

Yes	No	
❏	❏	Are you ready to make joint investments in the future by buying a home together, planning future trips, or sharing a savings account?
❏	❏	Are you willing to make concessions to accommodate your partner's needs and desires?
❏	❏	Are you ready to be his or her lifetime helpmate?
❏	❏	Do you want to make life easier for this person?
❏	❏	Are you able to put your partner's needs ahead of your own now and then?
❏	❏	Are you willing to share and trade tasks for the good of your relationship?
❏	❏	Do you monitor your lover's behavior to make sure that it is in accordance with a good relationship?
❏	❏	Do you share financial resources without a problem?
❏	❏	Do you want to create a relationship that complements you as individuals and as a pair?
❏	❏	Do you see the two of you as a family?
❏	❏	Do you give your love interest gifts?
❏	❏	Do you choose to be with this person despite the availability of other options?

Scoring: In order to evaluate whether or not this is an advanced, secure relationship, you must determine the mutual level of commitment. It should be equal from both ends! A lopsided commitment doesn't represent the kind you are looking for. That is not the level of commitment that will see you through thick and thin. To review how critical a commitment is to the quality and duration of your relationship, reread the discussion of commitment found in Chapter 3, "The Facts and Fictions of Living Together."

Part 2 ➤ *Coming Up with a Decision on Live-In Love*

> **Troubles A'Brewing ...**
>
> Signs of an unhealthy love relationship include: total absorption into the other person's life at the expense of your own, seeing your love interest through rose-colored glasses, and loving someone because that person fills your personal needs rather than loving him or her for who they are.

Mutually Exclusive or Mutually Necessary?

If you want a live-in who is a playmate and a sex partner, love and living together can be mutually exclusive, although the potential for danger is high. If you want to create a real partnership, to avoid common hazards, to maximize the odds of success, and to move down the road toward matrimony, committed love should be an integral part of your decision to live together.

There is no way to overcome the ups and downs of any relationship, whether live-in or married, unless both of you make a concerted effort to maintain a strong commitment and consciously determine that you will love your partner through it all.

Love is the glue that binds. As you have learned, there are all kinds of love and lovers. Hence, there are various grades of glue. The only one that offers the best protection against separation is the mature, advanced love that has been meticulously spelled out for you.

What you must decide is ...

➤ Are you in love?
➤ Is there enough of it to protect and satisfy you if you move in?

> **Love's Hot Line**
>
> Ninety-three percent of American men in a study claimed they would marry the same woman again. The poll must have been taken under a full moon, considering that the divorce rate is well over 40 percent. Or maybe these men were like a large number of the men I have interviewed who voiced regret over not staying with their wives.

➤ Is love necessary if you seek only a casual live-in relationship?

You must be the one to answer the questions. See if you can reconcile your level of love with a satisfying love arrangement and derive happiness from a live-in relationship. Not all types and degrees of love—married or cohabiting—work well together. You, however, have ways to measure your love as well as the benefit of information that gives ample clues about whether your future picture is sunny or gloomy.

Coming Up Empty on the Love Front

If you scored poorly on all of the tests in this chapter, you may not be in love but in lust. *Lust* in its fullest meaning is an intense and excessive sexual desire that is unrestrained in pursuing sexual gratification and finding physical pleasure. That doesn't sound like love or commitment to me. Lust alone just doesn't qualify as love.

Love and lust are easily mixed up. They both originate in the limbic system of the brain, the area that also governs the basic emotions of fear, joy, sadness, and hate. Furthermore, you can be attracted to someone you both lust after and love. Try to keep mind and body separate here. If it's lust, it's all in the body. If it's love, there is the matter of mind and body.

Troubles A'Brewing ...

Here's what is sure to snuff out love: affairs, lies, deceitfulness, lack of attention, sexual disinterest, selfishness, too much dependency, not enough space, lack of respect.

Love Stats

According to the *Janus Report on Sexual Behavior,* 96 percent of men and 98 percent of women believe that love *is* important. Of those couples who married, only 27 percent of men and 16 percent of women say they were initially attracted to their partners because of looks. Personality was the number-one overriding factor.

131

Part 2 ➤ *Coming Up with a Decision on Live-In Love*

> **The Least You Need to Know**
>
> ➤ There are a variety of love styles. Not all work well together or combine to form lasting love relationships.
>
> ➤ Men and women often have different love styles.
>
> ➤ You can't determine the direction of a current relationship without evaluating the love factor.
>
> ➤ Commitment takes two.
>
> ➤ Commitment on both sides is essential for lasting love.

Chapter 11

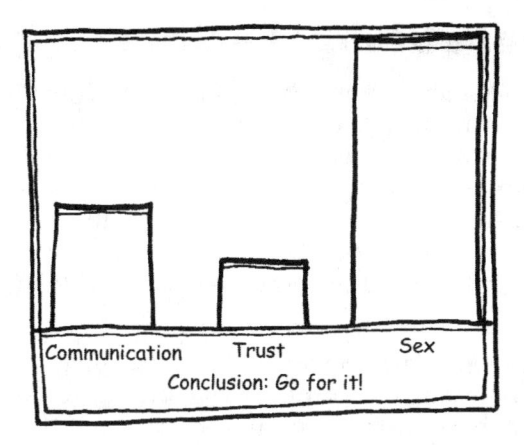

Partnership Potential

In This Chapter

➤ Are Dick and Jane compatible live-ins?

➤ Is sexual compatibility important?

➤ Why must you be both friends and lovers?

➤ Would you get an A+ in conflict resolution?

➤ Do you know the tricks for smooth communicating?

You will need every one of the elements in this chapter if you want to end up in the plus column for successful live-in lovers. Even if you get cold feet or determine that cohabiting isn't for you, this information will still benefit any other relationship, whether love, live-in, or marital, that you may wish to try.

By the end of this chapter, it ought to be glaringly apparent—even if you passed the love test—that you need more than love to keep you together. Compatibility in other aspects of your lives is number one. Staying compatible and maintaining a satisfying relationship is number two. To accomplish that requires expertise in conflict resolution and communication. Little else brings you through the inevitable highs, lows, problems, and ecstasies of all relationships like they do. And of course, good sex helps, too.

Once you have absorbed all of the helpful information in this chapter and are able to put it into action, you can feel more assured that your would-be live-in and you have real partnership potential.

Part 2 ➤ *Coming Up with a Decision on Live-In Love*

The Compatibility Factor

Many people talk about compatibility, but how many really know what it means? Actually, *compatibility* has a straightforward definition: the capability of two individuals to live harmoniously together. "Capability" and "harmoniously" are key words here. *Capability* implies the presence of a positive potential, and *harmoniously* depicts the condition that the two individuals could achieve.

Compatibility is predicated on a bunch of "ifs." If you have these qualities in your corner, if you can muster others, if you want to further acquire necessary ones, then you may consider yourselves a compatible couple.

There are different categories of qualities and characteristics that determine your live-in compatibility. Some are more important than others. We'll look at all of them.

> **Love's Hot Line**
>
> Ask yourself if this relationship is an equitable one. Inequity in a relationship usurps from one individual the power that, in an equitable relationship, keeps both parties protected, safe, secure, satisfied, and happy.

The Core of Compatibility

To ensure the optimum live-in compatibility, the following characteristics should be abundantly and mutually present. And should you eventually marry, as a large proportion of live-ins do, they are absolute musts in the marriage arena. All the characteristics are discussed in this chapter, except the last two, which were covered in earlier chapters.

- ➤ Friendship
- ➤ Respect
- ➤ Empathy
- ➤ Passion
- ➤ Shared values and similar backgrounds
- ➤ Love

Professor John Gottman, Ph.D., has investigated relationships for 27 years. His research at the University of Washington has led him to believe that the basis of a happy relationship is deep friendship. To Gottman, *friendship* means showing respect and understanding for the other person, as well as for his or her likes, dislikes, and quirks. Gottman found that couples with the highest relationship satisfaction have a strong presence of friendship in their romantic relationship.

In more than 100 interviews and questionnaires, I asked long-time happily married individuals for their marriage secrets. The vast majority reported becoming best friends with their spouse over the years. The kind of friendship they displayed toward one another involved support, acceptance, generosity, intimate familiarity, and trust.

Didn't your mother always say to pick your friends wisely? Well, be wise and pick your lover as a friend if you want to hang on to the relationship.

Empathy and Understanding

The qualities of *empathy* and understanding are the melody of compatibility. Someone who is empathetic has the ability to project his or her own personality into a partner's and see issues and emotions from the partner's viewpoint. Although empathy should initially be nurtured and developed, when that fails to take place not all is lost.

Despite a difference of opinion among experts, new evidence shows that empathy can be learned. Men as well as women can learn to be empathetic, say the authors of "Understanding the One You Love: A Longitudinal Assessment of an Empathy Training Program for Couples in Romantic Relationships" (*Family Relations*, 1999). According to the article, the results of a 10-hour empathy training program showed increased empathetic understanding and increased relationship satisfaction between romantically involved couples.

> **Sweet Nothings**
>
> Sociologists Letha and John Scanzoni believe, "**Empathy** means sharing another's thoughts, feelings, and experiences." To empathize they say means to emotionally and mentally "enter into their sufferings, worries, triumphs, or joys."

No Substitute for Respect

The kind of respect required for partnership compatibility isn't run-of-the-mill stuff. It involves reverence, honor, esteem, consideration, and courteous regard for a partner, as well as regard for the partner's opinions, decisions, and wishes.

Showing respect not only demonstrates partnership equity and affirms each individual's self-worth but is one of the best displays of true love. Real, genuine heartfelt respect keeps partners in line and discourages them from doing anything that would harm or hurt their loved one or their relationship.

Passion, the Love Potent

Without passion, your relationship is probably ho-hum and your partner expendable. Passion, the kind that makes two people capable of not just a harmonious live-in relationship but a great love relationship, is comprised of intense emotional and sexual desires for one another. Either it is present or it isn't.

Although passionate feelings cannot be learned, passion—like love—can wane or ebb. It must be nurtured and fed, tended and mended, to stay alive.

Part 2 ➤ *Coming Up with a Decision on Live-In Love*

The Compatibility of Daily Living

Now, let's get a little more practical. Compatibility extends to more than emotions; it includes practical issues, too. You and your partner should share similar attitudes about:

- ➤ Money.
- ➤ Work.
- ➤ Personal goals.
- ➤ Responsibility to family members.
- ➤ Partnership participation.
- ➤ Relationship responsibilities.
- ➤ Lifestyle.
- ➤ Individual space.
- ➤ Fidelity.

> **Love's Hot Line**
>
> Dollars and cents have a lot to do with your partnership potential. A partner's financial savvy is directly related to a couple's level of satisfaction. Your attitude toward spending and saving and the material wealth you aspire to are all part of this important issue of dollars and cents.

Summing Up Compatibility

Without a reasonable level of compatibility in all departments, moving in isn't a good idea—unless you are up for disappointment. Being in an incompatible live-in relationship can be like wearing a shoe that doesn't fit. Eventually your foot starts to hurt. A blister forms. The constant, annoying friction of the shoe on the blister makes it worse. Once your foot has been rubbed the wrong way long enough, the blister festers. Finally you jerk off your shoe and fling it into a pile of giveaways.

Sexual Compatibility: You Gotta Have It!

You don't have to have *sex* day and night to keep up with the national averages and prove your sexual compatibility. In fact, the National Opinion Research Center at the University of Chicago discovered in its social survey that less sex is going on in America than one would assume. The number of times a week you have sex isn't the primary concern here. Although if you are getting it on too infrequently, it is!

Good sex is mutually exciting and satisfying. If one of you is bored, failing to have orgasms and closing your eyes to fantasize about the identity of your partner, your sexual compatibility score is falling by the minute.

> **Sweet Nothings**
>
> Politicians have made it necessary to define the term "sex." **Sex** for the sake of this discussion means sexual behavior leading up to and including intercourse.

However, just because you and your partner are the greatest sexual partners ever, don't disregard the importance of the core components of compatibility. You can have fabulous sex for sex's sake with someone who would be disastrous in a love relationship.

Even that most platonic of teachers, Plato, might advise you to keep your coat and hat by the bed when engaging in this kind of sex. After all, Plato recognized that "There's no greater or keener pleasure than that of bodily love—and none which is more irrational."

Room for Misinterpretation

You know when you've had good sex, but does good sex simply mean a physical response to a good lover or does it signify something deeper? It probably doesn't mean the latter. There are enough studies to show that relationships founded only on the physical side are usually short-term. Therefore, moving in would probably be a wasted effort in such cases.

> **Love Stats**
>
> A research project at the University of Chicago found that Americans who have attended grad school have sex approximately 52 times a year. That is below the national average. Also, people who put in an average 60-hour workweek appear to be more sexually active than those working fewer hours. They are getting it at least 10 percent more often.

> **Love's Hot Line**
>
> Experts have measurable proof: Men do get turned on by curvy women. Scientists have even provided a formula for the most appealing waist size. Women who want to maximize their turn-on potential should go for a waist that measures no more than 60 to 70 percent of their hip size. For 36-inch hips, that computes to a 21$\frac{1}{2}$- to 25-inch waist. Wow!

What's going on could be as old as time. Men are turned on by a woman's appearance, passion rises, they have intercourse. On the woman's side, she is attracted to the guy, she becomes emotionally involved, and she interprets the act of intercourse as a validation of his deeper interest. Whether her viewpoint is primarily influenced by

Part 2 ➤ *Coming Up with a Decision on Live-In Love*

societal or physiological considerations, plenty of evidence does suggest that women attach an emotional component to sex.

Men are becoming more savvy to this fact. In fact, many men—both young and old—whom I interviewed told me that sexually transmitted diseases aren't the only reason they're cutting down on sex with uncommitted partners. They are actually avoiding intercourse in order to eliminate any misunderstanding about commitment and to prevent subsequent complications.

However, this old problem has a new aspect. The women out there today are different. Feminism hasn't just put women into the workplace; it has liberated them sexually. Need proof? Concurrently with liberation has been a recorded rise in women's sexual orgasms and sex partners.

Feminist leader Betty Friedan has said that sex is now a woman's choice. And it's a choice women are going for, though at times women do see sex as a form of exploitation. Most women prefer emotional arousal in conjunction with the physical. Nonetheless, women aren't ignoring their sexual needs.

In the absence of a partner and the belief that none is on the horizon, not all women are resorting to masturbation. On the contrary, Susan Crain Bakos, author of *Still Sexy* (St. Martin's Press, 1999), says that women are able to set aside their emotional agendas and find men whom they might not wish to marry or have a relationship with but whom they find desirable for sex.

Test Your Sexual Compatibility

How good is the sex you're having? Answer each question truthfully and find out. This could be a good exercise for you and your partner. However, I would wait to approach the subject until after you have mastered the art of communication and conflict resolution presented later in this chapter.

Love's Hot Line

Don't think something is wrong if your fiancé or spouse isn't your very best lover ever. Some very happily married women confided in me that their husbands weren't the absolute best they ever had. It's the whole package that counts when going for a lifetime love match. Nevertheless, don't scratch sexual compatibility off your list.

Chapter 11 ➤ *Partnership Potential*

	Positively Yes	Most of the Time	Hardly Ever	Absolutely Never
1. Do you agree on the kind and style of sex you like?	❑	❑	❑	❑
2. Are you attracted to your partner?	❑	❑	❑	❑
3. Does he/she know how to turn you on?	❑	❑	❑	❑
4. Do you share the same interest in sex?	❑	❑	❑	❑
5. Do you both want sex the same number of times a week?	❑	❑	❑	❑
6. Is your partner sexually responsive to your overtures?	❑	❑	❑	❑
7. Do you both reach climax when you have sex?	❑	❑	❑	❑
8. Can you be sexually honest with your partner about what you want and like?	❑	❑	❑	❑
9. Are you able to engage in experimentation?	❑	❑	❑	❑
10. Do you like to please your partner?	❑	❑	❑	❑
11. Does he/she like to please you?	❑	❑	❑	❑
12. Does your partner feel unrestrained and free when making love?	❑	❑	❑	❑
13. Do you feel happy and satisfied after having sex?	❑	❑	❑	❑
14. Are you content enough with your sexual partner not to go looking for extrarelationship sex?	❑	❑	❑	❑
15. When your partner isn't in the mood, can you understand and accept that?	❑	❑	❑	❑
16. Do you know how to get your partner going when he/she could take it or leave it that night?	❑	❑	❑	❑
17. Does your partner put you in the mood before getting really intimate?	❑	❑	❑	❑
18. Does your partner take enough time to engage in foreplay to please you and ready you for intercourse?	❑	❑	❑	❑

The "right" answers to this quiz ought to be apparent. You are on fire if all of your check marks are in the "Positively Yes" column. You also probably aren't telling the honest-to-goodness truth. There simply isn't time to be so hot. A complete chorus of "Most of the Time" is probably realistic and desirable because it represents sexual compatibility at a pace you can maintain. Too many "Hardly Evers" mean you need to work on this aspect of your relationship. "Absolutely Never" responses indicate something is going on, but it isn't compatible sex.

If you need help or spice drops to improve your sexual compatibility, an entire chapter awaits. Look for Chapter 21, "Sex, Sex, Sex," in Part 4, "Living Under One Roof."

A Tale of Sexual Incompatibility

Cybil, at 28, moved in with Joshua four months after they met. She says she was in love:

> "I was very attracted to Joshua. He was fun and had a great sense of humor. We built a good friendship that is intact today. I knew he was the kind of man I wanted to marry. Sex was our problem.
>
> "There were times I would visit him out-of-town before I moved in, and we would not make love. I wasn't sex-driven, but I was crazy about him and dying to sleep with him. When I moved in, we didn't make love frequently—maybe not even once a week. I was afraid that if I said something after we became engaged six months later he would change his mind about getting married.
>
> "I was the one to change the rules after we got married, but our sex life didn't change. I am embarrassed to tell you that sometimes we would make love once a month and always at my instigation. I felt terribly rejected and frustrated by our lack of sex. I finally asked him why we didn't make love more often. He said he just didn't get aroused. I told him it really bothered me and asked him to go to a clinic for sexual dysfunction. Joshua had no problem with that. He was more than willing to go.
>
> "We found out later that he had an incredibly low sex drive. We were given exercises that had to do with touching. A close friend and confidante told me to have an affair. Instead I went to a psychiatrist to determine if I could spend the rest of my life like that. In the meantime, I stopped taking the pill because we were making love so infrequently. Of course, I got pregnant. I wanted to have a child, but not then. I knew it would force me to stay married. Joshua wanted the child but agreed to go with me anyway to get an abortion.
>
> "Finally, a year later, when we were to move into the house we had just renovated, I couldn't go with him. We had been married three years, and I couldn't take it anymore. Nothing he did could make up for our lack of a sexual relationship."

> **Troubles A'Brewing ...**
>
> Approximately one in five adults is not interested in having sex. Low sex drives and impotence can be caused by physical conditions that physicians are able to treat. If there is an emotional component, therapy is also available. Not only does the person with the problem suffer, but so does the partner. A lack of adequate sexual participation could spell the end to an otherwise good love relationship.

Putting Out the Brushfires

Don't be smug just because you can make love better than Joshua and Cybil. Can you put out the brushfires, avert the wars, and benefit from the battles?

Conflict is inevitable any time you live with someone or something—even your dog. The difference is you can pick up Rover and dispassionately put him outside to do his business, whereas emotions are part of the territory of human disputes.

How you deal with conflicts in a relationship can become a matter of habit. Therefore:

- Develop a pattern that adds to, rather than detracts from, your overall relationship satisfaction.
- Avoid escalating the problem or conflict.
- Don't shout and scream so loudly that you discourage meaningful verbal interaction.
- Watch that your response to conflict is one you would want in return. There is evidence that your partner will reciprocate your behavior.
- Keep trying different ways to reach an agreement.
- Try to remain positive and view conflict resolution as something that will ultimately help your relationship.

> **Love's Hot Line**
>
> Conflict is a good thing. It means that neither of you is holding back or holding in opinions, demands, and complaints. That's positive. Otherwise, how else would you be able to resolve differences? Couples who argue well together, stay together.

> Do not use negative statements when trying to resolve a conflict. It makes you and your partner more pessimistic about the possibility for a happy ending.

> Defuse the situation by bringing up something in your relationship past that you know your partner will laugh at. (This is a new version of the kiss-and-make-up tactic.)

Positive conflict resolution according to Gottman.

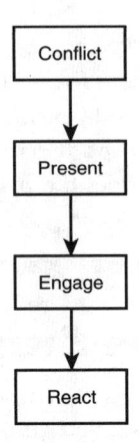

```
Conflict
   ↓
Present
   ↓
Engage
   ↓
 React
```

University professor John Gottman advises going for "positive conflict behavior." However, if, when solving a conflict or trying to communicate, one of the partners rolls his or her eyes, acts defensively, is critical, or tries to stonewall, chances are the couple's relationship is headed for trouble. Gottman calls these negative actions "The Four Horsemen of the Apocalypse."

Communicating with Purpose

The noncommunicator poses a problem for a would-be partner in or outside the home, and even in bed. And a lot of that noncommunication has to do with gender.

The most up-to-the-minute research continues to unveil gender differences in nearly everything we do, including communicate. Consequently, unless you and your partner are aware of this and make concerted efforts to bridge the gap when communicating, you may be affecting your partnership potential.

I can't tell you how many women have shown utter surprise when their live-ins, boyfriends, or husbands agreed to interview with me and spent hours pouring out their most secret thoughts. Their female mates would have bet the house that their guys weren't going to talk. It's all in the asking.

An Indispensable Communication Tip

Let's get down to basics. In the hierarchy of human needs, where does communication fall? Centuries ago, philosophers came up with the answer. Although they didn't have love relationships in mind, their answer still applies. Stated in terms of our discussion, their answer went something like this: Before you can successfully engage your partner in conversation of a more serious nature—whether to discuss important issues, resolve conflicts, or merely intensify intimacy—your partner's most basic needs must first be met.

The following ladder illustrates this point. Keep the ladder in mind and climb it before bringing up matters of love, life, and home.

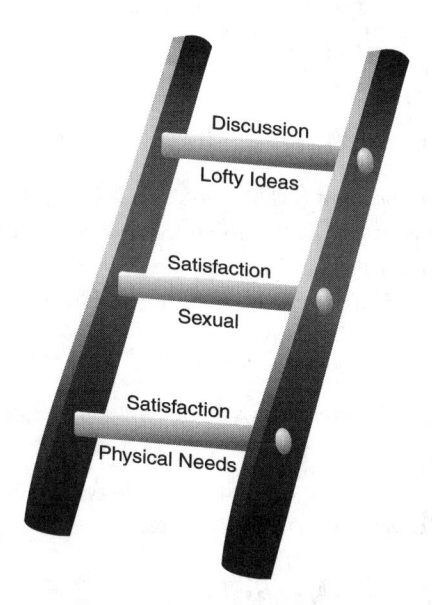

Climb this ladder to reach fruitful discussions.

Notice where sexual gratification is located on this ladder of basic human needs. Pure experience teaches that your partner will be more receptive to serious conversations when his or her sexual hunger has been fed.

Greasing the Communication Wheel

If you want to communicate in a way that will enhance your relationship, try to master these elementary skills first. The more you practice them, the more you will learn about communicating and the more you will know about your love partner. Getting at pertinent truths is what communicating is all about.

➤ Be a good listener.
➤ Make sure you are both talking about the same thing.

➤ Ask for clarification.
➤ Don't beat around the bush. Use language that can be understood.
➤ Don't interrupt.
➤ Be attentive.
➤ Be sure your tone of voice invites further conversation.
➤ Pick an appropriate place and time for more serious conversations.

> **Love Stats**
>
> According to Shere Hite's study *Women and Love* (St. Martin's Press, 1989), there simply isn't enough talking or communicating going on between couples who love each other. Ninety-eight percent of her female respondents said they desire more verbal closeness with their partner. Specifically Hite said, "They want the men in their lives to talk more about their own personal thoughts, feelings, plans, and questions, and to ask them about theirs."

Make talking to each other a pleasant experience. Set the scene with plenty of privacy and quiet, and sweeten it according to your own savoir faire.

Clogging the Communication Wheel

Shutting down communication doesn't take much effort and is usually done inadvertently. Here's how to prevent it:

➤ Be careful that you don't misinterpret what your partner is saying.
➤ Don't jump the gun and come to a conclusion too quickly.
➤ Don't become defensive.
➤ Make sure your perceptions are the same as your partner's.
➤ Don't say things that are hurtful or spiteful.
➤ Don't be stubborn or combative.
➤ Stop pointing the finger and laying blame.
➤ Don't withdraw.

Don't always buy into total honesty. For a long time, total honesty was touted as a prerequisite for couple communication. However, not all of our personal thoughts benefit from an exchange. If the information won't enhance understanding, could potentially damage your relationship, and ethically need not be voiced, think twice before saying it.

> **Love's Hot Line**
>
> "In this world, conversations are negotiations in which people try to achieve and maintain the upper hand if they can, and protect themselves from other's attempts ... to push them around," wrote Deborah Tannen, Ph.D., in her ground-breaking book *You Just Don't Understand: Women and Men in Conversation*. Women, she maintains, have a different understanding of conversations with their male partners than their partners do. If you want more information on this subject, check out her book.

Attention Grabbers

Part of the skill of communicating is knowing when to talk. If your partner is not receptive, your timing could be wrong. However, to garner the attention of the most hesitant conversant, you may need to grab his or her attention. Here's how:

1. Sit on top during sexual foreplay and begin a discourse, not intercourse. The chances of anyone getting up and walking away are pretty slim.
2. Open a bottle of wine, run a bubble bath, and get into pleasantly hot water together. Soaking relaxes the body and mind.
3. Go for a drive with a surprise picnic lunch or dinner packed away in the trunk. A romantic setting reduces resistance and breaks down barriers.

Learn to be inventive when it comes to communicating. You could teach a hesitant partner to enjoy it. Remember Pavlov's dog? Well, train or condition your partner by providing something extra pleasant for his or her communication efforts.

> **The Least You Need to Know**
>
> ➤ Being lovers doesn't necessarily make you compatible partners.
>
> ➤ Long-term relationships require a foundation of friendship.
>
> ➤ Sexual incompatibility can nix a relationship.
>
> ➤ You and your love interest must exchange ample amounts of empathetic understanding to make it as partners.
>
> ➤ Learning how to resolve conflicts and communicate can increase the odds of creating and maintaining partnership potential.

Part 3
Getting Ready to Move In

Okay, you have decided to take the plunge and live with him or her. No longer is staying over every night, keeping separate abodes, and playing peek-a-boo love enough. A thoughtful decision alone won't make the grade or give you your best odds at succeeding where many before you have not. Nonetheless, there is still more you can do to further your sound thinking. Make prudent plans!

That's what Part 3 of this book is all about: preempting disaster, making important legal decisions, figuring out where to live, creating house rules, building a sound live-in foundation, holding a critical economic summit, and setting precedents.

Once you have formulated specific expectations, filled out all of the worksheets, and checked every list, most of your preparation will be complete. The remainder you can do after you are under one roof.

Chapter 12

Pre-Empting Disaster

In This Chapter

➤ Confronting worrisome romantic pasts

➤ Power plays, ultimatums, and hard bargains

➤ What you can and can't change about your lover

➤ "Must discussions" before you move in

➤ The best place to set up house

➤ Your readiness move-in quiz

Living together is a whole lot more than putting the toilet seat down or assigning household chores. If that's what living together means to you, get out your childhood relics because what you're thinking of is called playing house. We're talking about something much more adult-like and serious.

In order to prevent the roof from caving in on your love nest, make sure you deal with all the issues discussed in Part 3, "Getting Ready to Move In," before moving day arrives. Use your newfound techniques for communication and conflict resolution to explore and deal with each of the issues. Granted, this may not be an easy assignment, but exploring and resolving each issue is absolutely necessary if you want to avert possible disaster.

Keep in mind that the purpose of this guide to live-in love is to create the optimum chance of success for a romantic, mutually satisfying partnership, should you and your pal decide to move in together.

Your Relationship Histories—Past, Present, and Future

Don't you envy those folks who never look back and say "That was then; this is now. It could never happen again"? Well, history *can* happen again.

We study history to learn about the present and to avoid revisiting distasteful parts of the past. History can help you determine future trends, too. In the financial markets, future trends are forecast daily, using history. You can apply this same kind of educated speculation to love as well.

If your would-be live-in has a worrisome romantic past, history may be about to repeat itself. If that happens, be wary of a potential partner who …

> ➤ Has broken more than one engagement
> ➤ Has participated in a string of live-in relationships
> ➤ Is addicted to love
> ➤ Engages in romantic love treks
> ➤ Has multiple divorces.

This person could be a *love junkie*. Historically speaking, the evidence points to failed love affairs possibly exacerbated by the need to experience new romantic thrills.

Sweet Nothings

Love junkies are individuals who become addicted to the high caused by body chemicals released in the presence of romantic, sexual, or passionate feelings. There is a particularly intense rush of these chemicals during the frantic, short-lived attraction and infatuation stages. One out of every 12 individuals is a love junkie, and two-thirds of those are men.

Charting Relationship Histories

A picture is worth a thousand words, they say. A chart of your partner's history of relationships may help you see what your heart may want to camouflage.

Your Partner's Historical Love Graph

Begin by adding the appropriate dots; then connect the lines. If there are too many peaks and valleys in your partner's love lines, you may have drawn a picture of a worrisome past.

Connect lines for each past partner or relationship that lasted over one month. Use a different color of pen for each one.

Chapter 12 ➤ *Pre-Empting Disaster*

	Months:	1	2	3	4	5	6	7	8	9	10	11	12	13	14	15	16	17	19	20	21	22	23	24
Evaluating the Relationship	Fabulous																							
	Great																							
	Good																							
	Okay																							
	Losing Interest																							
	Lost Interest																							
	Broke Up																							

Track your partner's past relationships.

Interpreting Your Partner's Historical Love Graph

What you are looking for are dubious love patterns. Watch for quick climbs, steep drops, and repetitions of love stories. It will be your job to make sure that your relationship doesn't look suspiciously like those that have come and gone before you.

Here's a blank graph. Fill in the progress of your relationship with your would-be live-in. Any similarities here?

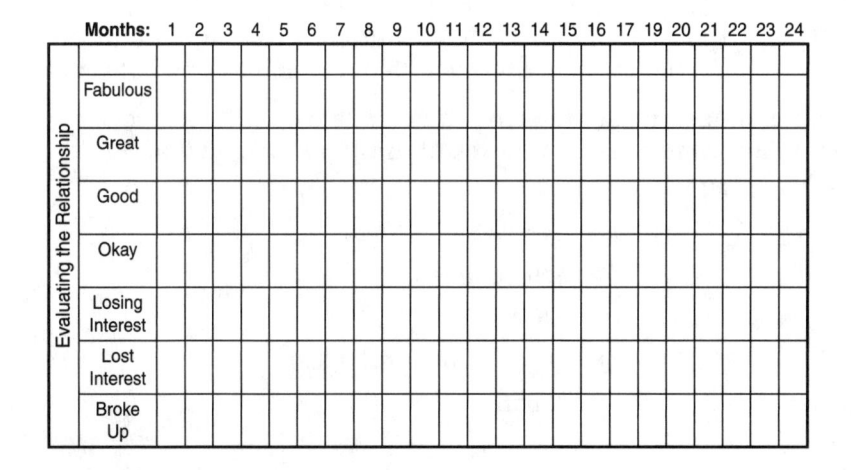

	Months:	1	2	3	4	5	6	7	8	9	10	11	12	13	14	15	16	17	19	20	21	22	23	24
Evaluating the Relationship	Fabulous																							
	Great																							
	Good																							
	Okay																							
	Losing Interest																							
	Lost Interest																							
	Broke Up																							

Track your relationship with your would-be live-in.

The Suspect Under Suspicion

Don't pronounce your love relationship over or toss your honey out just yet. You have two more steps to complete before you do that: Look closely and ask questions.

Try to determine whether there is something significantly new about your would-be live-in that might make the outcome of your relationship different from his or her previous ones. That includes you. What you bring to the partnership isn't what any other partner brought. Furthermore, don't dismiss the onset of maturity, a readiness for commitment, the power of true love, or a real effort to overcome previous relationship pitfalls.

My recommendation is to stay on the alert and don't ignore the signs. Always err on the side of caution. If need be, go back and review in its entirety Part 2, "Coming Up with a Decision on Live-In Love."

In the event, you are unable to objectively evaluate your would-be lover's intentions, get help. In complete confidence, discuss your concerns with a family member or a best friend. If you prefer, go to a counselor. The American Association of Marriage and Family Therapists can provide you with a list of qualified people in your area through their Web site at www.aamft.org.

> **Love's Hot Line**
>
> Certain details of past love affairs are best kept quiet. For instance, refrain from discussing the intimate details of sex in your past relationships or from giving verbal comparisons with your new partner. There is no need to spout insignificant facts that might engender jealousy later.

Some Things Never Change

Don't count on changing your partner's most basic outlook or fundamental personality characteristics. You don't have the power or ability to undo and remake him or her. Catch yourself if you say, "If only I could change this one little thing about Sally or Sam."

The truth is that, within each individual, numerous qualities are deeply embedded. Some qualities are particularly hard to alter. Your relationship history could be affected if your partner is …

- Lazy.
- Headstrong.
- An addictive-type personality.
- Selfish.
- Excessively stubborn.
- Bossy.
- Verbose.
- Self-centered.
- Mean.
- Emotionally unstable.
- A liar.

The preceding qualities are very difficult to change. You might have more influence when it comes to expanding interests, changing simple habits, or altering tastes.

Are Some Historical Facts Better Left Unsaid?

If you or your partner didn't spill all your beans or take all your skeletons out of the closet before hanging up your belongings, you aren't alone. However, you had better make sure that the secrets you left tucked away weren't toxic tales that could poison your relationship later.

Historical secrets become toxic tales when they are discovered if they …

➤ Diminish your partner's trust in you.

➤ Affect the quality of your relationship.

➤ Prove harmful to your love interest.

➤ Catch you in a lie.

Deciding what to tell or not to tell your love partner is best evaluated in the possible outcome. Don't be fooled by temporary peace and harmony in the face of silence. The long-term effect is just as important.

> **Love's Hot Line**
>
> "Honesty is at the cornerstone of every relationship …. Being aware of someone else's true intentions is undeniably valuable, often saving you time … and heartache. When you know a person's true intent, you have the power to control the situation, or at the very least not be taken advantage of."
>
> —David J. Lieberman, Ph.D., author of *Never Be Lied to Again*

The Art of Making the Deal

Getting ready to move in and set up a joint household requires tons of decision making. You will need all of your communication skills and resolution-conflict tools to wade through the issues.

Furthermore, each of you must be alert to the differences with which you approach a conversation. Deborah Tannen, Ph.D., a noted linguist and author, says gender is key. Men, she found, "jockey for status" in conversations and try "to establish a dominant position. Women, on the other hand, are more interested in "the negotiation of connections," said Tannen in her book *You Just Don't Understand* (Ballantine Books, 1991). Whether the other person is "trying to get closer or pull away" is of much greater importance.

Rules of Engagement

Because men and women's perceptions and interpretations of what is being said and what is on the table vary greatly, closing a mutually agreeable living-together deal can be complicated.

To ensure equal bargaining positions for men and women, check out these "Rules of Engagement" before you start conversing:

- Do not attack; talk.
- Don't give in on a point that goes against your convictions.
- Compromise when it is prudent, necessary, and mutually beneficial.
- Stand on equally tall pedestals to maintain equal bargaining platforms.
- Make sure your voice invites discussion.
- Know your bottom line and stick to it.
- Be specific.
- Do not allow room for misinterpretation.
- Use softening-up techniques.

Softening-up techniques are anything from cherry pie and sex to soft music and pearls.

Driving a Hard Bargain

With so much artillery on the field, be prepared, and don't back up as a defensive bargainer. Go on the offense. Here are a few tricks.

1. Learn how to *bargain* for what is less important to you. Write down seven things you want included in the bargain. You can either rate them numerically and agree to giving up the two least important or allow your would-be live-in to remove two that are most objectionable.

2. Rather than give in and accept a condition that is entirely unacceptable, don't give in and don't belabor the point. Go for an entirely new solution.

3. Maintain fairness and agree to consider a point you do not want to accept. Suggest that the two of you reconvene after you have had time to think about it and consider an alternative.

4. Keep time, control, and clear thinking on your side. If you are rattled or rushed, chances are you will default at the bargaining table.

> **Sweet Nothings**
>
> Live-in **bargains** are agreements regarding the sharing of space. Romantic live-in bargains are agreements about sharing a household, responsibilities, and lives.

The Matter of Ultimatums

There is some dispute over whether *ultimatums* are good or bad. Certainly I'll agree they should be used with caution. However, in my books they are definitely on the side of good. Here's the why and how of it.

Chapter 12 ➤ *Pre-Empting Disaster*

The idea of issuing an ultimatum comes up when one person in the relationship is aggravated and frustrated by something he or she thinks is unfair. Normally an ultimatum is a call either to end a lover's stalemate or to change a behavior that is unacceptable. However, just because you pose an ultimatum doesn't mean your partner has to make a decision that is against his or her will. Your partner gets to choose the poison.

State your ultimatum so that it gives your lover a legitimate choice between two actions. For instance, don't say:

> "Either you marry me or I will jump off the Brooklyn Bridge."

What you should be saying is:

> "If you don't want to get married within a certain amount of time, tell me so that I can move on."

Better yet, you should be asking for a timely choice. For instance:

> "Either decide you want to get married and let's figure out a time frame, or decide that you don't and let's end the relationship."

The purpose of the ultimatum is to alleviate your frustration and aggravation, even if the answer is not the one you hoped for. Ultimatums should be the final word, which means there are no ifs, ands, or buts, so you better have all your ducks in a row before you verbalize one. Adhering to the following guidelines will help you formulate a wise, meaningful, and enduring ultimatum.

> **Sweet Nothings**
>
> A romantic **ultimatum** is not a "demand." It is rather the very last "statement" that is made by a man or a woman regarding a set of conditions that must be met in order to keep a romantic relationship intact.

Ultimatum Guidelines

Make sure that your ultimatum is not prematurely issued. Check to see whether your expectations for decision making are reasonable at that point in time of your relationship.

1. Your ultimatum ought to be rational, thoughtful, and fair.
2. Before you give an ultimatum, anticipate your love interest's arguments against it.
3. Prepare your rebuttals before you enter the ring.
4. Be certain your ultimatum is warranted and works to solve your particular problem.

5. Do not present your ultimatum as if it were a matter of life or death. Be matter-of-fact and dispassionate. Try hard not to seem agitated or accusatory.
6. Explain clearly why you are issuing your ultimatum.
7. Select a time and place that will afford privacy when you give your ultimatum.
8. Allow your honey time to consider your offer. Don't press for an immediate answer, but do set a time for his or her response.
9. Vow to remain firm in your request for a decision.
10. Use an ultimatum with caution.

> **Love's Hot Line**
>
> Ladies, you normally give the ultimatums. So, if you are giving an ultimatum about marriage, be aware that men have a problem giving up their freedom and taking on new responsibility. Let him know you understand that he isn't hesitant over the commitment. He may genuinely love you but be scared about being corralled.

Important Discussions You Just Can't Afford to Put Off

If you aren't dealing with someone of unquestionable integrity and honesty, discussions aren't going to matter. I am going to assume that since you have come this far, you have no doubts about your partner's honesty and integrity.

Topics you shouldn't neglect to cover before you move in are presented here. Scratch each one off the list when you feel certain you have arrived at a level of agreement that won't compromise your relationship later on. Don't be afraid to ask the hard questions now.

Don't skip a beat on the last two items on the list. The next two chapters cover legal considerations and economic issues.

Chapter 12 ➤ Pre-Empting Disaster

The Agreement List for Would-Be Live-Ins

Agendas

Views on marriage

Attitude toward having children

Each person's professional or personal goals

Religious beliefs

Role of significant others

Parenting responsibilities if children are present

Independent time

Legal considerations

Economic matters

Love Stats

Actress Susan Sarandon and actor/director Tim Robbins, live-in partners for over a dozen years, appear to have established a good working family relationship. The two actively parent their two boys and Sarandon's daughter. According to *McCall's* magazine (January 2000 issue), Sarandon prefers cohabiting to marriage. However, Sarandon did tell her children that if the issue of marriage was important to them, she and Robbins would seriously consider matrimony.

Part 3 ➤ *Getting Ready to Move In*

Readiness Quiz

Take the readiness quiz by selecting a number from 1 to 10 in the answer column. Ten is the highest rating you can give and 1 the lowest.

	Numerical Answer
1. Do you have complete confidence and trust in your partner?	_____
2. Are you positive that you're doing the right thing?	_____
3. Can you be certain there is an equal commitment?	_____
4. Does your partner possess integrity?	_____
5. Are you both prepared to marry or commit exclusively to each other?	_____
6. Do you feel secure financially with this arrangement?	_____
7. Have you covered all doubts and reached agreement on important issues?	_____
8. Have you told family and close friends that you are moving in together?	_____

If appropriate:

	Numerical Answer
9. Have you had a family meeting with the kids living in your home, and have you provided all the necessary safety measures for their protection?	_____
10. If your ex-spouse is your child's parent, have you contacted him or her to get approval, and have you obtained a promise from him or her not to upset the apple cart of your new living arrangement?	_____

How to score: For the first eight questions, a score of 72 or higher constitutes a passing move-in grade. You need a pair of 10's on items 9 and 10 to advance to home.

Chapter 12 ➤ *Pre-Empting Disaster*

> **Love's Hot Line**
>
> To make single living more appealing, stop thinking of your home and everything in it as only temporary, suggests Michael Broder, Ph.D., author of *The Art of Living Single.* Fix up your present home, or buy one. Stop waiting for something to come along that will make you experience the joy of permanence. Get it on your own. Don't hold back because you are fearful and unhappy, Broder suggests.

Cold Feet

Don't be ashamed to admit you have cold feet. In fact, it's normal. But if you have the shivers, you may want to consider calling the whole thing off. If you have already moved in, you can still move out. You don't have to decide everything at once. But you do need to consider how returning the key or canceling the agreement is going to affect your relationship. You will want to know if your relationship can survive your uncertainty and your partner's possible disappointment and anger. You will also need to decide if you really care.

Madeline had the answers but did nothing about them. She moved in with the tide and treaded water until she moved out.

Madeline admits:

> "I knew I was fooling myself when I moved in with Rick. I was saying one thing and doing another. If I really thought we were going to get along and eventually get married, which is what I wanted, why did we keep two dining room sets, two couches, two of everything?

> "We had dated a year and a half when Rick was transferred out of town. We were both 25 years old and at a stage in our relationship where it was time to either get married or break up. There were lots of reasons why I knew marriage wouldn't work for us; we had different lifestyles, came from different backgrounds, and felt strongly about our own religions. And neither of us was madly in love. I followed him anyway and moved in. All it did was perpetuate a relationship that had become a habit.

"We lived together for nine months until Rick was transferred again. When he asked me to move with him again, I told him only as his wife. He didn't propose, so I stayed behind and was glad that I had kept my couch and dining room set."

Love's Hot Line

Okay, so you called it off. He or she just isn't going to make the grade as a matrimonial partner, and that's what you're after. According to *Men's Health* magazine, most adults think their best opportunity for meeting a suitable spouse is through family and friends or at church and religious activities.

The Least You Need to Know

- ➤ Your love interest's historical past may be the door to your future.
- ➤ Don't count on changing your partner's basic attitudes and personality, no matter how many "how to" books you've read.
- ➤ There is an art to love and romantic bargaining.
- ➤ Ultimatum is not a dirty word in the world of romance and fair play.
- ➤ In order to pre-empt live-in disasters, settle important issues before you move in.

Chapter 13

The Cohabitation Agreement and Other Sticky Legal Issues

In This Chapter

➤ Misnomers about common-law marriages
➤ Why you shouldn't count on palimony
➤ The in's and out's of cohabitation agreements
➤ Determining whether you need a legal live-in contract
➤ Creating a financially secure household arrangement
➤ Tips on avoiding legal hassles later

If you have decided that living together is more your style than marriage, you probably think that you are getting away from those conventional legal issues entailed by marriage. But, after reading this chapter, you may decide that cohabiting can be just as much of a sticky legal web as the marriage contract.

Laws and contracts aren't necessary for lovers. They are, however, definitely on the books to protect those who have stopped loving! The euphoria of *amour* and the generosity of spirit that goes along with love make the angry aftermath of a failed relationship unimaginable.

That is why it is important for you to consider whether or not a cohabitation agreement might be right for you. But don't stop there. You have other safety measures, such as rental agreements and home ownership agreements, at your disposal as well, should you wish to take advantage of them. Be aware, though, that the legal benefits and protection afforded live-in partners are still a "work in progress." The fact that this area of the law is not well-defined adds to the confusion and unpredictability for ex-live-ins.

Common-Law Marriage: a Relic of the Past

In the early American pioneer days, circuit ministers and judges made only infrequent visits to towns. Common-law marriages—a carryover from English law—were recognized to protect women from being taken advantage of by men. Today, however, common-law marriage is an option for a very limited number of men and women who cohabit. Fewer than a dozen states recognize common-law marriages. Where they do, some state legislatures are trying to get this archaic law removed from the books. The legislators want out of the business of deciphering the nature of live-in relationships.

Even if you live in one of the few remaining common-law states, such as Pennsylvania and Montana, merely living together doesn't mean you qualify as common-law partners. Nor can you decide you were, after the fact. Most of these states require that during the time you lived together, you presented yourselves as a married couple and conducted your lives as such in the community for a specified amount of time.

The moral of the story is: Don't rely on common-law marriages to save you. They are an antique from another era.

> **Troubles A'Brewing ...**
>
> Don't look to the "stars" for guidance when it comes to common-law partnerships. Although there are some highly publicized cases like that of a woman who had a daughter in the mid-1980s with New York Yankee Winfield Scott, don't pin your horoscope on these examples. The Texas courts awarded her $1.6 million, legal fees, and alimony during appeals. That was then and this is now! Each case is different but the legal experts agree that, without a credible contract, remuneration is very hard to come by.

Palimony: a Figment of the Imagination

If you think that being someone's "pal" entitles you to *alimony*, you've got it wrong, says Jared Laskin, a Los Angeles attorney with the firm that represented Lee Marvin in the infamous case that gave us the word *palimony*. "The term *palimony* is inaccurate insofar as it implicitly equates a 'pal's' rights with the rights of a divorcing spouse," Laskin states.

For those who fling the word around, thinking they can reap benefits akin to those sought by Michelle Marvin, you need to be filled in on the last chapter. Although Michelle Marvin was originally awarded $104,000 in "rehabilitative alimony," the decision was later reversed, and she got nothing.

Laskin explains that the importance of the landmark case was that the California Supreme Court upheld the right of "a nonmarital partner to sue to enforce an express or implied agreement for property division or support."

A palimony claim, in essence, Laskin asserts, is "a straightforward civil action based on a contract or quasi-contract."

Laskin and many others in the legal profession highly recommend a cohabitation agreement.

> **Sweet Nothings**
>
> **Alimony** is money in the form of an allowance to be paid by a man or a woman to a spouse after the divorce or dissolution of their marriage.

The Cohabitation Agreement

A cohabitation agreement is meant to remedy a host of situations that fall into the legal void for live-ins. Don't shortchange yourself. You may need to protect your bankbook by having a cohabitation agreement before you move in, even though the majority of younger live-in lovers have failed to do so in the past. Many unsuspecting live-ins harbor misconceptions about their rights and misperceive their partner's intentions.

Live-ins who don't have an agreement are taking a risk. Unlike the intricate and well-defined legal rights and obligations passed in state legislatures to afford married individuals protection, live-ins have no legal basis for compensation unless they have a cohabitation agreement. In other words, you can be a partner in a live-in union for years and still have no legal claim to your partner's assets upon dissolution of the relationship or death. You could be out of a home that was intended for you but that is legally not accessible to you.

It is to your benefit to seek qualified legal counsel—one for each of you—to write up your cohabitation contract. The legalities are complex, complicated, and in flux.

What Exactly Is a Cohabitation Agreement?

A cohabitation agreement should be a friendly, mutually agreeable contract. It is not meant to be an adversarial instrument of the law or of love. The living-together agreement is a relatively new legal concept. Before 1970 there was no such thing in the United States. In fact, prior to that date cohabitation was actually considered illegal in all states. You might be surprised to know that in a few states this same law has remained on the books, although it isn't enforced.

Legally speaking, a *cohabitation agreement* is a formal contract between two parties who are not covered by matrimonial law. It is a written document that bears both cohabitors' signatures and most often spells out the terms of their union and their possible dissolution as partners. When necessary, state courts interpret and enforce the terms of the contract.

Legal experts warn that without an existing body of law there are no guidelines for court decisions. The lack of guidelines makes it difficult for you to be absolutely certain how courts will respond when hearing your case, and there are states that refuse to enforce cohabitation agreements at all. Although laws have evolved in a variety of locales, they are not uniform. You can count on them being inconsistent for some time.

What a Cohabitation Agreement Isn't

Right now, no matter what you put into a cohabitation agreement, it will not entitle you to certain legal rights that are afforded a spouse. A cohabitation agreement is in no way a substitute for matrimonial law. Even with a cohab agreement, you will not be able to …

> ➤ Claim your partner's Social Security benefits.
> ➤ Demand health care and other similar benefits from your partner's employer.
> ➤ Transfer assets tax free.
> ➤ Apply for family insurance policies.
> ➤ Enjoy automatic inheritance rights.
> ➤ Assert legal jurisdiction over your partner should he or she become incompetent to handle his or her own affairs.
> ➤ Refuse to testify against your partner in a court of law.
> ➤ Make a health decision for your partner in case of an emergency.

The preceding rights are reserved for spouses, not for spousal equivalents. These are technicalities you should be aware of.

Why Do You Need One?

There are several reasons why you may decide to write a cohab contract, even though you may think it is unromantic and unnecessary at the moment. However, in many ways a cohab agreement accomplishes much of what couples seek to settle in the common prenuptial

---

Love's Hot Line

If cohabiting becomes as large a factor in American courtship as it is in the Scandinavian countries, it may well follow the Swedish path of becoming a social institution. In that case, cohabiting would garner legislative rules and regulations similar to matrimonial law, which covers child custody, inheritance, and alimony.

Love Stats

According to *Forbes*, firms such as Disney, Chevron, IBM, Microsoft, and Proctor and Gamble have chosen to include unmarried partners in their insurance plans. But, unlike a spouse who receives this paid benefit, a cohabitor partner must claim it as earned, taxable income, according to the Internal Revenue Service.

Chapter 13 ➤ The Cohabitation Agreement and Other Sticky Legal Issues

agreements that are popular between older and more-established couples. Whatever you want in the agreement, be sure to get it in writing!

A cohabitation agreement for wealthier individuals can …

- ➤ Establish a legal relationship with the live-in.
- ➤ Give peace of mind.
- ➤ Protect substantial assets.
- ➤ Protect the inheritance of children conceived from a previous relationship.
- ➤ Provide for inheritance benefits of your live-in.
- ➤ Spell out the division of joint property.
- ➤ Clarify each partner's position.
- ➤ Prevent costly legal problems later.

> **Love's Hot Line**
>
> I think it always pays to be practical. If you are a live-in who is paying for and supporting your partner while he or she is getting an educational degree, you may wish to include a payback schedule in your agreement should you separate.

A cohabitation agreement for younger individuals with fewer accumulated assets or wealth can …

- ➤ Spell out the couple's financial deal.
- ➤ Provide for the division of any accrued joint property.
- ➤ Clarify details of any loans assumed jointly.
- ➤ Determine the party ultimately responsible for a lease.
- ➤ Prevent undue financial problems later on.

Addressing the issues in a legal agreement will prevent disastrous economic consequences if and when a separation occurs.

Musts for Cohabs

The following is a list of items that are prudent to cover in any cohabitation agreement—between young, old, rich, or not-so-rich. These points and the preceding ones by no means include each and every possible item. Only you, your partner, and your attorneys can determine when your list is complete.

Everyone should consider including these issues in a cohab contract:

- ➤ Determination of ownership of capital items
- ➤ Determination of distribution of items and property

165

- Responsibility and settlement of debts
- Monetary value and compensation for services exchanged
- Arrangements for pets
- Financial obligations for children
- Responsibility for legal fees incurred in a split
- Determination of ownership of season tickets
- Settlement of joint leases

> **Troubles A'Brewing ...**
>
> To go for the fullest protection, avoid "Implied or Oral" agreements, advises attorney Jared Laskin. The problem with oral agreements, he says, is that memories fade. In the case of an implied agreement, there is an unspoken understanding. Not only may the two of you not be in agreement over that understanding, but the court may interpret it differently from you and can force you to fulfill the conditions of the agreement, even though it was implied and not written.

Imagine This Predicament

To further educate you on the legal limitations of live-in love, imagine being caught in one of the following predicaments.

Predicament Number 1

Sara and Ben were both widowers with sizeable wealth. They wanted to share their lives and were completely devoted to one another but did not want to marry or mix their assets. However, when Ben became ill, Sara was barred from the emergency room. She was not considered a family member by hospital personnel and could not act as Ben's agent in determining the course of his medical treatment despite their previous personal discussion along these lines.

Predicament Number 2

Tammy had lived with Joe for seven years during which time the couple had two children. Because they weren't married, she did not put his name down on the children's birth certificates. Now that she and Joe have split, he says he isn't so sure he is the father of the two and he refuses to pay child support.

Predicament Number 3

Mary and Tom had been divorced a number of years before she met Scott. When she and Scott fell in love, they decided to live together rather than marry, primarily to avoid having to give up Mary's alimony. Several months later, when they had made no attempt to hide the fact that they were living together, Tom stopped sending the alimony payments. When Mary called to ask about the money, Scott said that his attorney had informed him that he wasn't responsible for paying alimony now that she had a live-in partner.

Predicament Number 4

Phil and Pauline bought a house when they moved in together. Each put money down, and during their life together each equally paid the mortgage. When Phil died, he willed his half of the house to Pauline. Although neither thought they would ever have to sell the house, Pauline did. She had to put up the For Sale sign in order to have money to pay the inheritance tax.

Some may construe this as a federal anticohabitation law when in fact it was intended to be no more than a tax benefit for married partners in the event of the death of a spouse.

> **Sweet Nothings**
>
> **Anticohabitation laws** are those that have stipulations that deter people from moving in together. A few states have these laws, which decree, for example, that alimony payments can be discontinued when an ex-spouse becomes a live-in partner.

Getting Around Legal Shortcomings

There are ways to prevent the eruption of the predicaments just described. The following solutions must each be implemented in advance of the problem. Working backward from hindsight is very difficult.

Solution to Predicament Number 1

Had Sara and Ben been aware of the availability of a Durable Power of Attorney for Health Care, Sara might have been able to step in and exert more influence over the course of Ben's treatment and care. This is a real option today for committed, non-married couples.

Solution to Predicament Number 2

Tammy should have pinned paternity on Joe when she filled out her children's birth certificates. Now she is worried and afraid to try. Despite her need for financial assistance, she is concerned that Joe's intervention in her children's lives won't be worth the dollar support. She is making another mistake by thinking that child support and parental visitation rights are hooked together.

Solution to Predicament Number 3

Mary's big mistake was not checking the most up-to-date regulations governing cohabitation and alimony. Before moving in, always make sure that you are not putting any of your financial well-being in jeopardy. A visit to a lawyer could have prevented this predicament.

Solution to Predicament Number 4

Buying a house or any other joint property is tricky business when your goal is to obtain the same privileges of joint ownership as married folks. There is no way to get around all of the legalities. However, with good tax planning, at least you can minimize the dollar loss. Had Phil and Pauline and other couples realized that such a solution is obtainable, they surely would have made better provisions.

The Truth About Home Buying

According to Frederick Hertz, co-author of *The Living Together Kit*, "It's harder to break up co-ownership of a house than it is to get a divorce—longer, more expensive, and more difficult." Now that's a call for caution!

To avoid being responsible for one another's mortgage debt, you and your partner may be safer getting separate loans and establishing the percent of equity each partner owns in the home.

> **Love Stats**
>
> Laws are loosening up when it comes to unmarried couples, whether they are heterosexual or same-sex partners. In 1995 the Appeals Court of the District of Columbia ruled that unwed "committed" couples, heterosexual and homosexual, can adopt children. The case was brought by two homosexual men. The presiding judge, John M. Ferren, based his decision on the fact that the 1954 legislative statute was gender neutral.

Another way to protect yourself and your partner is to sign a "tenants in common" agreement, in which each live-in partner owns special shares of a property and may bequeath those shares to the other. You still have to pay taxes, however, if you're the surviving partner. However, the best rule of thumb is to get legal advice from a practicing attorney in your state who is aware of the latest laws, regulations, and court decisions on similar matters.

Chapter 13 ➤ *The Cohabitation Agreement and Other Sticky Legal Issues*

> **Love's Hot Line**
>
> **Durable Power of Attorney** is a legal document giving you the authority to be the "agent" for someone else, in the event that the person is incapacitated. A **Durable Power of Attorney for Health Care** bestows the authority to act as an agent specifically where health care is concerned. This power of attorney could detail a person's wishes in case of terminal illness or a comatose or vegetative state.

Practical Measures to Protect Life, Limb, and Pocketbook

If you and your partner are going to set up house, the two of you need to make some provisions for handling those day-to-day kinds of things you will undoubtedly encounter. The financial guidelines that follow will help you prevent trouble and turmoil later on—stresses that could tax your heart as well as your wallet.

The number-one measure is to keep your financial affairs in good order. Here's how to do it:

➤ Open a joint account for household expenses.

➤ Maintain a private, personal account for all other monies and investments.

➤ Keep detailed records, original receipts, and annotated check records in order to verify joint purchases versus gift purchases.

Some live-in lovers object to practical considerations and say they aren't necessary. If only love were such a certainty!

A Critical List of Nevers

You would be wise to take legal expert Jared Laskin's list of "nevers" to heart:

➤ Never "contribute money to the acquisition of a major asset, such as a house or a car, which is held solely in the name of your partner."

➤ Never "become so financially dependent on your partner that a break-up of the relationship or your partner's death would leave you financially devastated."

➤ Never "let your partner remain in doubt about your expectations and intentions."

➤ Never "refer to your partner as your 'husband' or 'wife,' adopt the same last name as your partner, or otherwise hold yourself out as married to your partner ...."

➤ Never "put money in a joint account—or hold title to other assets in your joint names—for 'convenience' or 'to strengthen our relationship.'"

In these instances, it's okay to say "never."

The Irony of Another Legal Web

Many men and women who live together in the United States attribute the appeal of their lifestyles to the fact that they are free from legal ties. Ironically, many of these same individuals will later need to seek assistance from the courts to protect interests that are similar to those of married couples. Whatever the rationale, the point is clear: Men and women need to consider the serious financial implications of cohabitation before they put their names side-by-side on the mailbox. Taking this precaution will, in turn, make moving out and moving on easier to handle if and when live-in love comes to an end.

The Least You Need to Know

➤ Very few relationships qualify as common-law marriages today.

➤ Palimony does not mean you get money from your pal just because you lived with him or her.

➤ It is a good idea to consult with a lawyer if you have any financial assets before you move in.

➤ Everyone is a candidate for a cohabitation agreement.

➤ There is a serious need to override the euphoria and optimism of love and to protect your personal financial well-being when becoming a live-in partner.

Chapter 14

Drawing Floor Plans

In This Chapter

➤ Choosing a substantial home front
➤ Selecting your financial plan
➤ Preparing an equitable budget
➤ Spelling out the meaning of "significant other"
➤ Setting the live-in clock

If you are patient and continue to walk slowly into a live-in union, drawing floor plans is the logical next step. Carefully deciding the best place to live, spelling out your partnership expectations, and holding an economic summit are musts. To help you in these endeavors and more, this chapter gives you ample worksheets and exercises.

Much of this chapter requires participation by you and your almost live-in lover. Now is a good time to begin working as a partnership. If you experience an impasse at this point, it will only get worse once you have taken the step of moving home and hearth.

I wouldn't recommend waiting and taking a chance on letting even one of these critical aspects of your live-in union evolve after you have moved in. Without making solid, mutually acceptable plans beforehand, you might have to engage in a cumbersome rearrangement later.

Whose Place? Yours, Mine, or Ours?

Where you live may have more impact on your live-in well-being than you might think. There is considerably more at stake here than an extra bedroom and bath.

Carefully consider these recommendations made by live-ins before you:

Recommendation 1: Go for a neutral place, one that isn't, or hasn't been, either yours or your partner's. Neutral turf dispels previous ownership and puts each of you in an equal seat of power. It prevents either one of you from naturally assuming you're the boss.

Recommendation 2: Select a place where you can both feel at home, secure, and comfortable. This may be hard to do if you are walking in someone else's shadow. It is also complicated by the presence of kids who have taken possession of all the empty space in their parent's home, leaving little room—figuratively and literally—for a live-in lover.

Recommendation 3: Use the period when you are getting your home in shape and preparing to move in as a time for joint effort. Not only are the preparations more fun that way, but the experience will be educational and good practice for working as a team. The goal of your work here is to make the chosen place "ours."

Recommendation 4: Asking someone to move in is easier than asking someone to move out. If you fail to select a place that the two of you will either mutually lease or own, you may find yourself in the unpleasant situation of showing someone the door. All kinds of emotions come into play that may compromise your security, comfort, and financial well-being when you don't have a joint interest in your new home. If you do move onto neutral territory, be sure to reread Chapter 13, "The Cohabitation Agreement and Other Sticky Legal Issues." It will bring you up-to-date on the legalities of signing on the dotted line.

> **Love's Hot Line**
>
> If one of you maintains a separate apartment as a safety net, does that mean you or your partner may have doubts about the outcome of a live-in union? Probably so. My recommendation is, don't make the move. Take the step of moving in together as seriously as you would a matrimonial pledge.

Learn by Example, Case Number 1

A Chicago man in his 30s isn't the only guy to find himself in the following predicament. He had entered into a relationship with a woman during his younger college years. They had traipsed around the country, having a ball, until he landed a serious-type job in the Windy City. With steady employment and an outstanding performance, he began to climb the corporate ladder. Before he knew it, he was attending formal affairs and buying an expensive Lake Shore Drive condominium.

Unfortunately, his lady love was not at all interested in settling down into a conventional lifestyle, nor was she particularly keen on finding a job and her own source of income. Although they decided to part ways, she wasn't the one who departed the condo. The young executive did, for nearly a year.

He felt so responsible for his ex-lady love that rather than endure pangs of guilt, he allowed her to stay while he lived in a less-impressive abode. After one year, he finally came to the conclusion she wasn't about to move. He sold the condo just to be able to make a fresh start.

Learn by Example, Case Number 2

Tish was into fashion and home decorating. However, when she moved in with a widower who was nearly twice her age and whom she eventually planned on marrying, she had to put her designs on hold. It seems he was penny-wise and pound-foolish about live-in matters.

After several months of sleeping in the same bed that he had shared with his now deceased wife, Tish begged him to at least redecorate the bedroom. Her guy thought that was foolish.

Tish and her widower didn't last until their wedding day. She knew she could never make his home feel like hers or feel free of his wife's ghost.

Worksheet: Picking an Address

This is the first in a series of worksheets in this chapter. Although you can fill in the blanks by yourself, you can achieve a dual purpose if you do it with your honey. Or, if you prefer, you could make three copies of each worksheet. Both of you could fill in a copy separately; and then the two of you could compare answers, negotiate, and finally use the third copy to complete one definitive worksheet together.

> **Troubles A'Brewing ...**
>
> Don't give it away for free. And I am not talking about sex. I am talking about rent. Unless you are in an advanced love relationship, paying all the rent and household bills is not a good idea. Your partner may learn to confuse love with comfort unless the two of you revise your arrangements into a more-equal exchange. This situation happens all the time, whether it is the man or the woman who is the workhorse.

Part 3 ➤ *Getting Ready to Move In*

Pick an Address

Unless the directions tell you otherwise, for each statement either choose the phrase that best represents your views or fill in the blanks.

1. We will each have an equal say in where we live. (Yes/No) _____

2. We will move into your place, my place, or find a neutral place to live. _____

3. We will rent month-by-month, take a year's lease, sign a lease for longer than a year, buy an apartment, purchase a duplex, purchase a home. _____

4. We will each sign the lease agreement, one of us will sign the lease agreement, we will assume one mortgage together, we will assume separate loans, one of us will assume an entire house loan. _____

5. We will be looking for a space that has one, two, three, four, five, six, or more rooms. _____

6. We have need for the following extra rooms (possible selections include nursery, office, game room, music room, guest room): _____

7. We will live within a _____-mile radius of each person's workplace.

8. We can spend _____ dollars on our housing per month.

9. We will decorate all rooms together or each assume responsibility for specific rooms. _____

10. We will each bring the following pieces of furniture with us:

    _____ _____ _____
    _____ _____ _____
    _____ _____ _____

11. We will not bring the following pieces of furniture with us:

    _____ _____ _____
    _____ _____ _____
    _____ _____ _____

12. We will purchase the following household items:

    _____ _____ _____
    _____ _____ _____
    _____ _____ _____

> 13. We will give extra keys to our house to best friends, renters, siblings, no one.
>
> 14. We will compose a complete household budget during an economic summit (Yes/No).

You don't have to stop with these questions merely because the worksheet has. Hopefully this exercise will open up discussion on your own unique issues.

Convening Your Economic Summit

By now, you shouldn't doubt the need for an economic summit. After all, plenty of examples have shown how the dollars and cents of living together can pull the plug on a live-in love relationship. Indeed, financial matters can wreak havoc on even happily married folks who have been holding annual summits for years.

Furthermore, the kinds of financial arrangements you make demonstrate your commitment—or your lack of it—and set important precedents should you move onto matrimony. If you aren't aware of the financial jeopardy that living together can pose, go back right now to Chapter 13!

Select Your Financial Plan

You have the following options at your disposal. My recommendations follow.

> **Love's Hot Line**
>
> Now that you want to live together like an adult couple, act like one. No more handouts from mom or dad. Assume your own financial responsibility!

- ➤ Split all living costs right down the middle.
- ➤ One person pays for everything.
- ➤ Go by the percentage each partner earns in relation to the whole.
- ➤ Come up with another option if you can.

The only way to truly make sure one person is not being taken advantage of is to go right down the middle—a 50/50 split. However, a fair way to work as a real team is to contribute according to your earning power.

Part 3 ➤ *Getting Ready to Move In*

Troubles A'Brewing ...

I don't care how old or young you are. Choosing a free ride will usurp your independence, put you under someone else's control, and affect your self-esteem. And *giving* a free ride certainly puts you in obvious jeopardy, as well. Buying love and companionship isn't worth the investment.

Worksheet: Developing a Live-In Budget

Now that you have selected a financial plan, you are ready to make a budget. You may want to post this worksheet in an obvious spot in the house.

Our Live-In Budget

Keeping in mind your financial plan, fill in the blanks.

Item	Total Cost	His Share	Her Share
Joint Costs			
Rent	_____	_____	_____
Utilities	_____	_____	_____
Telephone	_____	_____	_____
Food	_____	_____	_____
House repairs	_____	_____	_____
Furniture	_____	_____	_____
Negotiable Costs			
Entertainment	_____	_____	_____
Odds and ends	_____	_____	_____
Travel	_____	_____	_____
Pets	_____	_____	_____

Car payment	_____	_____	_____
Gas	_____	_____	_____
Car insurance	_____	_____	_____

Individual Costs

Children	_____	_____	_____
Family gifts	_____	_____	_____
Savings	_____	_____	_____
Medical expenses	_____	_____	_____
School loans	_____	_____	_____
Credit card debt	_____	_____	_____
Clothing	_____	_____	_____
Personal expenditures	_____	_____	_____
Totals	_____	_____	_____

Is this a fair and workable budget? Can you each meet the bottom line? If not, go back and make the necessary adjustments.

How Significant Is the Other?

When you move in, you should no longer be thinking me, me, me, me. You should be thinking me, him (or her), us. That's the minimum for acceptable significance. If you need to review the topic of significant other, go back to Chapter 3, "The Facts and Fictions of Living Together." Be sure to look over the "Checklist for a Significant Other."

Your actions are what count most of all. They demonstrate the other's significance in your life. What you do for, and with, each other and how these gestures measure up to your expectations are the crux of the matter. To make sure everyone is on the same page, you had best sit down and discuss how you plan to operate as a *spouse equivalent*. Cover all bases!

Sweet Nothings

According to the U.S. Census Bureau, the new up-to-the-minute name for a live-in lover, cohabitor, or significant other is **spouse equivalent.**

Worksheet: Defining Significant Other

To see how significant you and your partner intend to be to one another, fill our this worksheet. Be honest with yourself and your partner.

Rating Your Significance

	Will	Won't
We will/won't …		
1. Be equal social partners.	_____	_____
2. Attend family functions together.	_____	_____
3. Assume responsibility for one another.	_____	_____
4. Spend most of our leisure time together.	_____	_____
5. Expect others—family and friends—to treat us as a couple.	_____	_____
6. Share household responsibilities.	_____	_____
7. If children are present, assist with their needs.	_____	_____
8. Visit family members together on a regular basis.	_____	_____
9. Develop mutual friendships.	_____	_____
10. Attend business and social functions together.	_____	_____
11. Share in each other's wealth or lack thereof.	_____	_____
12. Help one another when help is needed.	_____	_____
13. Take joint vacations.	_____	_____
14. Make each other a priority.	_____	_____

Completing this worksheet is important so that each of you has a clear understanding of just how significant each is to the other and so that you both find that level mutually agreeable and acceptable. However, keep in mind that the greater the significance, the greater the love, the greater the commitment, and the greater the chance you will live happily under the same roof.

You'll find more on the topic of your relationship and how to build a lasting and meaningful one as you progress through the remainder of this book.

When Significant Expectations Aren't Met

If you aren't entirely satisfied with how significant your love interest rated you, go back to the round table for a discussion. When you do, be prepared and do not take anger along. If you need help in formulating your talk, the following step-by-step agenda may help.

1. On a piece of paper, write down the worksheet answers of your honey's that you find problematic.
2. Be able to explain why they are troublesome and provide an example.
3. Determine whether there are other areas in which you feel your expectations may not be met, based on your partner's answers.
4. Provide specific examples of things you might encounter as a couple that would define your significance or lack thereof.
5. Describe exactly how you would want your partner to react to these situations.
6. Have in mind how significant you expect to be.
7. Mentally draw a bottom line.
8. Be prepared to sit at the table until either your love interest complies, you set a further discussion date, or you call time-out to evaluate whether you should change your move-in plans.
9. Take time to think through this significance thing carefully.
10. Make a decision and stick by it.
11. Devise your own significant-other worksheet.
12. Be sure you and your partner agree on expectations inherent among significant others.

There is no room to hedge on this critical dozen. A consensus of opinion and understanding must be formulated when it comes to expectations in the union. This is a fundamental issue that affects all else in the living-together arrangement.

> **Love's Hot Line**
>
> If you feel comfortable with your would-be live-in and your decision, you won't have a problem telling your parents, family members, and friends about your plans before moving day.

Drawing Kids Into the Floor Plan

In Chapter 2, "The Scoop on Live-In Love," the precarious position of children within live-in relationships was discussed. If you have children, now is the time to figure out how they fit into the scheme of things. If you have drawn your house plans, you have already determined their physical place in the household. The following worksheet will help you and your would-be live-in come to terms regarding the children, whether yours or your lover's.

Part 3 ➤ *Getting Ready to Move In*

Troubles A'Brewing ...

At the first sign of trouble, remove your child and yourself from the household, seek shelter, and get help. If your child shows any signs of distress or discomfort, do not ignore them. In the event you are unable to handle or evaluate these concerns yourself, immediately find a qualified expert to assist you.

Making a Place for the Kids

Expectations	His Answer Yes/No	Her Answer Yes/No
1. My kids will be welcome in our household.	_____	_____
2. My kids will have a place to call their own in our house.	_____	_____
3. You will participate in family events with my children.	_____	_____
4. You will assume some of the parenting responsibilities.	_____	_____
5. You will assume some of the costs associated with having my children in our home.	_____	_____
6. You will not reprimand or punish my children without my consent.	_____	_____
7. You will not spank or physically jeopardize the safety of my children in any way.	_____	_____
8. You will be a friend to my children.	_____	_____
9. You will include my children in your family's functions.	_____	_____
10. You will afford me private time with my children.	_____	_____
11. You will agree to allow me to make my children a priority.	_____	_____
12. You will not begrudge the money I spend on my children.	_____	_____
13. You will always treat me with respect in front of my children.	_____	_____

14. You will not argue or shout at me in front of my children.   _____   _____
15. You will help me create a home in which my children feel secure, safe, and happy.   _____   _____

There is very little room when it comes to bargaining on these points. The safety of your child, and even the precariousness of the child's life, depends solely on you.

> **Love's Hot Line**
>
> Keep vigilant watch over your children, especially when a new love interest enters the picture and moves in. Watch for signs of distress or depression. Any change in mood or pattern may be significant. Do not delay. Talk with your child and get your child help if necessary. Prevent a minor problem from becoming a major one.

Dealing with the Ex-Spouse

This next worksheet is applicable only for those folks who have children with an ex-spouse or ex-live-in. Before your live-in arrangements are set in concrete, it's prudent to lay out the situation for your ex, explaining what the deal is and giving him or her a chance to air concerns. By informing all parties of the arrangements, you prevent any misunderstandings and anger on the part of your ex and your prospective housemate.

> **Troubles A'Brewing ...**
>
> Do not put yourself in a position where you could lose residential custody or visitation rights to your children. That is why it is absolutely essential that your child's other parent agrees to your live-in arrangement and also that your live-in arrangement is a totally safe haven for your child.

Part 3 ➤ *Getting Ready to Move In*

Complete the following two worksheets provided for your convenience and well-being. Then you can relax in peace and harmony.

Dealing with My Ex

Check off each item as you accomplish it.

- ❑ Position your ex-spouse outside the parameters of your new live-in relationship.
- ❑ Inform my ex-spouse of my decision.
- ❑ Ask for consent to take the children.
- ❑ Explain all living conditions.
- ❑ Make clear that all financial responsibilities and visitation rights remain the same.
- ❑ Ask him or her to voice any and all concerns now.
- ❑ Ask for my ex's cooperation.
- ❑ Take all precautions to ensure that your ex does not become an adversary.
- ❑ Determine a different plan of action if he or she disagrees.

Dealing with My Ex-Spouse and My Live-In

	I Will	I Won't

My live-in lover must pledge to …

1. Accept that my ex-spouse with whom I share children will be part of their lives. _____ _____
2. Cooperate and allow the nonresident parent to have access to their children. _____ _____
3. Abide by my decisions and that of my ex's when it comes to the kids. _____ _____
4. Facilitate communication between me and my ex. _____ _____
5. Refrain from feeling jealous of my ex-spouse's presence in our children's lives. _____ _____
6. Willingly do whatever is necessary to make it easy for my children to maintain a relationship with my ex. _____ _____

Setting the Alarm Clock on Live-In Love

Let's face it, unless you are a "true believer" in live-in love, you have an agenda. You have your sights set on something other than cohabiting for the rest of your life. To ensure you don't get stuck in the live-in phase of love, devise a time line and set the alarm. It is easy to fall into complacency or to tread water in a stalemate. To prevent these situations from happening, get out the calendar and affix your agenda to it now.

Compiling a Live-In Time Line

Fill in with the appropriate month/year.

I expect to get a ring by _____

I expect to set a wedding date by _____

I expect to be married by _____

I expect to move on by _____

Don't forget to write these dates in your calendar. Otherwise you've made out this worksheet in vain.

The Least You Need to Know

➤ Where you set up your new home may determine the success or failure of your live-in experience.

➤ You need to devise a financial plan that each of you feels comfortable and satisfied with.

➤ Spelling out your significant relationship is of the utmost importance.

➤ Creating specific plans for the welfare, safety, and happiness of children who live with cohabiting couples is a number-one priority.

Chapter 15

Finding the Best Building Materials

> **In This Chapter**
>
> ➤ What friendship, tolerance, and trust have to do with live-in unions
> ➤ A test of your live-in ability
> ➤ A prescription for household love
> ➤ A custom love calendar to create
> ➤ What constitutes a healthy relationship?

Everything about your partner is magnified when you live together—love, endearing qualities, and annoying habits. There is no escaping the latter by retreating to your own home or apartment.

You have already been given some tips on managing your relationship. This chapter will concentrate more on what you will need when you share space, especially if your goal is to turn this arrangement into a long-term union.

Don't expect every day together to be full of bliss. How to achieve your share of that comes later. Right now, let's settle for a secure household foundation in which harmony and satisfaction can grow.

What's in Your Tool Kit?

Let's review the items already in your tool kit. If you are missing any one of them, go back and get it!

- Romantic decision-making
- Real love
- Clear motives
- Compatibility
- Mutual agendas
- Sexual compatibility
- A golden opportunity
- Communication skills
- Conflict resolution know-how
- Power plays
- Ability to make a deal
- Ultimatum guidelines
- Cohabitation agreement
- Financial plan
- Mutual view of significant other
- Homesite

New Nuts and Bolts

The hallmark of romantic relationships that endure the test of time is *friendship!* I found that to be true in all of the happiest married folks whom I interviewed, from coast to coast, for *Marriage Secrets* (Birch Lane Press, 1993).

John M. Gottman, Ph.D., a leading research scientist on marriage, methodically uncovered this secret in his University of Washington "Love Lab." Although Gottman is talking about marriage, don't dismiss what he says. You need friendship for harmonious and satisfying live-in unions too. So plug in the word *live-in* for *marriage,* if it makes you feel better. Here's what Professor Gottman says about this necessary nut and bolt, known as friendship, in his book *The Seven Principles for Making Marriage Work* (Crown Publishers, 1999):

> "At the heart of my program is the simple truth that happy marriages are based on a deep friendship. By this I mean a mutual respect for and enjoyment of each other's company. These couples tend to know each other intimately …. They have an abiding regard for each other and express this fondness … in little ways day in and day out."

Sweet Nothings

Just in case you need a definition of **friendship,** commit this one to memory. A friend is someone you can count on to support you and wish you well in all endeavors. He or she is a person with whom you share an intimate and affectionate bond. Friendship is the mutual and active expression of friends.

Three Imperative Bolts, Three Accompanying Nuts

In construction and building vernacular, *bolts* are metal pins that are secured in place with a threaded metal *nut*. Consequently, a nut and a bolt make sturdy fasteners that keep pieces together. It isn't any accident that I have labeled the following qualities "nuts and bolts." Leave out just one of these qualities and your romantic structure could fall down!

Consideration: You don't have to be born with consideration, but you do need to acquire it. Considerate people deliberately take other people into account. You can train yourself to take notice of your live-in partner and consider him or her before you act.

An Example of Consideration: You are bringing home Chinese for dinner and can afford only one main dish. Your mouth is watering for shrimp with snow peas. Nonetheless, you go for lemon chicken, your second choice, because you remember that your partner is allergic to shrimp.

Tolerance: A tolerant individual is one who accepts another individual's imperfections without complaining and doesn't constantly try to change the other person.

An Example of Tolerance: Your partner is slightly overweight. It has bugged you because you thought it was a sign of laziness, something you simply could not tolerate. Initially you nagged him to go to the gym with you. Then you realize he is completely taxed by his vigorous efforts at the office. Reading is more relaxing for him. You quit trying to get him to exercise and decide to accept his flabby biceps and slightly rounded belly.

> **Love's Hot Line**
>
> Professor Gottman asserts that a way to show respect to your partner is to include him or her in your decision-making process. Not to do so shows disrespect, Gottman believes.

Respect: When you respect someone, you treat that person with consideration and courtesy. You regard the person highly, hold him or her in esteem, and do not devalue the person's differences. Real respect in a love relationship acts as a conscience that prevents a partner from doing any harm—in word or deed—to the other.

An Example of Respect: Eric's father has invited him to join the family business. Eric isn't sure what to tell his dad. The job would be a good deal, but he has reservations. It would tie him and Julie, his live-in fiancée, closely to his family. He tells his dad that he can't make a decision without consulting Julie first.

Sharing: Sharing isn't something that always happens naturally. It may take a little nudging to relinquish the idea of separate ownership when you first move in together. However, your mom or teacher won't be there to tell you, "Be nice, Johnny. Share your dresser drawers, your pool table, your space, your stereo, your time." If you feel the need to label everything "his" or "hers," you don't have the ability to share.

An Example of Sharing: You come home and notice that your tennis racket is on the couch. You saved for months to be able to buy that racket. When your honey comes

187

out of the kitchen, she has on her game shoes and your T-shirt, the one personally signed by tennis great John McEnroe. You are just about to scream when she puts her arms around you and tells you that she won the city championship with your racket. Your shirt added just the measure of good luck that put her over the edge. You give her a congratulatory kiss and tell her she is welcome to both the shirt and the racket when she plays in the district tournament.

Honor: Author Gary Smalley writes that honor is the most important principle in healthy relationships. "When we honor particular people we're saying in effect that who they are and what they are carries great weight with us." Hence, they not only are extremely valuable in our eyes but deserve priority in our lives.

An Example of Honor: You have a million and one things to do to complete a legal brief. The deadline falls one day after your partner's thirtieth birthday and the family dinner her parents have planned in celebration. You would love to have the liberty of staying late at the office and getting in a little extra work time, but your live-in means the world to you. You decide to stay two hours later each night for two weeks prior to her birthday so that you will be done well in advance of your deadline. With this plan, you feel confident you will be able to give her birthday the respect it deserves.

Conscientiousness: A conscientious individual is one who goes about life, work, and play making sure that everything is done in a thorough, complete way. An individual who is conscientious about a love relationship monitors his or her actions in order to enhance and perpetuate a mutually satisfying union.

> **Love's Hot Line**
>
> In a study by David M. Buss, professor of psychology at the University of Michigan, acts of sacrifice and concessions to appease a partner with regard to his or her parents are acts of love. I add, they are necessary acts of love to achieve and maintain household harmony.

An Example of Conscientiousness: Susan is afraid that she has been neglecting Fred. After all, she is finishing up her residency in surgery and spending nights at the hospital. Finally she has two full days off. Although she is dog-tired, she decides to surprise Fred at his office, take him out to lunch, and prepare an intimate, sexy, candlelight dinner for that evening.

Test Your Nuts and Bolts

Here's a chance to test your level of consideration, tolerance, and respect. How you react to each of these hypotheticals is a true measurement of these relationship builders.

Chapter 15 ▸ *Finding the Best Building Materials*

If your live-in partner …	Yes	No	Maybe
1. was sleeping in on a day off, would you keep the lights off in the bedroom and get dressed in the dark?	___	___	___
2. had a big project due and you had the day off, would you cancel plans and help him/her out?	___	___	___
3. got fogged in and couldn't fly back after a business meeting on a night your folks were coming to dinner, would you be understanding?	___	___	___
4. looked forward each week to drinking beer and watching Monday night football in his underwear on the couch, would you invite your girlfriend over on Tuesday instead of Monday so that he wouldn't have to get presentable?	___	___	___
5. was being given an award and you had yoga class or racquetball that night, would you give it up to attend the awards banquet?	___	___	___
6. asked you to go with him/her to visit family members you didn't like, would you go?	___	___	___

If you …

	Yes	No	Maybe
7. got a bonus and wanted to use it to take a trip, would you ask your live-in along and pay his/her expenses?	___	___	___
8. knew you weren't giving your live-in partner enough of your time, would you make the effort to change that?	___	___	___
9. found yourself in a situation in which you might possibly betray your partner's trust, could you walk away from temptation?	___	___	___
10. wanted to attend a family function to which your live-in was not invited, would you decline the invitation?	___	___	___
11. are asked to do a favor for your live-in, would you make every attempt to do it?	___	___	___
12. felt your live-in wasn't giving appropriate time and attention to the relationship, would you call his/her attention to it?	___	___	___
13. disliked your live-in's sister but she wanted to visit the two of you, would you be hospitable?	___	___	___

189

Interpreting Your Answers: There isn't room for any check marks in the No column. One or two "Maybes" at the most will pass. Flying marks go to those of you who said "yes" to every question. You are the ones who have the biggest supply of nuts and bolts.

A New Way to Look at Love

Misperceptions about love are counterproductive to its growth. The prevailing romantic, idyllic view of it oftentimes squeezes out the necessary reality that keeps love alive. You are now ready to look beyond this view and see love in a new way, one that will benefit serious romantic relationships, including your live-in union.

> **Sweet Nothings**
>
> **Romantic love,** according to Nathaniel Branden, a California psychotherapist, is a passionate spiritual-emotional-sexual attachment between two people that reflects a high regard for the value of each other's person."

Let's start with "Four Love Axioms":

1. **Love should reflect a choice.** Yours! Love isn't like getting stung by a bee. It doesn't happen regardless of your intention. When you consciously make the decision to love someone, you should vow with great determination to fulfill the responsibilities and the work that come with it.

2. **Love is not a state of perpetual perfection, nor is a loved one perfect.** Perfection is not something that can be achieved in love. Nor does it apply to the human condition.

3. **Love is finding happiness and ecstasy more days than not.** When Cinderella and her prince lived happily ever after, they weren't looking for a fairy-tale ending. They were willing to go with reality and settle for more good days than bad.

4. **Loving someone takes time.** Without giving love the house it needs, love withers.

Making Love Part of Your Concerted Efforts

In his article, "A Vision of Romantic Love" published in the *Psychology of Love* (Yale University Press, 1988), psychologist Nathaniel Branden describes isolated behaviors found in couples who maintained a deep love relationship for many years. They are efforts worth nothing. These lovebirds …

➤ Expressed their love verbally.
➤ Were physically affectionate.
➤ Expressed their love sexually.
➤ Demonstrated appreciation and admiration for one another.
➤ Engaged in mutual self-disclosure.

Chapter 15 ➤ *Finding the Best Building Materials*

- ➤ Provided each other with an emotional support system.
- ➤ Expressed love with gifts.
- ➤ Accepted demands made by each other.
- ➤ Put up with one another's shortcomings.
- ➤ Made time to be with each other.

Love is a verb; these actions are acts that demonstrate love. They should be part of your relationship behavior.

> **Love's Hot Line**
>
> The human needs that love fulfills, says psychologist Nathaniel Branden, include companionship, sexual fulfillment, an emotional support system, self-discovery, and value for oneself given by another individual.

Your Daily Planner

You won't do your live-in relationship any good if you leave your love efforts, your nuts and bolts, inside this book. Therefore, get ready to prepare your daily love planner. Fill in the following calendar with a daily expression of your love. Be creative, vary your efforts, and, while you're at it, have your partner fill out one, too.

A Month's Worth of Love Efforts: Your Sample Calendar

Monday	Tuesday	Wednesday	Thursday	Friday	Saturday	Sunday
Say "I love you"	Send flowers	Leave a card under the pillow	Meet for lunch with a kiss	Give a love gift	Surprise romantic dinner	Light a fire and open a bottle of champagne
A kiss and thank you for visiting the folks	Say "I love you"	Do not criticize the new hairdo	Ask how the job's going	Unwind with a bubble bath for two	Say "I love you"	Sex fest
Cuddle and ask how life is treating your partner	Suggest a movie your partner has been wanting to see	Say "thanks for making me so happy"	Quiet time for spilling what's on your mind	Say "I love you"	A night for his sexual pleasure	Forgive her for failing to show up at your tennis match
Send card to his office for a job well done	Say "I love you"	Call his mom to see if her cold is better	Buy the book he's been wanting to read	Agree to demand to have his kids for the night	Surprise night out: concert tickets	Go to a football game

191

Part 3 ➤ *Getting Ready to Move In*

Love's Hot Line

The person who doesn't believe in playing love games will have problems returning to the romantic stage of excited infatuation. Each relationship needs a dose of infatuation now and then. Your calendar of love efforts should be filled in with the intention of producing that high during the month.

Fill In Your Own Calendar

Monday	Tuesday	Wednesday	Thursday	Friday	Saturday	Sunday
_____	_____	_____	_____	_____	_____	_____
_____	_____	_____	_____	_____	_____	_____
_____	_____	_____	_____	_____	_____	_____
_____	_____	_____	_____	_____	_____	_____
_____	_____	_____	_____	_____	_____	_____
_____	_____	_____	_____	_____	_____	_____
_____	_____	_____	_____	_____	_____	_____

Chapter 15 ➤ *Finding the Best Building Materials*

> **Troubles A'Brewing ...**
>
> The little things you do to express how much you care for your partner will set the tone of your relationship. That's why there should be an equal exchange of such goodies. No one should do all of the giving. If you are the one who always gives, reevaluate the relationship and ask, "Is this person really worthy of my attentions?"

There Is No Substitute for a Healthy Relationship

You can't buy a healthy relationship at the local hardware store. A healthy relationship is something you build together, based on how your personalities and needs mesh, your abilities to give and receive love, and how your body chemistries work together.

If you have a healthy relationship, your partner and the love your partner shows for you will ...

- ➤ Enable you to feel empowered.
- ➤ Increase your self-esteem.
- ➤ Fulfill your companionship need.
- ➤ Meet your sexual needs.
- ➤ Provide the opportunity for self-growth and discovery.
- ➤ Provide emotional support.
- ➤ Help you reach your full potential.
- ➤ Make you happy, not sad.
- ➤ Make you feel more whole.
- ➤ Make you feel sexy.
- ➤ Make the world look brighter and better.
- ➤ Help fulfill your dreams of love.
- ➤ Add a richness to your life.
- ➤ Help you in unsuspected ways.
- ➤ Make life easier, not harder.

> **Love's Hot Line**
>
> One of the best ways to remind yourself and your honey how much you love each other is to say so every day. Sometimes we forget just how much someone means to us. By telling each other "I love you," neither of you will take your love for granted. And don't forget to keep in mind what loving someone means and the responsibilities it entails.

If these qualities describe you and your partner, congratulate yourselves on a clean bill of health. Nothing could make you feel better!

Troubles A'Brewing ...

Don't get carried away with all this love talk. "Real love" is seldom "ideal love." However, real love never defies the boundaries of a healthy relationship. If you get stuck on ideal love, you will never be satisfied with the real thing!

The Least You Need to Know

- ➤ Without respect, there can be no love relationship.
- ➤ Using materials that build love will make your household structure sturdy and durable.
- ➤ When you move in, be sure to set the sharing mode on high.
- ➤ People who love each other show it in their actions, thoughts, and deeds.
- ➤ A healthy relationship does not have to be a perfect relationship.
- ➤ A healthy relationship is full of pluses, not minuses.

Chapter 16

Beware of Poor Foundations

In This Chapter

- ➤ Why serious differences signal a poor foundation
- ➤ When your lover's bed is still warm from a previous relationship
- ➤ How to keep from flooding your partner with negative vibes
- ➤ How jealousy affects your relationship
- ➤ When to steer clear of the unfaithful
- ➤ Why there is danger in poor precedents

In several of the earlier chapters, you looked at some of the circumstances in which it is ill-advised to think of becoming live-in lovers. Now that you are on the threshold of forming your live-in union, you need to note certain problems that will interrupt the harmony and the love you look forward to having in your cozy cohab nest. There is no way of getting around the fact that any one of the issues in this chapter will create a wobbly live-in foundation.

If you think that many of these issues don't apply to you, that is fine—and a plus in your favor. However, don't gloss over the discussion on setting precedents. That's a topic that can rock anyone's abode!

Too Much Disparity of Style

We are not speaking of aesthetics or architectural style here. If your partner likes modern and you like Country French, the two styles can be effectively blended or alternated throughout a house.

Not so when it comes to the fundamental opinions and beliefs that affect your entire outlook on life. They are not so easily worked through and will continue to plague the long-term harmony of your relationship.

For instance, if you haven't figured out how to deal with issues like conflicting religious beliefs, opposing beliefs in marriage, and clashing views on children and family, your relationship is probably in *gridlock*.

Research shows that once this happens, the couple moves away from each other emotionally and the love tie has a very high probability of coming undone. Under those conditions, if you insist on going ahead and moving in, at least don't unpack your bags for a while.

> **Sweet Nothings**
>
> Researchers use the word **gridlock** to describe a situation in which there is no way for a couple to reach an understanding because neither partner will, or is able to, budge from his or her conflicting point of view.

Warm Beds Are Off-Limits

Some facts ought to be obvious, but in the throes of love you might not notice that the bed is still warm. Love relationships are tricky enough without throwing in added complications. Depending on the couple and the nature of previous relationships, the warmth of the bed could create a seismic crack in the structure.

The bed is still warm from a previous relationship if your lover …

1. **Exhibits signs of a "rebound mindset."** Moving in with a rebounder calls for caution. A *rebounder* frequently feels a need, even a panic, to experience a new love relationship that will confirm his or her desirability, lessen the pain, eliminate loneliness, and give hope of finding a life partner. Once your partner has shed this rebound mentality, his or her outlook about you may change too.

2. **Has not reached a state of closure from a previous love relationship.** Before the bed cools down to a comfortable temperature and is fit for a new partner to climb into without getting burned, the individual fresh out of a relationship must achieve closure. In order to achieve this, an individual must come to a determination about why a relationship ended. Thinking through the ending of the relationship closes the door on doubt, acknowledges truth, and frees a man or woman to resume dating and loving on a healthy note.

Chapter 16 ➤ *Beware of Poor Foundations*

In the event that either is true, it would be wise to stay out of bed and save your lovemaking for later.

Jealousy, Infidelity, and Mistrust

Jealousy, infidelity, and mistrust have no place in the structure of your relationship or your home. Let's tackle jealousy first.

Leave Jealousy on the Doorstep

There are two sides to jealousy, assert researchers Laura K. Guerrero and Peter A. Andersen. It can either be "an expression of love" that is valued by some or a "perceived paranoia" that causes distress for others. The latter is the hazardous one.

Romantic jealousy, according to researchers Gregory L. White and Paul Mullen, occurs in the real or perceived presence of a rival love interest. It is "a complex of thoughts, emotions, and actions that follows loss of or threat to self-esteem and/or the existence or quality of the romantic relationship."

In other words, romantic jealousy arises out of fear—fear of losing love and fear of losing the exclusivity one has with a romantic partner. Uncertainty, loneliness, and disapproval are all part of the process that makes a jealous partner feel insecure, confused, depressed, inadequate, angry, resentful, sad, and abandoned. Certainly none of these conditions affects a relationship in a positive manner, and if exploited they can result in serious harm to one or both partners.

> **Love's Hot Line**
>
> According to studies by psychologists who research the inner depths of relationships, the correlation between love and trust was higher among married couples than unmarried couples.

Infidelity Has a Venomous Bite

Sexual intimacy is a significant act of love. It spells commitment, ties the bond, and seals exclusivity between romantic partners. No wonder sexual betrayal is often the most painful and damaging act that a love interest can inflict on a partner.

Sexual betrayal cuts to the core of the partner's own sexual being, chips away at trust, brings enormous disappointment, awakens jealousy, shakes self-worth, and unleashes disgust.

Infidelity is considered a betrayal of love and in that sense represents the most excruciating element of the entire episode, some researchers say. That's why men and women who thought that their partners had had a sexual affair void of any attachment to another person found it easier to cope and get over the betrayal.

197

Cover-up lies, however, can make the betrayal worse, says Frank Pittman, psychiatrist and author of *Private Lies: Infidelity and the Betrayal of Intimacy* (W.W. Norton and Co., 1990).

Sadly enough for the state of love relationships in our society today, monogamy is extremely difficult to maintain, according to the information coming to the surface. The workplace, business travel, and finally men who follow their fathers' examples all contribute to the high probability of extrarelationship sex for men and women. In fact, Peggy Vaughan, author of *The Monogamy Myth* (Newmarket Press, 1998), believes that because our society is so entrenched in sexuality and influenced by a media that glorifies affairs, young adults as well as teens will find it nearly impossible to be monogamous.

If that's the case, an epidemic of distrust in serious love relationships is well on the way.

Distrust, an Outgrowth of Jealousy and Infidelity

Researchers Guerrero and Anderson conclude that as a consequence of romantic jealousy, partners become suspicious and distrustful.

The problem is a recurring lack of trust. Let's say we accept the concept put forth by family therapy founder Ivan Boszormenyi-Nagy: Every relationship includes a ledger of the give and take of trustworthy acts that affect one's residual trust.

If trustworthy acts do not counterbalance the distrust caused by jealousy and infidelity, the partners in the relationship will suffer a diminished amount of trust. The absence of this trust, some expects say, contributes to one partner's actively distancing himself or herself from the other, thereby contributing to relational dissatisfaction. Once the relationship is considered dissatisfying, who wants to stay in such an arrangement? Very few!

Troubles A'Brewing ...

Research shows that depression can result from feelings of jealousy. When depression occurs, an individual may feel not only sad but guilty, worthless, angry, and suspicious. Researchers Guerrero and Andersen believe that a jealous individual's sense of worthlessness can even lead the person into thinking that he or she deserves to be betrayed.

Shelving Your Jealousy

Although becoming jealous from time to time is a natural human reaction, it doesn't mean you have to succumb to jealousy's fatal blows.

Step 1: Ask yourself whether or not the eruption of your jealousy is warranted. Don't let it escalate without just cause.

Step 2: Guerrero and Anderson suggest that exposing your jealousy to your partner and dealing with it together can benefit your relationship. To do that, you must be able to engage in calm, quiet, constructive discussion that can enhances one another's understanding.

Avoiding Unfaithful Partners

If you want to eliminate a cause for jealousy and distrust, don't get involved with anyone who is most likely to be unfaithful. Psychiatrist Frank Pittman, author of *Private Lies: Infidelity and Betrayal of Intimacy,* says you can lessen the odds of having an unfaithful partner by someone who respects your gender, doesn't get kicks out of seducing strangers, values being sexually faithful, and whose parents have been faithful to each other.

Flooding a Partner with Bad Vibes

As I've said in previous chapters, the marital research done by John M. Gottman, Ph.D., has, I think, valuable implications for cohabiting partners. That's why it is worthwhile to look at his model that depicts why some couples fail to solve problems. This University of Washington professor is definitely onto something. With overwhelming accuracy, he can predict which couples will encounter serious marital problems based on observing the following process.

Observation 1: Couples who begin conversations with a "harsh startup"—that is, negative and accusatory, nasty or spiteful statements—are headed for trouble.

Observation 2: The communication that follows the startup is defensive, contemptuous, and critical.

Observation 3: In the wake of these negative exchanges, emotions run high, limiting the ability of the partners to process information, remain alert to what the other partner is saying, and respond productively. In Gottman's vocabulary, they are "flooded."

Observation 4: As a result of becoming flooded, Gottman says, individuals respond with the reflexive action either to fight or to flee. Either way, they have prevented the issue from being resolved.

The moral of these observations is to bury any trace of "harsh startups" in someone else's yard. Never make them part of how you interact with your live-in partner.

> **Love's Hot Line**
>
> If it is any consolation, there might be a cultural element to exhibiting jealousy. Americans aren't the most jealous folks on earth. Individuals in Spain, Germany, Portugal, Turkey, and the United Kingdom seem to have us beat in the amount of jealousy they show.

> **Troubles A'Brewing ...**
>
> Professor John Gottman says that in a conversation between partners, 96 percent of the time the outcome, whether positive or negative, will be determined within the first three minutes of their communication.

Blatant examples of harsh statements start with ...

"What a waste of money. Your movie selection sucked."

"We both agreed on that movie. You aren't smart enough to understand how good it was."

"Oh yeah? You're just a pseudo-intellect."

"Well, well. Do you even know what that word means?"

"Do you know what it means to be nice?"

"Nice? Look who's talking. You can't even spell the word."

"There is no use talking to you."

"Blah, blah, blah, blah."

"I'm drowning."

Love's Hot Line

Clinical psychologist and marital therapist Dr. William F. Harley Jr. recommends that couples discover one another's most important basic needs and learn how to meet them. That's how he suggests partners find and maintain love. Examples of basic needs are your partner's desire to excel in creative endeavors, to feel needed, to receive reassurance, or to experience love through sex. A partner who understands the importance of basic needs would then provide time and encouragement for creativity, verbalize how much they appreciate and require their partner's presence, let them know they are doing a good job as a parent, lover, or spouse, and demonstrate affection during sex. What one must be sure of are all their partner's real needs, not only the needs they assume they have.

Two Faulty Joints

As long as we're at it, let's build the sturdiest structure possible and eliminate all faulty joints.

> ➤ **Family disapproval.** A disapproving family could easily trip you up, enable your significant other to feel insignificant, and cause household strife.

When important family members don't quite get your live-in relationship, try to help them understand your decision. If your choice has been well thought out, they may be more likely to see it your way.

➤ **"Love busters."** Clinical psychologist and marital therapist Dr. William F. Harley Jr. says that angry outbursts, disrespectful judgements, annoying behavior, selfish demands, and dishonesty may bust up a marriage relationship. I say they represent a very serious and faulty joint if brought into your live-in household.

You have been forewarned. Family disapproval and too many love busters can make your house come tumbling down around you.

The Danger of Setting Poor Precedents

By this point, you may be getting impatient to move in, and you're probably saying, "Okay already. Why such a big fuss about this foundation stuff?"

The truth is that your foundation will affect not only your live-in relationship but your marital relationship, should you choose to move on to matrimony. The behavioral patterns set while you live together will follow you into marriage. Consequently, the precedents you set as live-in lovers are critical to your future well-being.

Therefore, make sure that your live-in foundation …

➤ Isn't deficient in commitment, the kind described in Chapter 3, "The Facts and Fictions of Living Together."

➤ Incorporates behavioral expectations appropriate for a lifetime relationship.

➤ Doesn't come up short on positive roles for each partner.

➤ Doesn't skimp on prudent guidelines for partnership behavior.

> **Love's Hot Line**
>
> Love coach and author Janet O'Neal says that "a commitment is an internal process, and for the relationship to really work, both people have to have undergone this process in their hearts, in their minds, and in their souls."

A Case of Poor Precedents

Kenny and Robin had been dating for about a year and had just moved in together when, at Robin's prodding, Kenny decided to go back to college and finish his degree. Robin, the great nurturer, suggested he quit his job in order to concentrate on school and finish the degree quickly. At every turn of the page, Robin was there to take charge, guide him in his course selection, get him to graduation, compose his resumé, and set up his job interviews. If Kenny had put on a blindfold, Robin might have passed for his mommy.

The couple made slow but noticeable progress in their individual endeavors during their lengthy live-in phase, with Robin continuing the role of nurturer. Eventually they married and within a year had become the parents of Kenny Jr.

The Backfiring of Poor Precedents

Shortly thereafter Kenny lost his job. The precedents set in their live-in days failed to change or accommodate Robin's expectations of a mature relationship. She grew weary nurturing Kenny Jr. and his dad, too. Although Kenny was bewildered by Robin's frustrations and her unwillingness to continually nurture him, her relentless nagging for him to grow up and get a job made him resentful and abusive in a childish way.

The Final Outcome

Unfortunately Robin learned too late that mothering is a poor precedent to set for an adult love relationship. Once the style had become fully entrenched in Robin and Kenny's live-together lifestyle, changing became impossible.

The last time I spoke with Robin she was in the midst of a terrible divorce and a tangled residential custody battle. Kenny claimed he was the proper custodial parent since he had been at home the entire last year taking care of Kenny Jr.

A Foundation Safety Recheck

Check off each item in this safety recheck.

- ❏ We have agreed upon our fundamental outlook of love, cohabitation, marriage, and family.
- ❏ Neither of us is suffering the lingering effects of a previous love relationship.
- ❏ We will not give each other cause to be romantically jealous.
- ❏ If one of us suffers a bout of romantic jealousy, the other is prepared to help lay it to rest.
- ❏ We have fully earned one another's trust.
- ❏ We have vowed not to be unfaithful.
- ❏ Harsh startups are not part of our communication modus operandi.
- ❏ Our family is on our side.
- ❏ We will try to avoid love busters.
- ❏ The precedents we set in our live-in relationship will be sound enough to serve us well in the future.

Congratulations! You have finished your preparation and are ready to advance to living under one roof. If you have thoroughly prepared yourself, you will be willing to undertake the efforts described in Part 4, "Living Under One Roof." These efforts will ensure your happy household.

> **The Least You Need to Know**
>
> ➤ Irreconcilable differences are rarely resolved within a live-in relationship.
>
> ➤ Moving in with an untrustworthy individual is like building your home on top of quicksand.
>
> ➤ A case of infidelity can strip a relationship of necessary trust.
>
> ➤ How you begin a conversation with your honey is the most critical phase of the exchange.
>
> ➤ How you behave in your live-in union shapes your marriage behavior.

Part 4
Living Under One Roof

You passed all the tests, jumped all the hurdles, and moved in together. As in any relationship when two people decide to reside under one roof, you need more than "good luck" as a house-warming present.

In fact, what you need is a new vocabulary to accommodate your new lifestyle, a living-together etiquette, some smart moves, tips on how to keep love's embers warm, and directions on stoking the fire with plenty of sex.

Those are the gifts that await in Part 4. They aren't frivolous, thoughtless, or random selections. They are offerings that have been proven to make a world of difference in the lives of all kinds of committed partners, including live-in lovers and married couples. They are your household essentials!

Don't leave them in their wrapping. Take them out, use them often, and heed the wisdom behind each. You will, no doubt, reap their benefits.

Chapter 17

A New Lifestyle Vocabulary

In This Chapter

➤ When "I" becomes "we"

➤ How to make your love nest "ours"

➤ Defining couplehood

➤ Casting your couple image

➤ How to combine "I," "you," and "us"

➤ Testing your level of interdependence

Now that you have moved in together, it is appropriate to start using an entirely new vocabulary. You'll need a little time to master the words that apply to this phase of your romantic relationship. This chapter will help you grasp their essence so that they can become a natural part of your verbal expression.

Don't think that because you have heard these words before, you know precisely what they mean. Until you use them in the context of your own relationship, you really can't begin to understand how complicated and essential they are to making love, especially live-in love, work.

Becoming "We"

You have lived through the "I" era of the 1980s and acted out its *cultural narrative*—a decade dedicated to self and bathed in entitlement. The focus of the "me" decade was on oneself and on self-satisfaction above all else!

Fortunately that period of time is over. It wasn't good for promoting long-lasting, devoted love relationships. Sorry, but you simply cannot successfully live with your dog, let alone another human being, without thinking beyond "I."

The 1990s brought a renewed emphasis on being a couple. The "we" regained significance. It is not possible for a good romantic relationship to operate on anything less. Nonetheless, with the advent of each new decade, social thought flows in numerous and varied directions affecting our individual outlook.

When you reside under the same roof with your honey, however, you cannot afford to be held captive by fickle social attitudes that aren't healthy for love relationships. That's why it is imperative to understand the nuances of the word "we." No matter what year it is, this two-letter word is essential to the well-being of your relationship.

> **Troubles A'Brewing ...**
>
> No one *is* telling you to leave "I" totally out of the equation. However, its usage has to be modified once you live under the same roof with your honey. If you persist in overusing "I" and underusing "we," your relationship will add up to unhappy nights and dissatisfied days.

An Elementary Lesson in "We"

Take a look at the words associated with "I" and "we." Commit them to memory and make sure they become an integral part of your vocabulary.

"I" Words	"We" Words
Mine	Ours
His or hers	Theirs
Singular	Plural
Individual	Couple
Me	Us
Independent	Interdependence
One	Two

Chapter 17 ➤ A New Lifestyle Vocabulary

> **Sweet Nothings**
>
> The **cultural narrative,** explain family therapists Michael Glenn, M.D., and Barry Dym, Ph.D., is the cumulative conventional wisdom of prevailing social trends and society's messages that prescribe how a couple should think, behave, and measure themselves. The cultural narrative covers a wide array of points from mate selection to financial considerations to timely reproduction.
>
> The cultural narrative for love relationships has changed greatly over the past decades, influenced in large measure by the new role of women. The subservient position of women has evolved from token jobs to junior partnerships to full equality. The result has been a big impact on mate selection and marital expectations. Don't fall behind the times!

Using "We" in a Sentence

"Sure, I would love to go to a movie with you and Kate. I'll tell Sue that's what I decided to do this Saturday. I don't have a thing to do. I'll tell her I made plans to meet you at 7."

What's wrong with this response? As you've already guessed, It's way too heavy on the "I" words. This speaker needs to use "we" words. The entire meaning of the sentences changes when the individual switches to the "we" words:

> We would be happy to join you for dinner.
>
> We usually go out for Chinese on Sunday.
>
> We prefer to spend Friday nights by ourselves, but let me check and see whether we might join you at the movie.
>
> Come on over to our house and spend the evening with us.
>
> The two of us will be happy to attend your party.

> **Sweet Nothings**
>
> If it was love at first sight or shortly thereafter, the French would call such an immediate, intense reaction a ***coup de foudre.*** Literally, that means "the bolt of thunder."

"We" implies consensus agreement and unity. And that is precisely why "we and not "I" is an important part of your new live-in vocabulary.

Making a Home "Ours"

Whether you took the advice to go for a neutral home or whether you stayed in your abode or his, it now belongs to the two of you. Separate ownership won't do. Maintaining control over a household that was your private domain relegates your partner to an inferior position, even if he or she is treated like an honored guest. Whoever had home before, it must now belong to "us."

There are practical steps you can take to merge households and bring "ours" into fruition. Consider these:

- Rearrange the furniture together.
- Shop for household items together.
- Make room for each of your favorite items.
- Change your living space to reflect the character of you as a couple.
- Remove most or all traces of the bachelor or bachelorette pad.
- Display photographs of the two of you.
- Include items in your home that are mementos of your history together.
- Create an area for each of you that is a private place
- Make concessions regarding the display of each other's prized possessions.
- Do not demand that a personal item to which your partner unequivocally objects remain in your common space.

Remember you are sharing a space called home. It should reflect your partnership, not your single self.

Committing to Practical Maneuvers

Now that you know what it takes to make your space into "ours," you have no excuse for not proceeding into action. To prevent you from forgetting to put "ours" into practice, fill out the following *punch list*—a builder's list of unfinished chores—to see what still needs to be done:

Chapter 17 ➤ *A New Lifestyle Vocabulary*

> I should remove _____ from the living room.
>
> I should add _____ to the living room.
>
> Removing _____ from the wall would be appreciated.
>
> Hanging up _____ on the wall would be a smart move.
>
> I want to tactfully recommend the following changes in our home: _____, _____, _____.
>
> Prudent additions to the bedroom include _____ _____.
>
> I should probably store _____ and _____ until there is room for my private space.
>
> Three items that might make both of us feel more comfortable with our home are _____, _____, and _____.
>
> To make the living space reflect more of our shared taste, we should add _____ _____.
>
> To make the living space represent our lives as a couple, we should display _____ _____.

Coupling: Unveiling a New Duo

It isn't appropriate now that you are living together to refer to yourselves as roommates or, for that matter, as significant others and lovers. You are, for all practical purposes, a *couple*.

According to family therapist and psychiatrist Michael Glenn, M.D., and Barry Dym, Ph.D., a clinical psychology professor at Harvard Medical School, co-authors of *Couples: Exploring and Understanding the Cycles of Intimate Relationships* (1993), the couple has become the ideal icon, romantically overplayed in the media. The repercussions of unrealistic coupledom expectations will be discussed in Part 5, "If the Roof Caves In." For the present, however, we are concerned about what these family therapists think being a couple means and how it changes your outlook and behavior.

Each couple, Dym and Glenn report, has a character and style that is separate and distinct from their individual personalities. Precisely put, "A couple's character is made up of regular, enduring patterns of thinking and feeling, acting and reacting."

The style by which a couple becomes known is a blend, a balance, and an interaction of their individual characteristics and developing history. For example, collectively you could be described as fun-loving, serious, romantic, and argumentative. Independently, you may not carry the same labels. In other words, your relationship develops a life and identity of its own when you become a couple.

> **Love Stats**
>
> Family therapists Michael Glenn, M.D., and Barry Dym, Ph.D., maintain that contemporary life has contributed to the evolution of couples. Because of our highly mobile society, close proximity to family is frequently missing. Couplehood compensates for the loss and provides many functions previously assigned to family and community. Consequently, there is a "frantic quest" in the United States today for individuals to find the right mate.

Growing Into the Word "Couple"

It is worthwhile to take a good look at what Glenn and Dym have to say about how you grow into a couple. Behind the word, there is plenty of substance. To begin with, Glenn and Dym have found that couples grow, develop, and evolve through the repeated revolutions of a three-stage cycle.

Being in love does not preclude the presence of this cycle. How you develop as a couple is not necessarily inclusive in the growth of love. Rather, love for one another is reflected in the way in which you join forces, adapt the sum total of our individual narratives, and move from "I" words to the "We" vocabulary.

> **Sweet Nothings**
>
> Each of us has an **individual narrative** that describes who we are. How we came to be that person and what values, ideas, and expectations we subscribe to are all part of this narrative. It is the personal counterpart to the cultural narrative.

The Expansive Stage

The *expansive stage* is characterized by the revelation of each person's individual identity and life story. This stage is similar in content to the development of intimacy in the growth of love. It is a somewhat idyllic period in which "we" takes hold, and the two individuals form an identity that binds them together as a couple. This stage is propelled by the desire for fusion.

The Contraction and Betrayal Stage

The expansive stage doesn't linger forever after. Rather, the *contradiction and betrayal stage* begins. Each person makes pilgrimages back to self and to separate spheres of life and functioning. Although this withdrawal is neutral and not a reflection of the relationship, one partner may feel betrayed or abandoned, say Glenn and Dym. The focus of this stage is a definite contrast to the expansive stage. However, this period of couplehood is normal and natural. The foray back to self and the differences that make each partner a distinct individual cannot be ignored. As long as they make it back to their *home base* their relationship is not in jeopardy.

> **Sweet Nothings**
>
> Authors and family therapists Michael Glenn, M.D., and Barry Dym, Ph.D., call the stage at which a couple resides most often and returns to frequently, their **home base.** The home base could be any of the three stages within the couple's cycle.

The Resolution Stage

In the *resolution stage,* couples compromise, negotiate, and accommodate the issues and feelings that arise within the stage of contraction and betrayal. The resolution stage is a period of growth, consolidation, and new understandings. How couples handle the resolution of this three-stage process will determine their success or failure as a couple and subsequently the duration of their union.

Defining Characteristics of Couples

The characteristics that define the character of a couple, say Michael Glenn, M.D., and Barry Dym, Ph.D., are …

- The rhythm of their cyclical revolutions through expansion, contraction, and resolution.
- Their "home base."
- How they talk with each other.
- How they make decisions.
- The way they manage household matters.
- How they choose to raise children.
- Their characteristic ways of showing and making love.
- Their interaction during conflict, play, or stress.
- Their shared goals, values, and ideas.
- How they fight.

> The way they meet differences.

> How they handle and solve crises.

The way in which each of these situations is met combines to form a unique fingerprint for each couple that reflects their identity as a couple.

The Blending Process

As two people strive to become a unit, the couple's character is being formed by sorting out individual elements that will be put into the final partnership. Authors Dym and Glenn call this process "organizing." I call it blending. Nonetheless, the process which we are describing is the same.

The best way to understand this process is to think of yourself—or your partner—and picture how you project yourself at work, in a group, or by yourself. Then take a good look at how you act with your partner in public and in private on a daily basis.

It is important to remember that the state of being a couple is not static. A couple does not reach a certain point and remain there forever. Instead, the blending process occurs, over and over again, reacting to changes in personality, experiences, and events. The more two individuals blend and mesh their pasts into one greater force, the more of a couple they become.

Love Stats

A **blended family** generally refers to a family in which children from previous marriages are combined into a new matrimonial family. As more couples choose to live together, we see blended families in nonmarital unions, as well. According to statistics, one in six American children lives with one natural parent and a step-parent. A large proportion of these families are blended families.

Fitting the Pieces Together

Patterns emerge from the way couples interact and blend. Dym and Glenn use the term *sequences* to describe this phenomenon. They claim that "Sequences create order out of chaos; they turn into patterns that limit, define, and focus our experience."

Sequences form predictable, interactional patterns that sometimes resemble a ready script. They enable a couple to project with almost absolute certainty how a partner will react. In turn, this knowledge makes couples feel safer and more secure in their relationship. Sequences are formed in nearly every phase and in most things we do together, Dym and Glenn say.

Identifying Your Sequences

Sequences become automatic. They can be both positive and negative. Because they are repetitious means of behavior, you should monitor your sequences to make sure they benefit your relationship and are not doing it any harm.

You could uncover conscious and unconscious sequences by taking note of how each of you repeatedly acts under the same circumstances. For instance, take notice of how you …

- Make up after a fight.
- Handle your weekend plans.
- Make joint decisions.
- React to each other's down days.

Once you uncover a sequence, follow it through to its conclusion. See how it plays out and affects your relationship and how it shapes you as a couple. If you need to make adjustments, make them now.

Interdependence: Converging Into One Now and Then

Deborah Tannen, Ph.D., linguist and author of *You Just Don't Understand: Women and Men in Conversation* (Ballantine Books, 1991), suggests that we make the mistake of thinking that there are only two critical viewpoints: independence and dependence. The latter is often construed as a negative, particularly by men who incorrectly see it as a threat to their independence.

What we seem to forget to use is the word *interdependence*. It implies a mutual degree of dependency and an intermingling of independence and dependence. The degree of interdependence is thought to be generated by *intimacy*—the extent and content of sharing, communication, warmth, support, and understanding that each generates toward the other.

> **Love's Hot Line**
>
> Think of a pair of socks, one left, one right. To have a complete pair, both socks must be present. In the same way, you and your partner are a pair of socks, mutually dependent on each other as a couple, yet separate individuals. When you act together, your sense of being a couple is greater.

There is a loss of self in accepting the responsibility of being a couple but not in the sense of lost freedom or individual identity. Rather, the loss of self one experiences as a partner within a couple is expressed in self-sacrifice for a loved one.

Picturing Interdependence

One way to visualize interdependence is to compare it to teamwork, whether that of a horse and carriage or of partners in a doubles' tennis match.

If you need a realistic picture drawn for you, read on to see how Ted pinch-hit for Samantha during a family crisis.

Part 4 ➤ *Living Under One Roof*

Samantha was working late one night when her mom called and told Ted that her husband, Samantha's dad, was very ill. Ted got on the phone, made plane reservations for Samantha, and then picked her up at the office. When she got home to pack, she found her suitcase open on the bed waiting for her to toss in a few things. By the time she closed the suitcase, Ted had made her a sandwich to eat on the way to the airport and had found a pad and pencil for writing down all the things she needed him to do while she was away.

For another example of interdependence, meet Ann and John.

John got a new boss he wasn't quite sure how to handle. Ann, who was much more perceptive about these things, suggested they invite the new boss and his wife over for dinner. She thought if she could observe him in a social setting she might be able to offer John some suggestions.

She helped John prepare a lovely meal that was meant to tell the boss they thought he was pretty important. During the evening, Ann was able to get the new manager to engage in friendly chatter. Not only had they lived in several of the same cities, but they realized that they had common interests.

By the end of the evening, John felt much more comfortable and natural around his new boss. He wouldn't have been able to accomplish that rapport without Ann's help.

Troubles A'Brewing …

Unless you willingly fill in for one another and are able to anticipate one another's needs, you don't yet have the hang of interdependence. True partners, couples, or lovers must demonstrate and develop this capability and capacity. Without it, they omit one of the essential vocabulary words required to describe harmonious, meaningful live-in love unions.

Rate Your Level of Interdependence

Take this little quiz to see where you and your live-in stand. Don't hesitate to have each of you respond. Remember, you are a duo now.

Put your check mark in the most appropriate column.

"Always" or "Usually" is what you are aiming for. "Sometimes" won't do. "Rarely" or "Never" means you aren't even in the same ballpark.

	Always	Usually	Sometimes	Rarely	Never
1. I cover for my partner when he/she forgets to do something important.	❏	❏	❏	❏	❏
2. If my partner forgets something, I try to remind him/her.	❏	❏	❏	❏	❏
3. I try to make my partner's life less stressful by helping him/her out.	❏	❏	❏	❏	❏
4. If my partner can't make a family function, I will go in his/her place.	❏	❏	❏	❏	❏
5. My partner's presence makes me feel more complete.	❏	❏	❏	❏	❏
6. If I have had a really bad day at work, I know my partner will help me put it into perspective.	❏	❏	❏	❏	❏
7. When my partner is down in the dumps, I am aware of it and try to do something to make his or her day happier.	❏	❏	❏	❏	❏
8. My partner and I can accurately call each other helpmates.	❏	❏	❏	❏	❏
9. My partner's problems are my problems.	❏	❏	❏	❏	❏
10. My partner's success is my success.	❏	❏	❏	❏	❏

The Least You Need to Know

- Residing under one roof means giving up a little of "you" in exchange for a lot of "us."
- You need to make every effort to make a home into "ours" and drop much of what *is* only yours.
- Becoming a couple is a complex and continual process.
- The identity you project is different and apart from your individual identity.
- Couples develop predictable patterns of behavior.
- A couple that does not exhibit interdependence is a poorly matched pair.

Chapter 18

Living-Together Etiquette

In This Chapter

➤ Why etiquette is important in live-in love

➤ Your etiquette starter set

➤ Etiquette for every room of your house

➤ Etiquette relationship tips

➤ Rules for socializing, visiting, and making introductions

Without a doubt, the earliest writings of Emily Post belong to a bygone era. Gentility for the sake of behaving in accordance with the "best society" is of little importance to those who aren't modern-day "social climbers." Nonetheless, the legacy of etiquette is very much alive and has a place in your live-in relationship.

"Manners are made up of trivialities of deportment which can be easily learned if one does not happen to know them; manner is personality—the outward manifestation of one's innate character and attitude toward life," Emily Post wrote. To her credit, and more relevant for the twenty-first century, she added, "Etiquette must, if it is to be of more than trifling use, include ethics as well as manners."

The ethics behind your relationship and live-in etiquette ought to reflect the values of respect, consideration, and common courtesy. If you already adhere to these values, living by the rules of etiquette ought to come somewhat naturally.

Etiquette for the Sake of Harmony

The etiquette of living together is every bit as important to our times as are the rules of etiquette we abide by in the athletic or business arenas. Sure, your home is the one place you are supposed to be able to let down your hair, be yourself, or grumble and groan. All of that is fine as long as your behavior doesn't make your partner swim in a pool of rudeness.

Judith Martin, alias Miss Manners, says etiquette is simply a matter of common sense and a way to make someone else feel comfortable. Etiquette is prescribed decorum that can prevent the rise of hostilities worldwide or within your home!

Drop all the childish protests. You need to master this chapter. Even children are expected to behave according to rules of etiquette that are the hallmark of civilized behavior. If you need to start over, your local library will surely have copies of the Muppets' or Barney's book of "please" and "thank you."

One of the most important things to remember is that you won't get the benefit of your partner's courtesy, respect, kindness, and consideration unless you offer the same. Without employing these rules of conduct, you will be moving into chaos. The chances of developing a peaceful, harmonious, satisfying, and workable living arrangement will be practically nil.

Love Stats

Emily Post, otherwise known as Mrs. Price Post, was born in 1873 and died in 1960. Her famous book, *Etiquette in Society, in Business, in Politics, and at Home*, was first published by Funk and Wagnalls of New York in 1922.

Peggy Post, author and wife of Emily Post's great-grandson, thinks that all too often we forget our best manners when interacting with those closest to us. Yet those are the folks who should be the beneficiaries of our kindest and most courteous self!

What Is Etiquette?

Etiquette is the learned elements of common courtesy and rules to live by, behaviors that differ according to ethnic background, culture, and time period. According to the updated and rewritten *Amy Vanderbilt's Complete Book of Etiquette* (Doubleday, 2000), etiquette keeps "self-centered instincts in check."

Chapter 18 ➤ *Living-Together Etiquette*

Judith Martin, syndicated newspaper columnist and author of *Miss Manners Rescues Civilization* (Crown, 1996), identifies three kinds of etiquette:

1. **Regulative etiquette.** Logical and functional rules of behavior that reflect thoughtfulness and orderliness. Examples include RSVPs to dinner parties, canceling a doctor's appointment, taking turns, and acknowledging receipt of gifts.
2. **Symbolic etiquette.** Arbitrary but individually and publicly scrutinized modes of behavior that are primarily symbolic respect. For instance, you wouldn't wear a baseball hat while singing the national anthem.
3. **Ritual etiquette.** Rules and customs for the ceremonious events in life. Ritual etiquette dictates the behavior for such events as weddings, inaugurations, and burials.

> **Love's Hot Line**
>
> Peggy Post said it *is* proper to notify your parents, family members, extended relatives, friends, mail carrier, and landlord when you move into your honey's abode.

It is proper etiquette to be polite and reserved during a funeral, and to be formally dressed when invited to a black-tie affair.

Starter Set of Etiquette, Live-In Style

From the moment you move in together, keep your manners and courtesy intact. To make sure you do just that, abide by these rules of living-together etiquette:

- ➤ Inform each other of your daily schedule.
- ➤ If you are expected home for dinner but won't make it, call as soon as you can.
- ➤ Let your live-in know if you will be late.
- ➤ Say please and thank you.
- ➤ Be polite when each other's friends call.
- ➤ Take thorough messages.
- ➤ Respect each other's space.
- ➤ Greet each other with a meaningful and sincere word or gesture morning and night.
- ➤ Don't open each other's mail.
- ➤ Don't pry into your partner's personal possessions or invade each other's privacy.

> **Love's Hot Line**
>
> It is always a thoughtful and loving gesture to stop what you are doing when your partner comes through the door, greet him or her with a welcoming smile, and always deliver a kiss. This is the kind of living-together etiquette that *is* wise to turn into habit.

221

- Pick up after yourself. Your live-in is not supposed to be a personal housekeeper.
- Don't eavesdrop or spy.
- Share, allocate, and agree on household responsibilities.
- Be ready to compromise.
- Put both of your names—or, alternatively, neither of your names—on your answering device.

Etiquette in the above form abets your love and encourages the niceties of living together.

Etiquette, Room by Room

Each room of your house requires different rules of etiquette. Each rule shows respect, courtesy, and consideration for the person living with you. Let's walk through your home, room by room.

Etiquette for the Bathroom

This is one of the most delicate spaces to share. Try to use these suggestions to ease into it:

- Keep matches close by and light one to help remove odors.
- Clean up the sink after you use it.
- Always flush the toilet and leave the seat down.
- Dispose of tampons properly.
- Hang up washcloths and towels. Put dirty ones in the laundry.
- Replace an empty roll of toilet paper.
- Clean out the tub or shower after you use it.
- Fill the soap dish if the soap ends up in tiny pieces.
- Do not use bubble bath fragrances that your partner finds offensive.

This list is a his and hers. Both of you should give it your best try.

Etiquette for the Dining Room

Apply these rules even when the pot roast is overcooked:

- Sit down and eat at least one meal a day with your live-in.
- Don't start eating until your partner sits down with you.
- Don't leave the table before your partner is finished eating.

> **Chapter 18** ➤ *Living-Together Etiquette*

- If the table is specially set or the meal preparation timely, make a nice comment or say thank you.
- Always help clear and clean up.
- Make mealtime count, and engage in meaningful conversation about each other's day.
- Don't leave dirty dishes on the table.
- Never read a book during dinner with your partner sitting across from you.
- Do not take the last piece of pie without offering to share it.

Use dining etiquette to show off how considerate and attentive you can be—a bonus of good manners.

> **Love's Hot Line**
>
> Peggy Post gives some pointers on handling your napkin. At an ordinary dinner, place it on your lap when you sit down. However, at a formal affair, follow the lead of your hostess and wait for her to place hers on her lap first.

Etiquette for the Kitchen

No one wants to live with a slob. Assume your share of kitchen duty.

- Don't leave your dirty dishes in the sink for your partner to wash.
- Start the dishwasher if it is full.
- Empty the dishwasher if the dishes are clean.
- If you get into the leftovers, wrap them back up to keep them fresh.
- Take out the garbage.
- Wipe up sticky spills.
- Don't leave the stove top a mess
- Deposit recyclables in the proper containers.
- Do not leave sacks of garbage sitting on the kitchen counter.
- Start the morning coffee if you are up first.

These little acts of common courtesy will get noticed. That should be reward enough.

Etiquette for the Living Room

The living room is probably the biggest room in your home and the most public. Be sure your behavior does not need to be censored. Simply …

- Pick up your dirty dishes and put them in the dishwasher. Put beer cans and empty potato chip bags in the trash.
- Don't leave food, personal items, or clutter lying about.

- If you spill something on the couch or on the rug, clean it up.
- If your partner's dog makes a mess, don't wait for your live-in to get home and clean it up.
- If your honey's friends come over, put on some clothes.
- If the card game is running late and your live-in has to get up early for work, ask your pals to keep it down so he or she can get some sleep in the next room.

Living room etiquette is a true measure of your joint efforts to make both partners feel pleased with their home.

Love's Hot Line

Emily Post called it "the old gray wrapper habit." What she was referring to was wearing old, dowdy clothes around the house and at the table. She didn't think that was good manners. Remember that you're trying to keep your lover alive and interested, so always aim to put your best face forward.

Etiquette for the Laundry Room

Dirty clothes leave a foul odor and a bad taste.

- Don't take clothes out of the dryer and dump them without folding them just because they aren't yours.
- Don't leave underwear soaking in the sink for days.
- Clean out the sink after washing the dog or scraping off muddy track shoes.
- Don't put items into the dryer that your pal doesn't want shrunk.
- If you use the last drop of detergent, buy another bottle or put it on your mutual shopping list.

You may need to use some romantic encouragement to get your honey to partake in laundry room etiquette. A reward or two ought to do the trick.

Etiquette for the Bedroom

Forget all the other rules of etiquette if you must. Here's where it counts the most.

- Always let your sex partner know if you have a vaginal or genital infection.
- The same goes if you have any kind of sexually transmitted disease.
- Engage in sex that is mutually agreeable.
- Don't complain when sex is less than thrilling.
- Don't accuse your partner of incompetence.

- Gently instruct your partner.
- Don't hog the covers.
- Keep the TV volume low if your live-in is trying to sleep next to you.
- Never assume the other is taking care of the birth control issue without confirming it.
- Don't invite anyone else into your bed.
- Don't make the bed if your live-in is getting back in it.
- Whoever is the last one up in the morning should make the bed.

> **Love's Hot Line**
>
> Miss Manners says "it's too much in your face" to discuss your sexual practices, restraints, or preferences at the dinner table. I imagine she means in front of others. Between the two of you, who could possibly object?

Etiquette for a Sound Relationship

Don't leave your etiquette behind when you leave home. Relationship etiquette should always be a part of your established behavior. Never leave home without these rules:

- Don't take each other for granted.
- Don't discuss your relationship in front of others.
- Don't air household fights in front of family, friends, or strangers.
- Wait to discuss your sex life out of earshot of others.
- Never make cruel fun of your partner or dismiss him or her in any way.
- Be ready to listen to your live-in partner.
- Make your home a private, special haven that each of you enjoys coming home to.
- Respect each other's needs.
- Don't embarrass your live-in in front of others.
- Don't shout or yell at each other.

The impetus behind these rules of etiquette is respect.

Unsettled Issues of Etiquette

Because living together is not a longstanding, accepted romantic tradition, many issues of etiquette that pertain to it are still evolving. Thus, you are the pioneers of live-in etiquette. However, you do have some notable and highly visible forerunners.

> **Troubles A'Brewing ...**
>
> Peggy Post thinks it is a good rule of etiquette to inform your children's teachers and schools when a live-in adult becomes part of the household. Educators who come into contact with the child should be aware of the person's name and role and should be told about any signs of distress in the child's behavior.

Jacqueline Kennedy Onassis lived with Maurice Tempelsman in her New York apartment with dignity, great style, and respect, despite their unmarried status. It is the way you conduct yourselves and the mannerly response you demand from others that largely determine the stature of your live-in arrangement.

Family Matters

Etiquette experts have some recommendations on how to interact with family when you take a live-in. Here is what they advise on a variety of issues:

- Before you move in with your honey, tell the people who care the most about you. Most likely you'll be telling your folks or your kids.
- When a cohabiting couple visits their children or their parents, they should abide by the rules of the house. If you are given separate bedrooms, you should sleep in separate beds while you are houseguests.
- The only events that parents and step-parents are compelled to attend together are weddings, graduations, and other special occasions of this nature.
- If your children already have a mom or a dad, it is not wise, fair, or proper to have them call your partner "Mom" or "Dad."
- If you are visiting your parents or your kids, keep down the noise and don't raise the roof while you are having sex.

Remember that others are affected by your actions. No one lives in a vacuum.

Sticky Introductions

Miss Manners has some help for those sticky introductions, whether it is your mother's or father's lover who has moved in, your grandmother's or grandfather's, your brother's or sister's, your son's or daughter's, or your own.

Miss Manners gives these guidelines:

- Avoid picking cutesy names.
- Don't be overly descriptive.
- Do not embarrass anyone.
- Select a title for the lover that has a neutral moral flavor.

> If "significant other" doesn't strike you as quite right, the columnist's readers came up with some new suggestions:

>> Meet Mom's committed partner.

>> This is my daughter's householdmate.

>> I would like to introduce you to Grandma's virtual spouse.

>> Have you met my son's sweetheart?

The point is to be sensitive to how others wish to be addressed.

Uncharted Territory

Country clubs, social functions, business conventions, and corporate incentive trips do not yet explicitly state the position or rights of your live-in partner. Therefore, it is up to you and your partner to pave the way if you want to be treated like a couple.

Here are my suggestions:

1. Determine ahead of time whether your partner will have the benefits of membership in your social, golf, tennis, or other private club. If your partner is not entitled to some member benefits, see if you can work out a package deal to include the two of you.

2. Avoid putting your partner in an embarrassing position. When the boss invites you to his or her cocktail party, explain that you live with a very important partner whom you would like to bring if other spouses are invited.

3. The same is true for conventions or incentive trips. Ask whether spouses are invited and whether you could include your significant other. Never bring your partner along if you have to leave him or her in the hotel room during dinner, or hide your partner in the closet.

4. Thank you notes should be written and signed by both of you when it comes to acknowledging a gift or dinner.

Wedding gifts, birthday gifts, holiday dinner gifts, or any of those gifts normally given by both husband and wife should be given from the two of

> **Love's Hot Line**
>
> Thanks to Miss Manners' readers, we have a suggestion for naming your live-in's parents. Try the "un-laws." It does seem to get the point across.

> **Love's Hot Line**
>
> It is important to communicate to your partner which points of etiquette you wish to incorporate into your household or love relationship and which slights of etiquette, if any, you wish to remedy.

you, and enclosure cards signed accordingly. The same is true of sympathy, Christmas, or any other special occasion cards.

Adding Your Own Rules of Etiquette

This chapter is still being written. You two are the writers. Therefore, I recommend sitting down together and adding some of your own live-in rules of etiquette. This is a simple but worthwhile exercise, so take time to fill in the blanks.

Live-In Rules of Etiquette We Both Want to Include

1. _____
2. _____
3. _____
4. _____
5. _____
6. _____
7. _____
8. _____
9. _____
10. _____

Live-In Rules of Etiquette She Wants to Establish

1. _____
2. _____
3. _____
4. _____
5. _____
6. _____
7. _____
8. _____
9. _____
10. _____

Chapter 18 ➤ *Living-Together Etiquette*

Live-In Rules of Etiquette He Wants to Establish

1. _____
2. _____
3. _____
4. _____
5. _____
6. _____
7. _____
8. _____
9. _____
10. _____

Live-In Rules of Etiquette That Do Not Apply to Us

1. _____
2. _____
3. _____
4. _____
5. _____
6. _____
7. _____
8. _____
9. _____
10. _____

The Least You Need to Know

➤ There is nothing outdated or stuffy about etiquette that is founded on respect, common courtesy, consideration, and kindness.

➤ Etiquette is not an affectation but a necessary part of a sound and harmonious relationship.

➤ Each partner in a live-in relationship should be cognizant of good etiquette that applies to every room in the house.

➤ There are no hard-and-fast rules for live-in etiquette. The best guide is your conscience and the love you have for your partner.

Chapter 19

Smart Moves

In This Chapter

- ➤ Simple do's and don'ts
- ➤ The relevance of space and solitude to the well-being of your relationship
- ➤ People who laugh together last together
- ➤ Foolish moves that get you tossed out the door
- ➤ Sorting out reasonable levels of expectation

This chapter continues to add to your store of information about practical matters. Love and sex follow in the next two chapters. Try to hold out for the fun and games. The household hints and smart moves provided here will get you through the day-to-day business of living together. I'll make this chapter short, sweet, and swift so that you can proceed to put the icing on the cake.

I think that it might be beneficial to consider this chapter in the same vein as the 1999 report, written by the Catholic bishops in the United States, on cohabiting couples. They alerted their colleagues that cohabiting should be more practically viewed as a "teachable moment" for the clergy. Instead of fighting the living-together trend, the bishops suggested that the clergy ought to better prepare cohabiting couples for marriage, thereby lowering the high divorce rate of former live-ins.

You would be wise to learn the lessons that follow. They have the potential to make your live-in experience more successful, whether or not matrimony is your ultimate goal.

Simple Do's

I'll give you the simple do's first. Although you may consider the items in this list self-explanatory or already explained in earlier chapters, they are important enough to be worth repeating.

- Continue to work on unresolved issues.
- Inform your partner if your feelings or agenda changes.
- Consciously develop your couple skills.
- Keep old friendships.
- Maintain self-control.
- Steer clear of the world of fantasy and make-believe.
- Guard and nurture your friendship.

None of the above are solo activities. They are meant to apply to each of you and encourage teamwork in your relationship.

> **Sweet Nothings**
>
> *Webster's* definition of teamwork says it perfectly. Teamwork is a "joint action by a group of people, in which each person subordinates his individual interests and opinions to the unity and efficiency of the group." Remember, teamwork can be carried out by a team of only two people.

Simple Don'ts

There are some elementary behaviors that should never cross your threshold. Here are a few of them. Do not ...

- Fake who you are.
- Forget the importance of sex.
- Stand for any emotional, verbal, or physical abuse.
- Use your partner.
- Let your partner use or take advantage of you.
- Give up all elements of your old life.
- Isolate yourself from others.
- Betray your partner's friendship or trust.

Love's Hot Line

According to my research, men who live with their honeys don't like women who are dogmatic, fickle, or angry. Nagging, procrastinating, failing to listen, and making men feel guilty aren't appreciated either. So watch yourself!

Guys, you aren't the only ones who find things about your lady love undesirable. Men who are messy, uncooperative, stubborn, overworked, or dogmatic had better mend their ways before they move in.

Four Essential New Moves

The following are good moves that will benefit you, your partner, and your relationship.

Time, Space, and Solitude

Psychologist Ester Buckholz, Ph.D., author of *The Call of Solitude,* writes, "Both the need to be alone and to engage others are essential to human happiness and survival with equally provocative claims."

What Buckholz says about these needs applies to your own relationships too. She says that alone-time can actually strengthen attachments. Solitude makes all of us happier persons by providing the atmosphere in which we can restore energy, sort out relationship issues, make necessary adjustments in our lives, and learn how to satisfy ourselves. Research found that the benefits of alone-time are lowered blood pressure, elevated mental functioning, increased positive outlook, and enhanced creativity.

The next time your live-in takes offense, is wounded, or feels threatened because you have expressed a desire to be alone or a need for space, explain these facts of life.

What Buckholtz and others consider alone-time may surprise you. The main criterion is an absence of outside stimuli or interruptions. Therefore, alone-time can mean that you're in the same room as your live-in, but you are reading a book and foregoing attentiveness to his or her presence. You may decide to soak alone in a hot tub of water or take a solitary walk. Or you may engage in one of four of Buckholtz's *m-word*

233

suggestions that will move you into your own world: meditation, massage, music, and masturbation.

Each individual needs a varying amount of alone-time. Therefore, as live-ins …

> ➤ It is your challenge to determine where your partner fits into the spectrum. Is he or she a loner who needs a great deal of solitude, or an extreme extrovert who requires minimal time alone?

> ➤ It is also your responsibility to make sure that you receive your share of alone-time.

> ➤ Each of you must make necessary adjustments to appease the other in this area. Neither of you should feel as if you have been sentenced to a jail term or left to your own devices for an inordinate amount of time. Allowing too little space may result in a rebellious, angry, resentful mate. But too much space may alter the kind of commitment required to maintain a truly satisfying, long-term relationship.

> **Troubles A'Brewing …**
>
> Don't wait until you are completely exasperated, are feeling hemmed in, or are in dire need of space or solitude. Try to get some solitude on a regular basis so that your partner has a chance to become accustomed to your habits. Expelling your desire for solitude in a loud combustion could create an explosion of peace and harmony at home.

➤ Communicate to one another your need for space and for time spent alone. Devise signs, verbal and otherwise, that the two of you can understand and that express when you want private time. Try to come up with signals that won't threaten or hurt the other.

Pick Your Fights

There are several reasons why you should learn to pick your fights. Constant fighting shows a lack of tolerance and a need for control that we have already said is contrary to a healthy relationship. Fighting over the little things will antagonize your partner and make him or her less receptive to the major areas of conflicts you may experience. Furthermore, if you learn to hold your tongue and temper for the really important issues, your grievances will carry more weight and be taken more seriously. Your goal should be to make your live-in your *ally*, not your enemy.

Try this little exercise to see whether it helps sort out issues that are worth fighting over. Ask yourself by answering yes or no whether …

➤ The problem is a threat to your well-being.

➤ The issue at hand seriously affects your happiness.

➤ The problem is important in the scheme of your long-term live-in relationship.

- This issue would top your list of five potential things to fight over.
- The issue could be resolved if you both gave in a little.
- The conflict has more to do with individual tastes, not values.
- A good night's rest will fix the problem.
- The problem is of little consequence to you and your partner's commitment to, and love for, one another.
- The problem would be more accurately described as an annoying habit, such as your partner's loud singing in the shower.
- The issue is that your partner failed to read your mind about what you wanted.
- The conflict is over your partner forgetting your favorite scent, food, or movie.
- The reason why you're angry is that your live-in honey neglected to pick up the cleaning, give you a message, or clean out the tub *once*.

Saying yes to the first four points would generally indicate that this is a battle worth fighting. "Yes" on the next four points means you could probably resolve the conflict peacefully. "Yes" on the last four points suggests you should take a second look because this may not be a major issue worth fighting over after all.

> **Sweet Nothings**
>
> An **ally** is someone with whom you have a relationship and share a united, not divided, front.

Befriend Your Partner's Pals and Family Members

Being friendly toward your partner's pals and family is just plain smart. If you don't befriend those who are important to your honey, you are missing out on making important allies and you are collecting potential enemies. The exceptions are those people who are not good for the well-being of your relationship and who refuse to think of your partner as anything but free, single, and ready to roll.

Here are a few tricks to making friends:

- Be genuinely interested in the other person.
- Ask questions.
- Refrain from being judgmental.
- Do not talk about your live-in, your live-in's pals, or family members.
- Invite them over.
- Include them in your social life.

> ➤ Don't lie, be false, or be overly aggressive trying to turn them into friends.
>
> ➤ Never try to come between your honey and his or her friends and family.

Not one of these suggestions is difficult to carry out, but the benefits are plentiful.

Your Home: A Comfortable Gathering Place

When your home becomes a comfy place to play, you will always know where your partner is and with whom he or she is playing. That isn't all bad, especially if you know how to play the able host or hostess. Extending hospitality while also maintaining ample privacy may take practice.

You may want to start practicing moves like these:

> ➤ Put a pool table in your well-lit basement.
>
> ➤ When the poker club takes their turn at your house, have plenty of food and beverages, but not so much that they stay all night.
>
> ➤ Don't hang around when your pal brings over friends for a jam session unless you've been invited to stay.
>
> ➤ Set up rules before the company arrives so that you and your partner don't disagree in front of the guests about what time they should leave.
>
> ➤ Be pleasant and welcoming, but don't outdo yourself and become the waiter or waitress for your honey's friends.
>
> ➤ Invite the romantic interests of your live-in's pals to go to a movie while your live-in is hosting the one-gender get-together.
>
> ➤ If your pal wants friends over every night because you are such a great host or hostess, remind him or her how much more fun you are alone.

> **Love's Hot Line**
>
> Primary ways of being hospitable include receiving strangers warmly, being generous, being open-minded to new ideas, and acting in a kind and warm manner.

With time and practice, you'll get the hang of it until it becomes a natural way of living. These suggestions will keep you in the safe lane.

Spoilers in the Fine Art of Living Together

Chapter 20, "Keeping Love's Embers Warm," and Chapter 21, "Sex, Sex, Sex," will tell you plenty about creating a deliciously artful live-in relationship. The three spoilers discussed next could easily spoil the taste of your live-in relationship if served in large doses.

Bah Humbug

Living with someone who has little sense of humor and is unable to laugh hampers the growth of a good relationship. Laughing isn't the only means of connecting with your partner, but it does defuse serious or touchy confrontations, add lightness and fun to all occasions, and act as a coping mechanism.

Studies by psychologists Herbert Lefcourt, Ph.D., and Rod Martin, Ph.D., reveal that individuals without a sense of humor are likely to be more depressed or anxious. Living with a new partner is tough enough, why add the hardship of a lack of laughter?

Drop the seriousness. It isn't recommended or necessary 24 hours a day. Go to a comedy club, catch a funny flick, turn on a sitcom, or do something goofy enough to make the two of you laugh! Actually, besides being good for your relationship, laughter has been shown to positively affect your health and your immune system.

> **Love Stats**
>
> Adults may not be laughing enough. Studies show that the average kindergarten-age child laughs 300 times a day. Adults, both men and women, fare dismally by comparison. They laugh only 17 times a day.

Nobody Likes a Whiner

Everybody whines, but those who do it to excess can drive you up a wall, especially if they use that silly grating, protracted, nasal sound that kids do.

The fact of the matter is that bona fide whiners are looking for sympathy or a pat on the head—not a solution to their problems, psychologists say. Furthermore, they are practically impossible to satisfy. Generally they are pessimistic, wishy-washy adults with a crybaby, victim mentality.

Living with a whiner is a real downer and can make you crazy. If you yourself are tempted to start complaining and to cross the bridge into the land of whining, ask yourself what you are truly seeking—sympathy from your pal, or input for a solution. Only the latter is acceptable.

If you think you might be too close to being a whiner, ask your partner. Just don't lapse into whining if the answer is yes.

Uncontained, Runaway Stress

There is nothing to be ashamed of and nothing wrong if you frequently become stressed. It is an understandable response to the enormous pressures that are part of contemporary society.

> **Love's Hot Line**
>
> It won't do you any harm, and may do you some good, to commit to memory what your partner likes in the opposite sex. Women like living with men who are sensitive, responsive, caring, understanding, patient, honest, loving, and loyal. Men like women who are loving, caring, attentive, strong, independent, intelligent, sexy, and pretty. These traits are present in abundance in a good relationship.

However, whether it is your job, your classes, your boss, or your mom that causes you stress, it's a big problem for you and your live-in lover when you don't know how to handle the stress or get rid of it. Stress can affect both your health and your relationships.

Many people who are stressed can't get themselves to shrug off the trials and tribulations of the day when they leave for home. They walk through the door angry and revert to being either uncommunicative or uncivil to their partners.

When two people live together, each must recognize his or her own level of sensitivity to stress and also recognize the partner's level. Then each must learn to deal with the stress in a way that doesn't alienate or antagonize the other.

The solution may be as simple as allowing ample time for the stressed partner to simmer down. This could be accomplished in the moments it takes to change clothes, sip a glass of wine, or take a long, hot shower. Without controlling stress, the chances of building a wall between you and your live-in seem likely. (Check out Appendix B, "Stress Busters," for more information.)

Reasonable Expectations

One of the smart moves that live-in or marriage partners often neglect when they begin sharing a home is considering the level of expectation on which they should set their sights. Years ago, when I researched and wrote *Marriage Secrets: How to Have a Lifetime Love Affair* (Birch Lane Press, 1993), it became clear to me that the most satisfied couples had very high expectations of one another.

Expectations reflect one's acceptable standard of behavior. If you ask for a minimum, that is likely what you are going to get. For instance, if you expect your child to make his or her bed once a week, do a half hour of homework daily, and walk the dog every other day, the child will interpret this minimum as acceptable behavior. There is little pressure to perform at a higher level. If you have low expectations of a romantic partner, that, too, is precisely what you are likely to get.

John Gottman, Ph.D., co-founder and co-director of the Seattle Marital and Family Institute, warns in his book *The Seven Principles for Making Marriage Work* (Crown, 1999) that high expectations are not a cause of marital unhappiness, as some experts in the field claim. Nor will lowering expectations prevent a partner's disappointment.

In fact, his research on newlyweds demonstrates that those individuals who refused to accept the negative behavior of a partner, who called the partner on it, and who insisted on reform were the most satisfied couples down the road.

Precarious Live-In Expectations

Setting elevated levels of expectation is trickier for live-ins who do not have a strong commitment to each other. Live-ins who have high levels of self-esteem, feel secure with their partners, and see each other as equally committed to a long-term relationship find it easier to set elevated expectations.

They are not afraid to challenge a partner who is …

- Contributing to their unhappiness.
- Negatively impacting their love relationship.
- Diminishing their live-in satisfaction.

> **Love Stats**
>
> "All lovers swear more performance than they are able, and yet reserve an ability that they never perform; vowing more than the perfection of ten, and discharging less than the tenth part of one."
>
> —William Shakespeare

An Exercise in Expectations

If you are concerned about your future romantic outlook, be certain and firm in your expectations; then monitor your own and your live-in's behavior. Follow this exercise:

1. Nip unacceptable behavior in the bud.
2. Don't let expectations slide.
3. Tell your partner in specific and explicit language what you consider acceptable in a given situation.
4. Discuss expectations that either of you feels are excessive or insufficient.
5. Make only those adjustments in expectations that benefit your relationship and your mutual well-being.

> **The Least You Need to Know**
>
> ➤ Your live-in relationship requires a ready supply of smart moves.
>
> ➤ Living together is not a replacement for your own time, space, and being.
>
> ➤ Choose your battles; don't let them choose you. Only go to war on the important ones.
>
> ➤ A sense of humor and doses of laughter are essential household supplies.
>
> ➤ Don't be afraid to have the highest expectations of your romantic partner.

Chapter 20

Keeping Love's Embers Warm

In This Chapter

➤ How to stir the fires of love

➤ The magic of love talk and romantic overtures

➤ What responsive love acts add to your relationship

➤ How men and women respond differently to love talk

We are done for now with the practicalities, so to speak, although in my experience love talk and the like are practical measures that help ensure the survival of a relationship. It's just that love talks and acts are a lot more fun than conflict resolution, cohabitation agreements, and economic summits. Learning when and how to launch these babies takes the same kind of skill and know-how you have been acquiring throughout this book.

You might find that there is an absence of "explicit" sexy details and directions in the pages that follow. However, that is entirely intentional. Sex requires its own spotlight and will be more thoroughly addressed in Chapter 21, "Sex, Sex, Sex."

Beginners Guide to Love Talk

Before you start using all of the categories of love talk, it is important to remember several things as you read about and launch love messages, romantic overtures, responsive love acts, and stimulants that stir dormant emotions.

The purpose of these gestures is to show your love and to demonstrate to your partner how terrific the two of you are together.

University of Wisconsin professor Deborah Blum, Ph.D., author of *Sex on the Brain: The Biological Differences Between Men and Women* (Viking, 1997), said that delicacies like love talk help stimulate a delicious return to the infatuation stage. It is important for the sake of love to feel the same rush of bodily chemicals that caused the initial urgency and rage of sweet desire.

> **Troubles A'Brewing ...**
>
> If you don't derive pleasure or enjoyment from giving your honey "love bites," something is seriously wrong in your relationship. Love bites include sexually craving your partner, giving him or her gifts, showering your honey with love and affection, or being comforted by your partner's presence.

➤ Don't use the same treats all the time. They will lose their effectiveness if they become routine, rote, and insincere. Go for new stimuli or variations of the tried and true.

➤ Never waste your time and efforts offering such bounties to an unworthy or unappreciative romantic partner.

➤ While you are on the receiving end, make an adequate, appreciative fuss to reinforce the use of love talk.

➤ If you use all of the components of love talk with some degree of frequency, behaving toward one another in this endearing way will become an enviable habit.

➤ Love talk doesn't have to spell dollars. According to a report in *Psychology Today,* the results of a poll of 250 individuals showed that 62 percent of the respondents considered a bouquet of wildflowers spontaneously picked along the road side preferable to a dozen expensive long-stemmed roses. A candlelight dinner at home instead of a costly night out was the preference of 66 percent. Love talk doesn't have to take money, only effort and enthusiasm.

➤ It is important that all love messages, romantic overtures, responsive love acts, and stimulants to stir dormant emotions be tailored to your partner's likes, dislikes, and needs. They should demonstrate your understanding and knowledge of your pal. In other words, for an "I love you" gift, don't get her a tennis tee if her sport is skiing. And don't get him a multicolored, high-fashion European sweater if he prefers button-down oxfords and cable V-necks.

> **Sweet Nothings**
>
> **"I love you" gifts** are offerings that don't signify a special occasion like a birthday or anniversary. They are surprise packages meant to show affection. Whether large or small, they carry an extra measure of meaning because they are prompted by thoughts of love and generosity, not duty.

> Devise expressions of love that no prior romantic partner has ever used. For instance, an article on love in a popular magazine described a young woman who carried in her purse a bottle of the hot sauce her honey liked to put on everything he ate, but that wasn't readily available at most restaurants.

> We aren't talking about only hearts and flowers. Blum uses an example from her own marriage. The fact that her husband went to three grocery stores to find the kind of milk she likes counts big, she says. So do thoughtful phone calls, compliments, and holding hands.

The Power of Love Messages

Love messages can be large or small. They are gestures of generosity and expressions of affection that work magic on married folks, live-ins, or singles.

Take Phil, a 32-year-old eligible, but confirmed, bachelor who couldn't see himself settling down—until he found Meagan's love messages irresistible.

Phil says:

> "Meagan was determined to make things work after we started dating. I couldn't help but be swayed by the energy she put into our relationship. She sent me packages, cards, and flowers."

Meagan never stopped putting that kind of energy into her relationship, including their engaged live-in period and their marriage. When I last checked, their seven-year journey into matrimony was heavenly. They are a couple envied among their peers for their devotion, loyalty, and love.

> **Troubles A'Brewing ...**
>
> According to a 1999 *Cosmopolitan* article, showering lavish attention (what I call **love play**) on a beau could be exceedingly dangerous if it's overdone in the first stages of dating. Why? You could just as easily overwhelm and scare off a guy as you could turn him on by giving these obvious signs of your love.

Sending Messages of Love

Trade your love secrets with friends, and use your creative brain to come up with a multitude of recyclable love messages. In the meantime, you may want to run through this list:

> Smiles, hugs, kisses, and unexpected teasing or playful groping

> A box of Swiss chocolates

> A photo of the two of you that oozes with good memories

> A picnic in front of the fireplace

- Cards at the office, on a bedroom pillow, or in his or her attaché case
- Homemade love tapes left in the car with a note that says, "Play Me"
- "I love you" gifts
- Affectionately rubbing your body up against your partner's in public
- As your honey drives down the road, leaning over and rubbing his crotch—just don't run off the road!
- Saying "I love you" and meaning it
- Preparing a football feast for his favorite game
- Sex
- Flirting with your partner
- A romantic walk in the woods or by the beach
- Breakfast in bed
- Using words like "adore," "love," or "my guy"
- Lunchtime quickies
- Granting wishes and fantasies
- Dedicating a song over the radio
- Printing a love message in the personals

> **Love's Hot Line**
>
> If you have been negligent in sending love messages, here's the way one young man caught up. For his honey's thirtieth birthday, he supplied a gift, card, or expression of love for each of the 30 days preceding her birth date.

Men, Women, and Love Messages

Gender plays a part in how your partner will respond to, hand out, and interpret love messages. Men and women show distinctly different preferences and interpretations.

For instance, *Psychology Today* found that men and women rated the following gifts this way: Women preferred tickets for a show or concert over a gift certificate, a night out over roses, and a cashmere sweater over a "friendship ring." Men, on the other hand, thought that sending roses was the best way to express affection, a ring was second, tickets to an event third, and a cashmere sweater and gift certificate equally appropriate.

Furthermore, don't expect your honey to react the same way you would have if you had received a love message. Women will be more emotional in their responses and more overt. Although men do like receiving gifts, attention, and affection, they don't react as quickly or as effusively to them. Nonetheless, love messages perform their magic.

Patrick's lover, Kelly, is the mistress of love talk. Here's what Patrick says about her:

> "Our relationship is a 10. Kelly makes me feel she is glad to be with me. I have never felt so loved before. All her tricks keep me straight. I am definitely content with Kelly and couldn't love anyone more. I wouldn't jeopardize that."

Professor Blum would probably congratulate Kelly on her effort. Here are Kelly's own words:

> "Although some may scoff at these treats and other tricks, you have to put energy into it. I really get impatient with some of the feminists who must say it is not necessary to cater to a man. This isn't catering but saying, 'What relationship do I want with a long-term partner, and what do I have to do to get that?'"

Time for Creative Thinking

To get your creative juices flowing and to make sure you understand love messages, try to list at least five measures you can devise by yourself as a treat for your partner.

1. _____
2. _____
3. _____
4. _____
5. _____

Romantic Overtures

Surveys show that respondents believe there is a distinction between love and romance. Love, the respondents said, was about feelings; whereas romance was about acting out the feelings. In my book, *romantic overtures* are those actions that express love and create an atmosphere for it. Oftentimes romantic overtures become a prelude to sex, but they don't have to be. There are different kinds and varying degrees of romance. Remember, variety is the spice of life. No relationship can do without variation or romantic overtures!

Romantic Suggestions

The following list provides some examples of what I mean by romantic overtures. You will find plenty of sexy ones in the chapter that follows. These are a bit more fundamental. To turn down the lights and turn up the heat, try …

- Sexy nightgowns.
- Tantalizing daytime teasing on the phone, through e-mail, or via a note.
- A surprise weekend away.
- Picking up him or her at work with nothing on under your coat.
- Dim lights, candles, a bottle of wine, and whispers of love.
- Preparing a treasure hunt that ends up with your partner as the treasure.

- Meeting at a favorite restaurant (your treat) or at a local hotel.
- Packing up dinner and taking it to your honey's lonely private office on a late work night.

Roxy's Bag of Tricks

Here is one lover's creative romantic overture that also effectively quenches any thirst her live-in partner might have for extra sideline sex. Roxy thought her guy might be envious of his friends' multiple sex partners, so she decided to play mistress and told her partner exactly that. They were not allowed to have sex at home for a while. Instead they had to meet for what seemed like discreet rendezvous in hotels, parking lots, their friends' empty apartments, or any private place they could think of.

Roxy confides:

> "I could tell the excitement in his eyes from the first time I mentioned that his mistress was going to call. It's kind of silly but we are both so attentive at our rendezvous that we don't want to give them up, although we are having sex at home too."

Create Your Own Overtures

The possibilities are endless. It is just a matter of getting into the swing of it. Listen for things your partner says or does that might give you a hint about what would definitely strike his or her fancy. For the football aficionado, a cheerleading getup might get you tackled. If your partner is swayed by moonlight, take her out to see the brightest moon in the most private place you can find. It wouldn't hurt to pack a blanket, her favorite beverage, or a CD with background music.

Before you continue, do your work. Come up with at least two romantic overtures, including the day and the time you plan to set them in motion. Do not delay.

Romantic Overture	When	When	How
1. _____	_____	_____	_____
2. _____	_____	_____	_____

What to Do About Dormant Emotions

It isn't good for your romantic emotions—lust, love, sex, desire, and passion—to remain at rest and undercover for too long. Nonetheless, all of us get rusty at times and need to relight those fires.

Daily pressures and activities cause us to take the easy road, mumbling thoughtless "luv ya's" and throwing goodnight kisses into the air. And habit, complacency, and proximity all abet our inclination to take each other for granted and neglect our love relationship. Under these conditions, critical emotions that maintain love relationships may fall into a deep retreat and sleep. Once you have a case of *dormant emotions,* you may have a case of neglect and cause for dissatisfaction within your romantic relationship.

How to Wake Up Dormant Emotions

With a little thought, you can think of stimulants that have the potential to arouse and renew interest, desire, and love. Here are some suggestions:

➤ Celebrate the anniversary of the day you first professed your love or moved into your home.

➤ Repeat a favorite vacation or return to a favorite restaurant. Such places hold a special romantic reminder of the love you share. Recalling those magic moments is always enjoyable and effective.

➤ Flip through photo albums or other meaningful romantic memorabilia in a private, cozy atmosphere. Besides being a gentle reminder of your shared history, this walk down memory lane shows your appreciation of each other.

➤ Call an appreciation night in which you each reveal several things you love about the other. Singing your partner's praises is a great way to say thank you, make your partner feel special, and show how much he or she is cared for. It is also worthwhile to mention how much certain things meant that he or she did for you.

Naturally, all forms of love messages, romantic overtures, affection, and sex have awakening affects.

Creative Thinking to Combat Dormant Emotions

Jumping on your partner, whispering "I love you," and slapping up a photo of yourself to give him or her isn't exactly the kind of creative thinking that you should have in mind. First, you must address the issue of why emotions are dormant. Are they

> **Sweet Nothings**
>
> **Dormant emotions** are those that are in a state of inertia—slumbering, quiet, and still. The seeds of these emotions are present and possibly underdeveloped, but they are definitely at rest.

> **Love's Hot Line**
>
> Don't become so overzealous in your use of love talk that you squeeze out any room for your partner to reciprocate or initiate treats of his or her own. Love acts should look fairly equal on a balance sheet.

asleep from natural causes, or is there an outside influence? Second, once you have determined that these are normal dips in your relationship, you can proceed with suggestions like those given in the previous section.

If you suspect that your partner's dormant emotions are under the influence of something more serious, address that with real talk and understanding.

However, let's not be pessimistic; let's assume instead that all is well and just the normal course of daily living has put the squeeze on your romance. If you want to try more-novel attempts and have some ideas of your own, try them out, one at a time. To make sure you don't forget these ingenious creations, write down at least two of them here:

_____

_____

Responsive Love Acts

"Responsive" is the key word here. *Responsive love acts* are specific, well-directed reactions to your partner that are meant to demonstrate your love, devotion, caring, and understanding.

A lover who is responsive generally appreciates his or her partner, anticipates the partner's needs, and desires to make life easier and happier for him or her. Responsive acts are born out of intimacy and contribute to it. In that way, they strengthen the bonds of love. This may not be an easy concept to grasp without the aid of specific examples.

Increasing Your Understanding of Responsive Love Acts

These three scenarios ought to be sufficient to teach you the meaning of responsive love.

Example 1: Tim was having a tough time dealing with the death of his father. He was at a new job, and no one there realized how close he and his dad had been. Sherrie could tell how down in the dumps he was when she spoke with him over the phone, especially since there was no understanding friend in the office to give him a pat on the back or a sympathetic nod. To make Tim's day a little brighter, Sherry showed up at his office minutes before lunch. She took Tim to a quiet place around the corner for lunch where he could talk and laugh. It was just the medicine he needed. She was planning another dose when he got home from work.

Example 2: Sherrie's dog was hit by a car on a Saturday. Tim was playing golf. While Sherrie frantically drove the dog to the veterinarian's, she tearfully called Tim to tell him where she would be. Within a half-hour of her arrival at the vet's office, Tim walked in.

His reply to her quizzical look was:

> "How could I keep playing, knowing how scared and upset you were? I wanted to be here with you."

Example 3: Sherrie's folks were coming for a visit. They weren't really excited about their daughter's living with Tim—or any guy for that matter. The whole idea of having them in her home made Sherrie really nervous. Tim didn't have any problem figuring out what was worrying her. Consequently, he offered to pick up her folks at the airport. He promised to be exceptionally nice and overlook any derogatory remark her mother or father might make about their live-in relationship.

He even added a few words of understanding and encouragement:

> "I know your folks are important to you and so is what they think. I want them to like me. Would you object to me telling them on the way home that after you meet my folks we are going to get engaged?"

Planning Ahead for Love

When it comes to responsive love acts, it is hard to plan ahead. You never know when an occasion might arise where a love act is needed. Still, with creative thinking, you can be prepared and on the lookout for just the right moment.

Sometimes it's helpful to consider when in the past you might have inserted a responsive act but failed. Then figure out what you might have done in that situation so that you are ready should it happen again. On the other hand, give yourself credit for any time in the past when you responded appropriately with a love act.

Improving your awareness might be the only lesson you require to become a responsive, loving partner.

> **Troubles A'Brewing ...**
>
> Lovers, live-ins, wives, and husbands who never react to a responsive love act with a "thank you," a sign of appreciation, or a reciprocal act, risk receiving only the dying embers of love. And they probably won't be on the receiving end of too many more of these goodies.

The Least You Need to Know

- ➤ Love talk isn't only fun; it is essential for the well-being and continuation of a romantic relationship or partnership.
- ➤ Keeping your live-in arrangement satisfying, loving, and ongoing requires skill and know-how.
- ➤ Love talk ushers in those vital returns to the pleasurable, exhilarating feelings that are part of the infatuation stage.
- ➤ Doing things that make a partner happy shouldn't be a chore but a matter of love.
- ➤ Love talk is interpreted and dished out in different ways by men and women.

Chapter 21

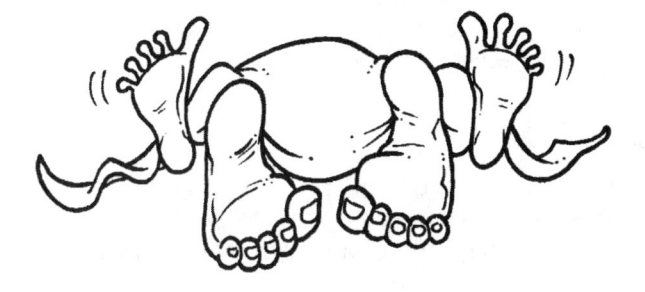

Sex, Sex, Sex

In This Chapter

- ➤ Special challenges for long-term committed sex partners
- ➤ Tastes and pleasures, men's way, women's way
- ➤ Sex facts you can't live without
- ➤ New sexual treats
- ➤ Improving your orgasm record
- ➤ Sex rules

Sex is indisputably important! Practically speaking, David Reuben, M.D., author of the new edition of *Everything You Always Wanted to Know About Sex* (HarperCollins, 1999), says none of us would be here if it weren't for s-e-x.

Romantically speaking, Ellen Berschied, a professor of psychology at the University of Minnesota, believes that romantic love is about sexual desire—90 percent of it to be exact. We all know that sex can be and often is an expression of romantic love, as well.

Pleasurably speaking, some experts believe that sex is the most exhilarating and rewarding act of human life.

Consequently, this chapter is designed to help you achieve satisfaction in the boudoir—or wherever you choose to make love—and reach delicious, memorable peaks of sexual ecstasy. Without sex that is mutually enjoyable and that quenches desire, your live-in relationship will lack critical intimacy and expressions of love. A great live-in sex life can't be calculated by the number of times you have sex in a week. It is much more complex, demanding your conscious attention and effort. Increased understanding will enhance your intimate moments and prepare you for many sexual repair jobs, should that become necessary.

The Challenge of Couples' Sex

True, most surveys and research show that sex with a committed partner is the best sex you can have. Actually, the heralded Kinsey Report stated that sex between committed partners nurtures "a sense of well-being, happiness, and perhaps even physical health."

And no wonder! A partner who knows what turns you on, who caresses you with love, and with whom you feel secure not only satisfies you but makes you feel wonderfully accepted. Under these covers, the emotions of intimacy, closeness, pleasure, and love have optimal conditions in which to flourish.

However, so much in a couples' relationship hinges on sex that Barry Dym, Ph.D., and Michael L. Glenn, M.D., say that the loss of one partner's sexual desire is the most difficult problem experts confront in treatment. Indeed, some men and women have admitted that once sexual desire has gone—whether as a result of sexual dysfunction or a lack of attraction—their entire relationship changes.

In fact, noted expert Dr. John M. Gottman says, "No other area of a couple's life offers more potential for embarrassment, hurt, and rejection than sex." However, don't jump ship prematurely.

First of all, there is plenty of help out there for committed couples. Such couples have more going for them when faced with a major or minor sexual crisis than do less-committed couples without a vested interest, love, and mutual support.

> **Love Stats**
>
> The newly opened Museum of Sex (nicknamed "MoSex") in New York mounted its first major permanent exhibition in the spring of 2000—"Sex in America: From Puritans to Cybersex." The museum focuses on the history and evolution of human sexuality and will provide educational resources for the study of sex. The building that houses the museum won the 1999 Progressive Architecture Award.

Second, committed long-term lovers have to face facts:

- ➤ The frequency of sex between committed couples declines over time. One study showed that it dropped 25 percent after four years.
- ➤ Not all sex is going to set the stage for fireworks. There is ordinary weekday sex, and then there is weekend magic. The challenge for couples who are intimately

familiar with one another is to avoid getting stuck in the rut of workaday sex, where an orgasm is reached but thrills are not.

➤ What they cannot neglect is a weekend workout that expresses love, shows affection, and reaches satisfying heights of pure pleasure.

Gender and Sex: Let's Get the Record Straight

You simply can't get away from gender issues when it comes to sex. The vast majority of research that is being done on sexual stimuli, physical chemical responses, evolutionary reproduction, and the brain indicate different responses in men and women.

"There is that element of male biology. Women are not designed to be as sexually driven as men. Never the twain shall meet on this issue," Blum pronounces.

> **Love Stats**
>
> According to a recent *Glamour* magazine poll, 97 percent of interviewed couples had sex before their wedding night. Only 3 percent of those respondents admitted to being virgins. Seventy-six percent felt relaxed, not pressured, about their wedding night performance; but only 16 percent said they had great sex that night.

Consequently, the sexual needs of men and women are the hardest to reconcile in long-term love relationships. The 20s and 30s are the most critical decades for sexual differences, says Dr. Theresa L. Crenshaw in *The Alchemy of Love and Lust* (Pocket Books, 1997). Biological forces come closer and do not appear to drive couples apart as much in their 40s. By the 50s, once women are not concerned with reproduction and when testosterone levels drop in men, hormones and sexual motivation are more perfectly matched, Crenshaw explains.

Varying Sexual Tastes and Practices

For proof that men and women differ in their approach to and practice of sex, check out the following facts. They are also worthwhile tidbits to consider the next time you have sex with your partner.

➤ According to *Sex in America* (Warner Books, 1995), 83 percent of men find vaginal intercourse very appealing, whereas only 78 percent of women do.

➤ Men find more pleasure in watching a partner undress than do women.

➤ Men get more pleasure out of receiving and giving oral sex than women.

➤ *The Janus Report on Sex* claims that 89 percent of married men and 75 percent of married women think intercourse is the best way to achieve orgasm.

253

- Eighty-two percent of men and 69 percent of women prefer intercourse. Ten percent of men and 18 percent of women prefer achieving climax through oral sex.

- Least-appealing sex practices for women aged 18 to 44, according to *The Janus Report*, are anal-stimulated sex, stimulation of a partner's anus, and anal intercourse.

- The least-appealing sex practices for men of the same age are passive anal intercourse, vibrators, and active anal intercourse.

- Ninety percent of women close their eyes during sex, but only a third of men do.

- Men are aroused more easily by visual stimuli than women.

- Men masturbate more frequently than women. Fifty-five percent of the men in the poll masturbate regularly, compared with 38 percent of the women. (Nearly 66 percent of both groups agreed that masturbation was natural and continued into married life.)

> **Love Stats**
>
> The average erect male penis is four inches long, and the average vagina measures three and a half to five inches. Although the penis is much larger than the clitoris, which is the female pleasure center, both have about the same number of nerve cells and nerve fibers. They are just more compactly packed in women.

A Distinctly Different Outlook

Here is where women can get into trouble. Women who are too concerned and self-conscious about what they consider to be their defective body parts are cheating themselves. A survey at Old Dominion University in Virginia found that women who were self-conscious about the way their bodies looked reached orgasm only 42 percent of the time during sex, whereas women who felt more comfortable with their bodies reached orgasm 73 percent of the time.

The silly thing is, ladies, that guys aren't concerned about your cellulite, your slightly bigger boob, or your buttock dimple during sex. They are much more focused on their sexual performance, achieving climax, and knowing from your moans and groans that you are squirming with pleasure. According to *The Janus Report*, 53 percent of men said that their sex partner's pleasure is more important than their own. (Only 34 percent of women voiced the same opinion.)

My advice is, don't hold back, ladies. Enjoy. Worry about the excess weight or less-than-perfect body part later.

Turn-Ons Male/Female Style

Naturally, it is best to find out what particularly turns on or off your honey. However, to get a clue on tastes in general, look these over.

Women's Turn-Ons

A poll by *New Woman Magazine* found that women think men look sexiest in jeans. Only 8 percent of the 16,000 women in the study thought that men looked sexiest nude.

➤ Women are most attracted to men's eyes. Next in order come their smile, mouth, hands, and butt.

➤ Qualities that turn an average guy into one who is irresistible to these women are a sense of humor, kindness, sensitivity, and sincerity.

➤ Verbal expressions of love are a woman's aphrodisiac.

> **Troubles A'Brewing ...**
>
> Fellas, watch out. Women don't like guys who are arrogant, self-centered, rude, disrespectful, or egotistical. You won't get anywhere with that approach.
>
> Ladies, you don't stand a chance, guys say, if you have bad breath or a vaginal odor.

Men's Turn-Ons

Here are some basics on what turns on most men. Each guy, however, has his own preferences that you should learn about later.

➤ Once men are attracted by a woman's youth and beauty, they are ready for sex. (Fortunately for all, this is a subjective judgment!)

➤ Watching X-rated movies gets them started.

➤ Seeing a woman getting excited and climax is their big turn on.

➤ Watching women masturbate is their pure delight.

➤ A woman who wants him!!!

➤ A woman who enjoys sex.

This should get the fires going!

Sex Facts You Should Be Familiar With

Even a good, natural lover can stand some education. Each of these facts could benefit your understanding of your sex partner or your sex life.

1. It is natural for sexual intensity to vary with your partner. A quickie, like intense, timely lovemaking, has its place.
2. Women have natural sexual swings. In some women, they are related to progesterone levels.
3. The busiest people are having the most sex, say the authors of a University of Chicago study. And the busiest people are married folks with long work hours and children living at home.

4. Married men and women report that sex is more gratifying after marriage.
5. Men and women agree that simultaneous orgasm is not necessary for sex that is satisfying.
6. Sexual pleasure zones in women are more abundant than those in men. In addition to breasts, the entire lower torso of women is more sensitive than in men, whose pleasure is centered in the testicles and penis.
7. Sex is healthy for you. It improves breathing, circulation, and flexibility. It also aids the immune and cardiovascular systems and has the potential to relieve anxiety and depression.
8. Love is one of the finest aphrodisiacs.
9. Women can have ejaculations that are so small they are hardly noticeable.
10. A large proportion of men and women express the desire to have more sex and a greater variety of sex with their partners.

> **Love Stats**
>
> So you thought having breast implants was the only body enhancement that people undergo. The truth is that both men and women can experience feelings of organ inadequacy. Some resort to fat injections in the labia, pubis, and penis to increase the size of their genitalia, even though the injections are surgically questionable and the motivation suspect.

> **Sweet Nothings**
>
> **Aphrodisiacs** are substances that get sexual juices flowing and begin lubrication in women and an erection in men. In a broad sense, aphrodisiacs may be any form of stimuli, ingested products, or substances applied to the genital area that arouse passion, increase excitement, and intensify the desire for sex.

Common Complaints, Simple Answers

Don't think you are the only one out there complaining about your sex life occasionally. Loss of passion is normal; so is boredom. To complicate matters even more, sociologist Pepper Schwartz, Ph.D., says that couples are more secure in long-lasting equitable partnerships. Great; but she goes on to tell us that they exhibit less lust and passion than do couples whose relationship is more tense and insecure.

Nonetheless, this shouldn't be an excuse to put sexual desire on hold. Work on jump-starting your lust and breaking the routine. In addition to the male and female turn-ons mentioned earlier in the chapter, try a few *aphrodisiacs*. To jump-start female sexual desires, serve up chocolates, diet drinks, and artificial sweeteners.

If your complaints have to do with the fact that all too often one of you is the pleaser and the other the pleasee, play fair and turn it around. The same goes for initiating sex. It isn't just one partner's responsibility.

Tips to Alleviate Boredom

When you anticipate every move and can determine exactly how long sex is going to take from start to finish, it's a wonder that you don't fall asleep from boredom before you climax. Fortunately, you don't have to change partners to add excitement into your sex life. A little creativity will do just fine. Suggestions are limitless and so are the resources that supply them. Before you go seeking them, I dare you to try and get through my list first.

Category Number 1: Change Sexual Maneuvers

- Build suspense. Tease each other for a week through your clothes before you take them off and have sex.
- Double your amount of foreplay. Take him or her to the brink. Make a game out of it.
- Serve up several courses of sexual foreplay before you finish each part of your six-course dinner in bed.
- Locate spots in your house where you haven't had sex and give them a go. Give a prize to the partner with the biggest and most creative list.
- Try counter sex. If you, your partner, and your counter are just the right height, the woman sitting on the counter and the man standing can be a terrific fit.
- Cook dinner naked together. See how many courses you can get through before you get to your sexy dessert.
- Bathtub sex is relaxing. Candles, wine, soft sponges, and fragrant bubble baths add to the entire effect.
- Build suspense. Call him or her at the office and tease about the pleasures awaiting later that night. Your live-in won't be late.

> **Love Stats**
>
> According to a 1998 global sex survey, the average lovemaking session in the United States was 28 minutes, France 16 minutes, and Italy—the land of lovers—a mere 14 minutes.

Category Number 2: Sexy Surprises

- Create your own deck of sexy playing cards, and let your partner take a blind pick.
- Exchange sex wish lists and have a night of granting wishful thinking.
- Act out a sexual fantasy.

- Try the old whipped cream and other food treats. Apply, spread, and lick where your libido desires.
- For a month's worth of pleasure, fill in your own sex calendar. If you can't figure out 30 days of various delicacies, you are free to use the calendar provided for you here.
- Welcome your guy with nothing on but a strand of pearls.
- Bring a sexy new manual to bed.

A Month of Sexy Surprises, Treats, and Sweets

Sunday	Monday	Tuesday	Wednesday	Thursday	Friday	Saturday
Anywhere but bed—partner's choice.	Five minutes of foreplay before TV football.	A.M. counter sex.	Her pleasure only; make her come.	His pleasure only; make him come.	Naked candle-light dinner.	Rub a dub dub—two in a tub before date night out.
Start early and hunt for new erogenous zones.	A quickie and early to bed.	Selfish sex, his choice.	Selfish sex, her choice.	Rest up for the weekend.	Boudoir feast.	Show-stoppers from an afternoon of shopping.
A quickie in the closet or bathroom while the guys are in the den watching the big football game.	Trip to Fantasy Island.	Find a new place for sex.	Touch only; no sex.	Body massage with lotion; no sex.	If you can can stand it, touching only. Go to a funny film.	You're ready to explode with desire. A Saturday afternoon matinee and marathon. Climax by oral sex first, then together with intercourse.
Show time, x-style.	Bonus night; a half hour of your favorite foreplay before intercourse.	Make it easy; use a vibrator.	Massage, sans hands.	A quickie in a new position.	Her fantasy night.	His fantasy night.
Breakfast sex.	A night of rest before a new month begins.					

Chapter 21 ➤ *Sex, Sex, Sex*

> **Love's Hot Line**
>
> Help your partner explore your body and then you be the explorer so that each of you is attuned to the likes and dislikes of the other. Couples' sex should be mutually pleasing and satisfying. No one has a corner on the market.

Category Number 3: New Tactile Sensations

Try these to add variety, increase excitement, or reach *orgasm:*

- Try a lot more kissing, teasing, and touching before hopping to it.
- Explore and see whether you can find new sensitive spots on one another.
- Massage his or her body with the side of your cheek only. No hands allowed.
- If you usually give oral sex by going up and down, go for, or alternate with, tongue and sucking action.
- Use two hands for his pleasure. Gently grasp his testicles in one and rub his penis with the other. Another trick is alternating hands in a downward massaging motion instead of an upward pumping motion on the penis, one after the other.
- Men, you may want to learn how to effectively use a vibrator for foreplay with your partner.
- A number of sources recommend pillow play. Put a pillow under the woman's hips during intercourse so that her pelvis has an upward tilt, exposing the G-spot more readily for stimulation.
- Use warm oils for genital stimulation and menthol products for body stimulation.
- Pay attention to a man's testicles by licking, stroking, or sucking them.
- Although there are sexier parts, sucking on a woman's finger, her neck, or earlobes and down her spine are tactile treats often forgotten.

Becoming More Orgasmic

Interestingly, there is no correlation between the ability to have frequent orgasms and the amount of love one expresses for a partner. That might be comforting for partners to know, since many women don't regularly climax and many men wish they could have multiple orgasms.

259

However, there are ways you and your partner can achieve orgasms more readily and more often. Here are a few suggestions from a variety of experts:

- Masturbate to improve upon the orgasmic response system.
- Develop greater pelvic muscle control to hold back orgasms.
- To accomplish this, contract and squeeze muscles that hold back bladder flow for several seconds, release, then repeat.
- Alternating between high and low levels of arousal will intensify sexual responsiveness. Some say this optimizes the release of endorphins.
- For women, in the missionary position during intercourse, push down on your skin right above your pubic area to give greater exposure to your G-spot.
- Another way a woman can assist her partner to help her reach orgasm during oral sex or clitoral manipulation is to pull apart her labia and open her vagina for maximum exposure.

David Reuben, M.D., author of the new edition of *Everything You Always Wanted to Know About Sex* (Harper Collins, 1999), believes that women aren't wired to have orgasms as easily as men and therefore need to use their brain. Think orgasm!

Sexual Communication

You will never arrive at the level of sexual pleasure you are seeking without talking to your partner. No matter who starts the conversation …

- Be open minded.
- Express yourself confidently and clearly.
- Ask for what pleases you.
- Do not be critical of your partner.
- Be positive.
- Say "no" to something that makes you uncomfortable.
- Accept your partner's opinions, decisions, likes, and dislikes.

> **Sweet Nothings**
>
> Sex researcher Barbara Keesling, Ph.D., defines an **orgasm** as "a reflex that occurs when muscle tension and blood flow to the pelvis reach a peak and are dispersed, and when the muscle group that supports the pelvic floor spasms rhythmically."

> **Troubles A'Brewing …**
>
> You'd better pay attention to solving your sexual problems. According to a global study, the United States has a higher percentage of male and female partners who cheat than do Australia, Britain, France, Italy, or Hong Kong.

Your Sexual Rule Book

These rules are golden. They protect you, your partner, and your relationship.

1. Anything goes as long as it isn't objectionable to either partner.
2. Coercive sex is way off-limits and out of bounds.
3. Lies about one's physical health that could affect your partner are entirely outside the rules of fair play and should not be tolerated.
4. Sex is never to be consummated in a fashion that is demeaning to either partner.
5. It is each partner's goal to provide sexual satisfaction to the other player.
6. Sex should never be used as a weapon or means for control.
7. Players will modify and improve technique to become more expert in the field of play.
8. Each player will willingly and honestly seek help and information that might correct sexual problems.
9. Despite the demands of daily living, work, or play, each player will make time for the game.
10. The winners are those couples who enjoy their partners and experience intimate sex that enhances and solidifies their relationship.

Troubles A'Brewing ...

A 1999 study in the *Journal of the American Medical Association* revealed that 31 percent of men and nearly 43 percent of women report sexual dysfunction (problems with erections and orgasms or limited sexual pleasure). The libido can be dulled by birth control pills, antidepressants, and blood pressure medications, and by alcohol, emotional problems, and frequent changing of sex partners.

> **The Least You Need to Know**
>
> ➤ To be a good lover, you have to be willing, able, and educated.
>
> ➤ Live-in lovers, no matter how long or how short a time they have been living together, should not ignore the implications of a good or bad sex life.
>
> ➤ It is imperative that each partner attempt to understand, explore, and appreciate his or her partner's sexual tastes and needs.
>
> ➤ Men and women agree and disagree on a host of sexual issues.
>
> ➤ All sex lives could use a spicing up now and then.
>
> ➤ There are endless possibilities to expand your sexual repertoire.

Part 5
If the Roof Caves In

You thought you would move in with your honey and live happily ever after. That's the stuff fairy tales are made of, not real life. Living with someone is never easy. At times it is a bundle of fun. At best it is satisfying and fulfilling despite those momentary bumps and inevitable monumental humps.

You, however, aren't sure exactly what's going on. You thought you knew your partner well enough to detect and interpret any and every sign of trouble. Yet things changed when you started to live together, and now you think you may be at a critical juncture in your relationship.

The first thing you must do is pinpoint the source of your unease. Second, determine whether or not the trouble you think is present is real. Without these first two steps, any attempt to employ household survival tactics or use patching materials won't work. Application depends on the problem at hand.

Learning the dynamics of how couples change will serve you well in the present and the future. It should enable you to look more objectively at your relationship and more positively at conflict. If, however, you determine after the first two chapters in this section that your problems are insurmountable, you will be given ample direction on how to move out and begin to move on.

Chapter 22

Sensing Trouble in Hearth and Home

In This Chapter

➤ How happy are you in your live-in relationship?

➤ Laying the blame for the blahs on you, your honey, or your relationship

➤ Pinpointing areas of your discontent

➤ Revealing troublemakers

➤ What does synergy have to do with it?

➤ Finding out about common relationship breakers

Something is out of whack. You can't quite put your finger on it. You simply have this nagging sensation that all is not well. However, you don't know if this vague feeling is all in your head, between the sheets, or for real. If you've been thinking these thoughts, you must get to the bottom of whatever is causing those butterflies to flutter in your stomach and your mind to reel with doubt.

Could be you are analyzing things too much, experiencing that first loss of magical infatuation, facing natural disappointment, and traveling the peaks and valleys of normal adjustment, or perhaps you are facing a serious dilemma. Sensing trouble in hearth and home is a danger sign that merits investigation. This chapter will help you pinpoint the culprits of your discontent.

Part 5 ➤ *If the Roof Caves In*

Measuring Live-In Happiness

The first step in your investigation is to arrive at the level of your live-in happiness. The following quiz is designed to measure just that.

Love's Hot Line

For all you doubting Toms and Tinas, here's a warning and a suggestion. Before you jump the gun and declare that your live-in relationship is in serious trouble, go back to Chapter 6, "Playing It Safe," and make sure this isn't a case of romantic misunderstanding!

Your Live-In Happiness Test

Check the column with the appropriate answer.

		Yes	No	Sometimes
1.	When I come home, I enjoy finding my partner there.	❑	❑	❑
2.	I look forward to the evenings and weekends when we can spend time together.	❑	❑	❑
3.	My partner's presence makes me happy.	❑	❑	❑
4.	I am having fun sharing a household with my partner.	❑	❑	❑
5.	I feel at ease and comfortable in my new home.	❑	❑	❑
6.	I am happier now than when I was living alone.	❑	❑	❑
7.	Living together has fulfilled my initial objective.	❑	❑	❑
8.	I feel more secure about our relationship.	❑	❑	❑
9.	My lifestyle has improved since we moved in together.	❑	❑	❑
10.	My sex life with my partner is more than satisfactory.	❑	❑	❑
11.	I am satisfied being in a monogamous relationship.	❑	❑	❑

Chapter 22 ➤ Sensing Trouble in Hearth and Home

		Yes	No	Sometimes
12.	My partner and I are loyal and committed to one another.	❏	❏	❏
13.	I wish I could walk into an empty house.	❏	❏	❏
14.	I feel lonely at home.	❏	❏	❏
15.	My partner is intruding on my space.	❏	❏	❏
16.	We are bickering over finances.	❏	❏	❏
17.	There is a power struggle brewing in our household.	❏	❏	❏
18.	One of us is avoiding sexual contact.	❏	❏	❏
19.	I feel constrained in my own home.	❏	❏	❏
20.	I find my partner's habits and quirks more annoying than endearing or palatable.	❏	❏	❏
21.	I prefer spending time with friends over doing an activity with my live-in.	❏	❏	❏
22.	I laugh infrequently when the two of us are home alone.	❏	❏	❏

Love Stats

A study on the balance of power in heterosexual relationships by researchers Susan Sprecher and Diane Felmlee had significant findings. They found that men who believed that their relationship reflected an equitable balance of power, except perhaps in decision making, reported the highest level of satisfaction. Other studies show that when the balance of power is greater in the woman's corner, men express relationship dissatisfaction.

Evaluating Your Test Results: Let's look at the answers to your first 10 questions. If all fall into the "Yes" column, you must be ecstatically happy and you must be taking this test on a day when all of Cupid's arrows are lined up just right. A few

"Sometimes" responses are probably okay. The fewer the better in this case: Even two or three "Sometimes" might indicate a drop in happiness ahead. A stray "No" for the first 10 questions is cause for serious concern and tells you that you aren't as happy as you could or should be.

If the last 10 questions get a "Yes," you must be miserable. What a sorry state of affairs. A healthy relationship and beneficial live-in union aren't supposed to generate those kinds of answers nor that much unhappiness. A straight line of "No" answers is the best you can do for max in the happiness column. One or two "Sometimes" are probably realistic and won't compromise a satisfactory level of live-in happiness.

Obvious Troublemakers

When the following troublemakers start firing, they can cause plenty of friction. You may want to consider whether one of these five troublemakers could be the cause of your discontent.

1. **Meddling outsiders.** Outside meddlers may or may not be well-intentioned. Nonetheless, family and friends who continually badger you about cohabiting or press you to come up with a wedding date can create serious dissension and doubt between you and your partner. If your decision to move in was well thought out in the first place, you will probably find their meddling less disruptive, and you will not allow it to shake your confidence in your decision.

2. **Financial mishaps.** Someone isn't pulling his or her own weight, isn't living up to the financial agreement, and is spending more than his or her share—or not sharing at all. Being a drag and draining your partner's resources catches up sooner or later in live-in love.

3. **Household heavies.** One of the duo changes the rules of living together. It no longer is a fun and satisfying arrangement. Rather, cohabiting has turned into a heavy load of burdens. For instance, the allocation of duties in caring for children, tending to household responsibilities, or contributing financial resources may be giving one partner the edge on leisure and personal time. That's the stuff resentment, discontent, and anger are made of.

4. **Changing agendas.** A change in agenda happens all the time and creates major trouble at home. Let's say that the stated and agreed-upon agenda by both parties on moving day was to

> **Love's Hot Line**
>
> Relationship expert John M. Gottman, Ph.D., says the matter of money requires a pragmatic balance of the freedom, empowerment, security, and trust that money provides in a relationship. If a lack of money contributes to an individual's emotional inadequacy, then money will likely be a prac-tical cause of trouble in a relationship.

enjoy their romantic relationship, test out living-together compatibility, and consider matrimony. Suddenly, he is content to let things ride where they are and lets marriage slip entirely from his future outlook. She, on the other hand, is done with the testing and wants an engagement ring—now.

5. **Incompatibility.** When couples move in with the assumption that they are compatible, they envision being able to live together in harmony, united by those things they have in common. However, if they have misjudged one another or misrepresented themselves, what was supposed to bring them together now moves them apart.

   Unlike the other troublemakers, once couples determine that the two of them are incompatible, thoughtful remedies won't do much good.

You may need to return to Chapter 11, "Partnership Potential," for a review of compatibility before making a final judgement.

Searching for the Roots of Trouble

Your live-in relationship may be troubled by something that is not readily visible but is simmering below the surface. In that case, it is definitely prudent to recheck your level of commitment, love, coupledom, and friendship. The four tests provided in this section will help you make a reliable diagnosis of the ailments in your relationship.

Where Does Your Commitment Stand?

Use a scale from 1 to 10 to indicate your response to these statements. Ten represents the most, 1 the least.

> ### Love's Hot Line
>
> You can have bouts of not loving your partner that aren't actually serious signs of love's decay. The trick to a long-term relationship is behaving and acting as if you still love your honey during these emotional fallouts. This effort prevents you from doing irreparable harm to your partnership and helps to usher in the eventual return of love. If love is gone forever, well, that's another story.

Part 5 ➤ *If the Roof Caves In*

	1 to 10
1. We willingly, eagerly, and readily try to meet one another's needs and desires.	_____
2. We are emotionally invested in our relationship.	_____
3. We have made joint financial investments.	_____
4. We have invested time in each other's friends.	_____
5. We have invested time in each other's family.	_____
6. We readily make concessions to one another.	_____
7. We participate in gift giving.	_____
8. We divide tasks and make accommodating changes in them when necessary.	_____
9. I monitor my own behavior and my partner's to make sure that it doesn't negatively impact our relationship.	_____
10. We share resources.	_____
11. We present ourselves as long-term partners to the world outside our home.	_____

Scoring: The higher the score, the greater the commitment you and your partner have to this relationship. If your score or your partner's is less than 50 points, your commitment is ailing. A radical difference in partner scoring is also a sign of root rot. Should you doubt the impact that commitment has on your relationship, refer to Chapter 3, "The Facts and Fictions of Living Together," where the concept was first introduced.

What's Your Take on Love?

Indicate your agreement with the following statements by checking the proper column.

Your Live-In Happiness Test

Check the column with the appropriate answer.

	Yes	No	Sometimes
1. My partner's love is suffocating and doesn't allow me to grow or feel energized.	❏	❏	❏
2. My partner's imperfections are becoming more apparent and bothersome.	❏	❏	❏
3. My partner gives criticism that is hurtful and irrelevant.	❏	❏	❏
4. I fail to give my partner criticism that is constructive and could help him/her and our relationship grow.	❏	❏	❏

	Yes	No	Sometimes
5. I don't see my partner as a person worthy of admiration and respect.	❑	❑	❑
6. Our relationship lacks passion and excitement.	❑	❑	❑
7. Our relationship fails to encourage me to see life with deeper meaning.	❑	❑	❑
8. Our relationship reduces my level of self-esteem.	❑	❑	❑
9. We don't engage in disclosure of our deepest thoughts together.	❑	❑	❑
10. We rarely please and appease one another.	❑	❑	❑

Scoring: If you have racked up a perfect score of "Yes" answers, your love is already in the minus column. There isn't a shred of it left. A majority of checks in the "Sometimes" column means that your love is wavering in the wind. A solid degree of love would be indicated by a "No" to every statement. If your love isn't performing at a satisfactory level, I recommend rereading Chapter 10, "Is It Love?" Then it is up to you to determine whether your love is salvageable or not.

How Bonded Are You as a Couple?

Use a scale from 1 to 10 to indicate your response to these statements. Ten represents the most, 1 the least.

	1 to 10
1. My partner and I use the words "we" and "ours" when referring to ourselves in the presence of others.	_____
2. Our home is a reflection of both of us.	_____
3. My live-in is a significant partner and treats me the same way.	_____
4. We behave like teammates.	_____
5. We are able to move away and come back to one another without repercussions.	_____
6. We have developed a predictable and satisfying style of resolving conflicts.	_____
7. We can anticipate one another's reactions.	_____
8. We share goals, values, and ideals.	_____
9. We have developed an unstated but reliable pattern of joint decision making.	_____
10. We show love in our own way, and each of us understands it.	_____

Part 5 ➤ *If the Roof Caves In*

Scoring: Your coupledom is solid as a rock if you scored 100 points! Anything less than 50 means you aren't close to the definition of a couple. A healthy, growing relationship with a sunny future outlook must exhibit substantial proof that you and your honey have become a couple. If no blending has yet taken place, see Chapter 17, "A New Lifestyle Vocabulary," for a detailed discussion on coupledom.

> ### Sweet Nothings
>
> Friendship is given three definitions: *Webster's* says it is "a close acquaintance, a sympathizer," or "a person whom one knows well and is fond of" and is on "the same side of a struggle."
>
> Men define friendship as someone with whom they engage in an activity. Women define friendship as having a relationship that allows for sharing emotional intimacy and disclosing secrets.

How Firm Is Your Friendship?

Use a scale from 1 to 10 to indicate your response to these statements. Ten represents the most, 1 the least.

		1 to 10
1.	My live-in partner and I spend a lot of our leisure time together.	_____
2.	We confide in each other.	_____
3.	We feel as if we are teammates.	_____
4.	We are there to pick the other one up after a fall.	_____
5.	We don't take each other for granted.	_____
6.	We recognize when a special pat on the back is needed and give it to the needy partner.	_____
7.	We attend activities together when one of us prefers going with the other instead of with friends.	_____
8.	We do special favors for each other without the other one having to ask.	_____
9.	We are loyal to each other.	_____
10.	We are ready and willing to be each other's cheerleader.	_____

Scoring: The importance of friendship in a relationship cannot be overstated. It is the basis of the best relationships. If you haven't tallied up points in the 90 range, you'd better start working on being a better pal or expecting your live-in to improve his or her friendship skills. You can't live happily with someone for very long who fails to pass the test of friendship. Chapter 11 advises you on the importance of friendship as the foundation of compatibility.

Too Much or Too Little Synergy

Relationship experts have started to use the word *synergy*, which literally means to work together. Synergy is a word often applied to the perfectly combined efforts of human organs that perform a complex task. Another example of the word's use might describe two medications that work in tandem with each other. In other words, different entities that build positively on one another's responses are synergistic. No wonder the word fits so well into the realm of interpersonal relationships.

Psychologist and professor of clinical psychology at Harvard University Barry Dym and physician and psychiatrist Michael L. Glenn, co-authors of *Couples: Exploring and Understanding the Cycles of Intimate Relationships,* believe that the synergistic process is an ongoing, integral part of a healthy couple's relationship. Dym and Glenn describe synergy as feeding off of one another's energy in a way that expands a relationship upward, bringing the pair closer together and enhancing their performances both as individuals and as a couple.

It's kind of like teamwork that draws on each other's strengths, diminishing individual weaknesses and producing an energetic and sound effort that is based on a richer and fuller picture.

> **Love's Hot Line**
>
> Richard Buckminster Fuller, noted inventor, poet, architect, and engineer, wrote, "Synergy means behavior of whole systems unpredicted by the behavior of their parts." Although he wasn't referring to the behavior of romantic couples, his words could explain how a couple's behavior deviates from the partners' individual behaviors.

An Example of a Couple's Practical Synergy

Let's take a perpetual, pragmatic worrier and a carefree, free-wheeling pal who are thinking about making a life change and moving to a new city. The worrier, though feeling unhappy and stuck, sees only the risk factor in moving to a new city. The free-wheeling partner is inclined to focus on the excitement of new horizons. Together they lean on the positives of each other's predisposition and make a list of interesting cities that offer the best employment opportunities. In the process of working well together, they glean individual energy.

Runaway Synergy

As wonderful as synergy can be for two people to experience, it does have a downside. Runaway synergy could be your problem.

According to experts, synergy that is too intense can overwhelm fresh partnerships. The process of intermingling one's separate characteristics with a live-in honey's could begin to take on the weight of demands if misunderstood and could threaten the sensitivity of an individual's separate and important being. Synergy must settle into a comfortable zone, not too much or too little. It takes flexibility and experimentation for couples to arrive at just the right combination.

> **Love Stats**
>
> Experts say it's okay for an optimist to be romantically involved with a pessimist as long as they operate more optimistically as a couple! In fact, feeding off of each other's energy can mean balancing caution with daring and coming up with a broader picture of reality. In this sense, a couple could demonstrate real synergy.

An Exercise to Evaluate Synergy

Here is a three-step litmus test of the energy or synergy you and your live-in generate.

1. Think of concrete examples that demonstrate how you and your partner act as vital parts of a whole. Write them down.

   _____
   _____
   _____

2. Do these actions produce energy (Yes/No)? _____
   (The answer best be Yes.)

3. Does the energy result in positive action, behavior, or outlook (Yes/No)? _____
   (The answer best be Yes.)

Signs of Troubles

In researching my book *The Complete Idiot's Guide to Handling a Breakup* (Alpha Books, 1999) and other books, I discovered signs and signals of a troubled relationship. Here are some that you should pay attention to if they crop up in your live-in relationship. Their presence is pretty certain evidence that you aren't imagining trouble in hearth and home.

- A demise of sexual intimacy coupled with abundant excuses.
- Coming home late without reasonable explanations.
- Sudden concern over appearance and extra primping before leaving home alone.
- He or she doesn't look you in the eye.
- An absence of those once-delicious, affectionate gestures.
- Disappearances at parties with other guests.
- Preoccupation with everything but you.
- Deliberate attempts to start fights.
- Canceling important plans that leave you hanging.
- Not the slightest show of jealousy or interest if you mention bumping into an old flame.
- Catching him or her in a sudden rash of lies.

Any of the above should put you on the alert for trouble. Get to the root of the problem at once.

> **Love Stats**
>
> Debbie Then, Ph.D., author of *Women Who Stay with Men Who Stray* (Hyperion, 1999), says that research shows that men's quest for sexual variety and novelty makes them stray. Women, on the other hand, go looking for other sex partners for the purposes of sexual experimentation and fulfillment of emotional needs.

Absolute Relationship Breakers

The results of polls are telling, and reveal precisely what is apt to cause a split in your relationship. The most certain breakers appear at the top of the following list. (I'm not talking divorce here, but rather "relationships." The reason I have made the distinction is that the number-one relationship breaker is not ordinarily the number-one motive for divorce.)

1. Infidelity, including *transaction sex*
2. Lies and deceit

> **Sweet Nothings**
>
> **Transaction sex,** according to Debbie Then, Ph.D., is a short-term sexual liaison in which an emotional connection is minimal. She classifies one-night stands and weekend or holiday flings as forms of transaction sex.

3. Inattentiveness
4. Little sexual interest
5. Illegal activity
6. Depression in a partner
7. Lack of job or status
8. Sudden weight gain

> **Troubles A'Brewing ...**
>
> According to a mid-1990s investigation by *New Woman Magazine*, men who go for a cheating one-night stand once do it again. And it doesn't stop there. Guys who cheat on their wives do so repeatedly. One expert estimated that 25 percent of married men will engage in four affairs during the course of their marriage. Men most likely to cheat have higher incomes and ample opportunities.

What's Best for You?

The ball is in your court. Are you taking the blame for problems at home, or are you laying them on your partner or attributing them to a relationship that has proven to be inadequate? Before you decide, you may want to recheck whether or not you made a good decision in the first place. Turn to Chapter 7, "Devising Romantic Motives and a Lovers' Agendas," for help with that question.

The important issue here is what's best for you. Ultimately, only you can make that decision. Are the relationship and the live-in union worth saving? Again, that's your decision to make. You have plenty of other chapters to lead you through that question.

If you want to work on these issues, then turn to the next chapter, where you'll be able to try your hand at household survival tactics and patching materials. The material imparted thus far in Part 4, "Living Under One Roof," will also help.

The Least You Need to Know

➤ If you want to save a decaying relationship, you have to first discover the root of the problem.

➤ Looking at your level of love, commitment, friendship, coupledom, and compatibility are good places to begin secondary investigations.

➤ Live-in couples need the energy supplied by synergy but they cannot endure the smothering loss of individual action.

➤ Infidelity is not only a major relationship breaker but often a repeated offense.

Chapter 23

Household Survival Tactics and Patching Materials

> **In This Chapter**
> - Is your lover lying?
> - Personality-based or situational-based problems?
> - How conflict creates positive change
> - The do's and don'ts of calling a lover's meeting to order
> - Ways to check and balance your relationship
> - Improving the home-front atmosphere

Now that you have verified that something is awry in your live-in relationship, you need to rectify the situation. This is a two-person job. You cannot make things right all by yourself. Nor is it a good idea to suffer discontent in silence. There is no substitute for getting down to the real issues, no matter how difficult a task that may appear to be.

How you approach your partner and deal with the problems you have uncovered could be tricky. Done thoughtlessly or impulsively, such an encounter will only lead you down a darker path. Love talk and sex may help set the mood, loosen up your partner, and make him or her more receptive to touchy discussions.

This chapter will tell you precisely how to ease your honey into a house meeting, give you the required survival tactics once you have each other's attention, and provide sufficient materials to patch up the cracks.

Objectivity Is the Critical Factor

After learning about the body's chemical response to an attractive partner and the way love influences mental functioning, you may think I'm asking for the impossible when I ask you to introduce the element of objectivity into your romantic relationship. Nevertheless, you need to be objective and set your emotions aside. If you don't, any attempt to confront your partner could easily deteriorate into a high-tempered exchange of angry, indiscriminate, and harmful statements.

This is the time to employ control and logic. Without them, you will have a difficult time getting your live-in relationship back on track. You must be open-minded enough to see the problem clearly, understand both parties' roles in it, and figure out precisely what you are asking your partner to do.

Three-Part Objectivity

There are three requirements of objectivity. You haven't approached the objective state until you …

1. Turn on a neutral mindset.
2. Stop listening to your heart or your libido.
3. Rely solely on the facts.

You will need to address the remainder of this chapter with an air of objectivity. Take time to make sure that your objectivity is turned on high before you continue.

When Emotions Take Charge

Unless your emotions remain in control, you will be unable to discern fact from fiction. David J. Lieberman, Ph.D., author of *Never Be Lied to Again* (St. Martin's Press, 1998), says that without *objectivity*—the state of divorcing oneself personally and emotionally from a problem—an individual loses perspective on reality and interprets events based on his or her own hopes, desires, and wishes.

This form of self-deception is easy to fall into, Lieberman says, particularly for the individual who cannot, or does not, want to see the truth.

Love's Hot Line

Don't let fear of the outcome or worry over what will be said stop you from addressing problems in your relationship. It is too easy to allow things to slide by in live-in love. Fix what is fixable now, and don't linger too long in the house if your relationship is beyond repair!

Troubles A'Brewing …

Thinking subjectively is the opposite of being objective and fair-minded. Subjective individuals look at everything from their own points of view and with their own interests in mind. People who use this approach at the bargaining table of love are bound to fail in the short or long run.

Who are among the most vulnerable self-deceivers? You guessed it—lovers. The desire to be liked, loved, and valued is so overwhelming that logic often loses and self-deception prevails. You have been forewarned.

Detecting Your Lover's Lies

Just as important as maintaining objectivity is making sure that your partner deals in the same degree of honesty, as the two of you begin to patch up your relationship. Dory Hollander, Ph.D., and author of *101 Lies Men Tell Women* (HarperPerennial, 1995), says that "men lie to women much more than most of us acknowledge."

Fortunately, you don't have to rely on intuition alone to detect lies that cover up empty promises and sabotage attempts. Lieberman's research has revealed signs that help you spot deception. Someone who is lying is likely to ...

> Avoid eye contact.
> Lack bodily animation.
> Shrug his or her shoulders.
> Quickly change facial expressions.
> Slouch rather than stand erect.
> Avoid touching you.
> Protest too much.

Be on the lookout for these signs, especially if you have a gut feeling that your partner may be lying to you.

> **Love Stats**
>
> "Under the influence of strong feeling we are easily deceived. The coward under the influence of fear and the lover that of love have such illusions that the coward owing to a trifling resemblance thinks he has seen an enemy and the lover his beloved."
>
> —Aristotle (322 B.C.E.)

In Which Bed Does Your Problem Lie?

How you resolve a problem is dictated by where the problem lies. Before you can proceed, you must make an objective determination. You have two choices. Does the problem with your relationship lie with you or with the situation?

Bed Number 1: Personality-Based Problems

For those whose relationship problems are personality based, the problems will be related to their own desires, needs, or goals and can be remedied only by the individuals themselves. If yours is a personality-based problem, keep in mind that the problem can be either yours or your partner's.

Let's take an example.

Shirley feels a strain in her relationship. Recently Pete has been leaving the dinner table before they are finished eating and seems to hide behind a book or magazine most of the evening. His behavior provokes Shirley into angry confrontations that often lead to her going to bed alone and in tears.

Once Shirley is able to sit down calmly, evaluate what is happening, and ask Pete a few questions, she has a significant revelation. She sees herself coming home from work each evening angry and out of sorts. If Pete begins an enthusiastic accounting of his day as a medical researcher, she jumps into a sarcastic, bitter description of hers. If he describes a victory on the racquetball court, she combats it with a failure at work. If Pete suggests they get a humorous video, Shirley retorts that there was nothing funny about *her* day.

"Why shouldn't he go and hide," Shirley finally concludes, realizing that Pete is actually trying to avoid what has become a perpetual stream of arguments started by her.

As Shirley furthers her objective exploration of this chain of events, she sees that the problem doesn't really have a thing to do with Pete. She is miserable at work because she doesn't feel that she is doing anything worthwhile. There is nothing rewarding or challenging about her day, yet she hasn't examined any of the options.

Only Shirley can get herself out of this jam. Once she decides to make a career change, she feels optimistic and invigorated. The mood in the house changes entirely. Pete brings her flowers with a card that says, "I'm glad the Shirley I know is back," and listens attentively to her plans.

> **Love's Hot Line**
>
> Destructive conflicts tear things apart as opposed to ushering in greater understanding and resolution. Such conflicts generally produce feelings of exploitation, hopelessness, disappointment, and disillusionment that cause one partner to leave.

Bed Number 2: Situational-Based Problems

The situational-based relationship problem lies in a particular set of circumstances. It can be eliminated only by resolving to change the problematic situation.

Let's take an example.

Ellie was miserable and didn't like feeling unhappy from sunup to sundown. It hadn't been that long since she and Bill had moved in together and had been ecstatically happy. She had felt confident and excited about their future engagement.

Nine months lapsed, and there was no ring. Ellie was becoming depressed and feeling inadequate, unappreciated, and rejected. When Bill stopped saying he loved her and asked instead, "What does love mean?" and when he refused to continue putting money into their house-buying fund and asked her not to attend his grandmother's funeral because it was a closed, family service, her self-esteem plummeted. She felt insignificant. When she caught Bill in bed with his co-worker, she completely lost it and tried to make him swear to be faithful and start treating her with love.

However, after her temper cooled and the tears dried up, she realized that her unhappiness and her feeling of having fallen into a dark pit were due to the way Bill had been treating her ever since they had started living together. The negative feelings she had didn't have anything to do with anything else in her life. Although she hated to admit that things weren't going to work out the way she had planned, she determined that the only way to resolve her problem was to remove herself from the problematic situation—Bill.

How Couples Change

Don't get overloaded with pessimism just because something is wrong. Conflict isn't all bad, nor is it avoidable. The good thing is, the hard time your relationship is going through could actually propel it into better territory. If handled properly, conflict may strengthen relationship bonds and cohesiveness.

I like the terminology that Barry Dym, Ph.D., and Michael Glenn, M.D., use to explain this concept. When you encounter a problem and feel shaken up, you are in a state of "disequilibrium" in which your personal organization is more loose and you are more open to looking for help.

To alleviate the disequilibrium and return to a state of "balance" requires readjustment. In this way, these experts, and others, see conflict as a condition for change, particularly when old solutions don't quite fix the problem. An inability to deal with each other in familiar ways introduces an opportunity for learning and growth. New solutions create changes in a relationship that bridge previous gaps in understanding.

Even the threat or the idea of separating can actually become a *transformational experience* for you, your partner, and your relationship, Dym and Glenn suggest.

> **Sweet Nothings**
>
> **Transformational experiences** alter the way we see ourselves and situations by providing moments of unprecedented clarity, say authors Dym and Glenn. These experiences are generally ushered in by chaos, confusion, and despair but dissolve into light that gives us a new perspective, reorders our priorities, and engenders a sense of joy and relief.

Calling a House Meeting

The purpose of the house meeting is to put your cards on the table and respond to the hand you have dealt.

Be smart. Living together can be pretty tenuous and the outcome not all that successful. So if you want to attempt to salvage your relationship in the house meeting, follow these guidelines:

➤ The very nature of a meeting implies participation. Think of yourself as a facilitator—not as a dictator and not ever as a leader. Each of you has a stake and a responsible role in the meeting.

➤ To make the most of this peace talk, you have to know your partner well enough to select a prudent time to initiate the meeting.

➤ Frustration levels may be running high. Remember all you have learned; and be calm, collected, and objective before you call the meeting to order.

➤ You want your partner's undivided attention, so stop yourself from impatiently rushing into the discussion while your honey is engaged in doing something else.

➤ On the other hand, don't make the meeting sound so serious and somber that you add more tension to the atmosphere.

➤ Before you begin, refresh your communication and bargaining skills. (Check Chapters 11, "Partnership Potential," and 12, "Pre-Empting Disaster.")

➤ Have all your ducks in a row, and plan what you are going to say. Don't bring up too many issues at once. State the easy ones first.

➤ Be an astute participant. Read all of the signs, and consider each of the cards out there before you make another play.

➤ Don't expect your partner to have all the answers. He or she hasn't had a chance to consider the situation as you have.

➤ Get ready to hear some surprising things come out of your partner's mouth.

> **Love's Hot Line**
>
> Pick a time and place when you know your partner will be receptive to your message. If you don't want to sit around a table for your house meeting, consider a picnic under a tree, a walk along the beach, a stroll in a scenic park, a soak in a hot tub, or coffee in a quiet outdoors café. Don't choose a crowded restaurant with a high noise level.

The Do's and Don'ts of Expressing Your Frustrations

Keep these do's and don'ts in mind when you and your honey have your meeting. They will keep you in line and on track. They enhance your chances for surviving the meeting and patching things up.

Chapter 23 ➤ Household Survival Tactics and Patching Materials

Don't …

- Make accusations.
- Use negative words.
- Overwork the "I" word.
- Come across as dependent and weak.
- Beat around the bush.
- Interrupt your partner when it's his or her turn to talk.
- Lie or shout.
- Be afraid.
- Be judgmental.
- Come to any rash decisions.
- Attack your partner's ego.
- Place all the blame for the problem on just one of you.

> **Love's Hot Line**
>
> Attention all male live-in lovers. Women want the truth. When you come up with lies, whether you think you are saving your honey's feelings or saving your hide, you are behaving in a demeaning and condescending fashion. Give it to them straight. They can handle it.

Do …

- Ask your partner to take equal responsibility for the problem.
- Use neutral words.
- Stay objective.
- Use inclusive words and phrases.
- State how you think things could be better.
- Ask your partner to do the same.
- Explain why something bothers you.
- Be strong.
- Use diplomacy.
- Try to honestly hear what your partner is trying to say.
- Take time-outs—get something to drink, go to the bathroom.
- Give your live-in time to think.
- Ask your partner to be honest and forthright.
- Allow equal time at the podium.
- Be genuinely curious about your partner's opinions and receptive to his or her ideas.
- Keep in mind that relationships and individuals are complex.

Check yourself to make sure you are using the do's and not the don'ts. Each is an important point to remember and employ.

Three Quick Steps to Improving Home Atmosphere

These three steps probably won't fix your problem all by themselves. Nonetheless, they are the collected wisdom of a number of experts, and they include my own observations of relationships under duress. Used with other suggestions in this chapter, they will give you a potent remedy.

1. **Prioritize your priorities.** It might be a good idea to reevaluate your priorities. You might find that your relationship is too far down on the totem pole. That's okay when you are a participant in a casual fling, perhaps even a live-in relationship that was meant to be a loose, no-strings kind of a thing. For anything else, your relationship won't work if it's sitting under a pile of other priorities. If you are on the marriage track, you ought to know that in the happiest of marriages, each person puts his or her spouse as either number one or number two on the list of priorities. You might consider making a list of your own priorities and then making any necessary adjustments.

2. **Try ego-building.** Building up another person's ego makes the recipient feel powerful, successful, and desirable; and it isn't all that hard to do. It just takes a little show of admiration, attention, and pampering. In a relationship, ego-building shows your partner just how special he or she is in your eyes. Ego-building acts like honey and always attracts the bee.

3. **Reduce stress.** Therapists, authors, and partners Wayne and Mary Sotile say that people under stress back away from intimacy and that stress can squelch the comfort and closeness that a couple once had together. Talking, altering lifestyles, allotting more playtime, and slowing down are a few of their remedies. Letting your partner know that his or her behavior is not normal or acceptable is another.

> **Love's Hot Line**
>
> Psychologists have conducted studies proving that in the best relationships the partners communicate the positives to one another. For those of us who are practical in our approach to love, this next statistic is just as worthwhile: The partners also communicate the negatives but slip in only one for every five positives. Sounds like a good, workable ratio!

Designing Checks and Balances

In every good partnership, someone must monitor the course of the relationship, keep it on solid ground, and makes sure each participant is acting in the best interest of the live-in union.

A good monitor becomes adept at paying attention, looking for negative signs, and finding ways to move the relationship forward. For the monitors out there, here are two more ways to keep your relationship in check and in balance.

Effective Emotional Management, a product of the Sotiles, calls for "a fenced-in territory" for you and your partner in which you can exert control. The purpose is to alleviate stress, learn how to lovingly cooperate, and develop a distinction between the worlds in which you act as individuals and as a couple. If built well, your territory should be nurturing and affirming for you and your partnership.

For the couple who needs formal training on relationship behavior, you're in luck. Experts are now using the word "education" instead of therapy. The current school of thought promotes the idea that good relationship behavior is learned. A number of researchers have put together courses specifically designed to enhance relationships, handle conflict, teach empathy, prepare couples for challenges, and teach skills needed for marital unions. (Check out Appendix C, "Premarital and Relationship Courses," to get a list of them.)

> **Troubles A'Brewing ...**
>
> Wayne M. Sotile, Ph.D., and Mary O. Sotile, M.A., authors of *Supercouple Syndrome* (John Wiley & Sons, 1998), have found that people who respond to stress with certain types of behavior patterns do not comprehend the obvious: Their behavior has negative repercussions on their relationship.

The Least You Need to Know

➤ Take prudent action. You can't wait for your relationship to return to balance on its own.

➤ Without an objective point of view, you may be trying to solve the wrong problem.

➤ It is imperative to determine whether the problem lies with you, your partner, or the relationship.

➤ Problems aren't all bad. They can present the condition for change.

➤ Be thoughtful before sitting down with your partner for "the talk."

➤ You can't afford to jeopardize your future happiness by being afraid to address your relationship fears.

Chapter 24

Getting Out the "For Sale" Sign

In This Chapter

- ➤ The dynamics of breaking up
- ➤ Getting straight what happened
- ➤ Determining whether time is on your side
- ➤ Wasted time, his and hers
- ➤ A stuck-in-the-muck test
- ➤ Stargazing, a last resort

Things haven't worked out quite the way you hoped they would. Your relationship has fizzled, and your live-in partner turned out to be either a jerk or a sad version of Prince or Princess Charming. You've tried all the tools provided for you in Part 4, "Living Under One Roof," and you've tried the suggestions in the previous chapter for resolving relationship problems.

You are left with little choice. It's either tear up the lease or put up the "For Sale" sign. Someone is moving out!

No one will deny that you are at an emotionally difficult crossroad. Breaking up is full of pain, guilt, heartache, and anger. Nonetheless, call upon your courage, fortitude, and good sense. You have tried live-in love and lost. It happens more often than not. This chapter gives you the kick in your derrière you may need to get out and get on with it.

The Dynamics of Breaking Up Your Live-In Relationship

If you are bewildered about how your relationship came apart, the dynamics of breaking up discussed here may put an end to your confusion.

Normally your partner will have gone through an *intrapsychic phase* of questioning before asking for a split.

Most breakups are actually perpetrated unilaterally, that is, by one partner. Too often this person won't engage in direct, open, and honest conversation. Instead the desire to separate is made through complaints and hints. Nonetheless, this isn't the only way things can come apart at the seams. Some breakups are gradual, with protracted negotiations, and others appear to be over so suddenly that one partner is left stunned and bewildered.

A Mental Model of Breaking Up

Here is a mental model for a gradual breakup: One or both partners begin to experience disappointment over their relationship. Living together isn't as fun or as satisfying as they had thought it would be. Eventually one partner acknowledges in his or her private thoughts that this simply isn't going to work out and stops trying to make the relationship better. This person slips off into a state of resignation and sadness and *psychologically departs* the relationship. There isn't a reason anymore to try to correct the situation, to blame the other partner, or to punish the other for the disappointment. Yet, despite the disillusionment, no one is moving out. Instead, both parties hold on to the relationship out of fear. Eventually they are able to disengage themselves from each other mentally and emotionally.

Although disengagement affords a person a new point of perspective, the relationship may or not dissolve then and there. It sometimes take an extra boot to physically disengage from a partner and the home that the two have shared.

> **Sweet Nothings**
>
> Psychologists have given a name to the period when one partner feels dissatisfied, begins to search for what is wrong in the other partner, tries to determine whether satisfactory adjustment can be made, and considers what it would take to make himself or herself happy. This period is called the **intrapsychic phase**.

> **Sweet Nothings**
>
> When a partner decides that he or she wants out, that there is no longer any romantic interest, and that he or she has given up on the relationship, this event is called the **psychological departure**. The actual relationship will usually unravel over time.

Chapter 24 ➤ *Getting Out the "For Sale" Sign*

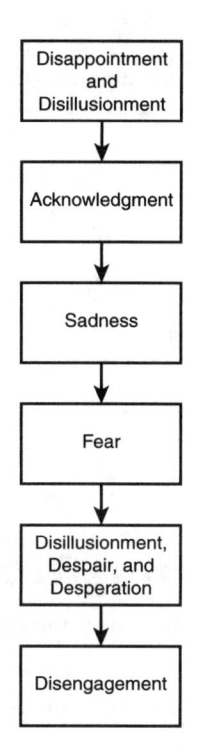

```
┌─────────────────┐
│ Disappointment  │
│      and        │
│ Disillusionment │
└────────┬────────┘
         ▼
┌─────────────────┐
│ Acknowledgment  │
└────────┬────────┘
         ▼
┌─────────────────┐
│     Sadness     │
└────────┬────────┘
         ▼
┌─────────────────┐
│      Fear       │
└────────┬────────┘
         ▼
┌─────────────────┐
│ Disillusionment,│
│  Despair, and   │
│  Desperation    │
└────────┬────────┘
         ▼
┌─────────────────┐
│  Disengagement  │
└─────────────────┘
```

Feelings leading to breaking up.

Getting the Partner Involved

The steps in the breakup process when the partner gets involved have been given various names. The verbiage is plentiful. You have the dyadic phase, the social phase, and the grave-digging phase; or, alternatively, there is the exposure, negotiation, resolution, and transformation.

No matter the terms, the situation boils down to much the same thing. You or your partner have stayed away from exposure, fearing confrontation, arguments, battles, hurt feelings, blame, recriminations, and guilt—all of which are inevitable when ending a live-in relationship. Suddenly, you've had enough, and you get it out in the open and decide what to do.

> **Love's Hot Line**
>
> If after reading the chapters in this part of the guide, you still can't make up your mind and you're still not certain you want to break up, check out my book, *The Complete Idiot's Guide to Handling a Breakup* (Alpha Books, 1999). It has tons of quizzes, questions, and explanations that may assist you in your decision-making process.

289

Part 5 ➤ *If the Roof Caves In*

Steps in the breakup process.

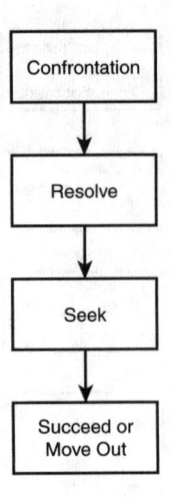

```
Confrontation
     ↓
  Resolve
     ↓
   Seek
     ↓
Succeed or
 Move Out
```

Stop Wasting Time!

Don't hem and haw any longer. You're wasting your time if …

- ➤ You've already established that the problem cannot be resolved.
- ➤ You are on divergent paths.
- ➤ Your relationship is degrading to you.
- ➤ You've made monumental compromises and your partner hasn't made any.
- ➤ There isn't a ray of sunshine in the picture.
- ➤ The live-in relationship is lowering your self-esteem.
- ➤ You have lost control over your future.
- ➤ You are being taken advantage of financially.
- ➤ You are being emotionally, sexually, or physically abused.
- ➤ Your partner has repeatedly been unfaithful.

Do not hesitate. It may be difficult now to call it quits, but you'll be happy you did later.

> **Love Stats**
>
> A precise definition of "codependence" has not yet been uniformly agreed upon by members of the research community. Nonetheless, nearly all who study this behavior agree that behaviors considered codependent are negative. An example of codependent behavior is the situation that occurs when one partner tries to increase his or her self-esteem by controlling or excessively nurturing the other partner.

Telling Time

Determining whether time is your friend or enemy can be complicated and depends primarily on what you are waiting for.

If you are waiting for things to improve in your live-in relationship but there haven't been any positive changes over the last six months, time is probably your enemy. Your partner may be *stonewalling*. Stop looking for excuses to stay.

If it's a proposal for marriage or a definite wedding date you are waiting for, what has gotten in the way? How long are you going to be stalled by a potential new job or the necessity to put a little more money in the bank? Granted, sometimes these are legitimate excuses for holding off matrimony. Other times they aren't. Check out these "time pieces" to help you determine whether time is a friend or an enemy in your living-together waiting game.

> **Sweet Nothings**
>
> **Stonewalling** is a defensive measure to gain time and put off making a relationship or marital commitment because of ambivalence, uncertainty, or an inadequate degree of mature love.

Time as a Friend

The hours are on your side when …

- ➤ Your partner is showing progress in meeting his or her conditions.
- ➤ You and your partner are willing to work on the relationship.
- ➤ Love is growing.
- ➤ You share the same goals.
- ➤ Your agendas are in sync.
- ➤ There is evidence of commitment.
- ➤ You are happy.
- ➤ There are sufficient reasons to trust your partner's word.
- ➤ Neither of you is in a hurry to walk down the aisle.
- ➤ You're not quite sure that your partner is the right marriage partner for you.

Time as an Enemy

The hours are not in your favor when …

- ➤ Your partner is deliberately trying to stonewall.
- ➤ Love has left the picture.
- ➤ Live-in motives, agendas, and goals are not compatible.
- ➤ Biological clocks are ticking.
- ➤ You are into self-deception.

- ▶ A partner has already psychologically departed the relationship.
- ▶ Living together is preventing you from finding a better, healthier, and more satisfying relationship.
- ▶ You have lost sight of your own goals.
- ▶ Your growth is being stifled.
- ▶ The relationship is making you unhappy.

Three Images of Wasted Moments

Just in case you need things drawn out in more detail, these three examples clearly make the point about relationships that waste your time.

Wasted Moment 1: I like to call this the case of "circular reasoning." By the time I finish this saga, you'll know what I mean.

If you have to ask what it means to be in love, chances are that you're not. And if you have to work at falling in love with your live-in companion, chances are you won't. Yet, capturing the elusive, inexplicable passionate love bug is what Billy tried to do during the first four years he lived with Donna.

In all fairness to Billy, it is Donna who in the beginning moved in strictly as a roommate, though it didn't take her long to fall for older, charming Billy. But he does admit that there was an attraction on his part, too. "We are like two peas in a pod. I love sharing things with her. We have the same aesthetic outlook and appreciation of things."

What they didn't have was a great sex life. Billy explains:

> **Troubles A'Brewing ...**
>
> All of the research indicates that negative behavior by a partner begets negative behavior in return. A reciprocal cycle is easier to fall into and more difficult to climb out of. The repeated exchange of negative behavior will, over time, cause a romantic relationship to crumble.

"Donna is angelic. I love that part of her, but it doesn't satisfy me sexually. It isn't my ideal of a sexual woman. I had an affair before we got together. It was very intense and very powerful and passionate. I was in love the very moment I saw this woman. There wasn't that immediate attraction to Donna. I don't want to hurt Donna, but I won't marry her without it being there. It is really difficult to admit that I love Donna, but I am not in love with her. If all the ingredients for the kind of relationship I want were there, I would probably want to have kids. If I were a betting man, I would give this relationship 50/50 odds."

Evidently those odds were good enough for Donna to hang onto. And hang on she has. Donna says:

"I have made it clear that I want children in my life. Now I am waiting for Billy to decide if that's what he wants, too. It is hard to put a time limit on the relationship. To be honest, even if Billy says he doesn't want children, I don't know if I will be able to walk away from him."

Several years later, I found Donna and Billy still together—unwed and without children.

Wasted Moment 2: This couple began their two and a half year live-in relationship in college. The sex was great, she was emotionally and financially needy, and he was willing to share the rent. She transferred from a top-notch school to one of lesser reputation, formed no outside friendships, and decided the love she and her guy shared was the real thing. So did her fella.

But, after graduation she moved out and across the country. When he personally delivered an engagement ring, she put it on but then took it off when she dropped him off at the airport. She was still playing the dating game.

When I peeked in on her two years later, she still had his ring. It had become collateral for the money he owed her. Nonetheless, the shining diamond in her jewelry box did not stop her from taking a new live-in lover.

Wasted Moment 3: Far too many women, particularly between the ages of 19 and 29, may identify with this story. Nearly four million American women suffer violence at the hand of an intimate partner within a 12-month period. And a recent survey of 3,500 women who had come to emergency rooms in Pennsylvania and California indicated that 37 percent had been sexually or physically abused by their intimate partners.

Wanda's live-in union was typical. She and Howard hooked up early in their 20s. There weren't any problems to speak of until she turned up pregnant two years later. After a baby was on the way, Howard changed entirely, Wanda said.

> "Howard would come home after work and grab a beer. Once he got done telling me how fat I was becoming, he kept me running

Love Stats

York College social psychologist Perri B. Druen, Ph.D., found that men and women who think love is the foundation of a relationship had shorter romantic partnerships. Those who exhibited greater willingness to work on a relationship and focus less on choice of a partner had longer relationships.

Love's Hot Line

Sexual coercion should not be tolerated between live-in and married partners any more than in courtship relationships. Coercive sex is the result of persistent pressure, deception, threats, physical restraint, or physical force.

> **Troubles A'Brewing ...**
>
> According to research by Chris Segrin reported in *The Close Side of Dark Relationships* (ed. Brian H. Spitzberg and William R. Apach, Laurence Erlbaun Associates, 1998), mental health problems such as alcoholism, schizophrenia, loneliness, depression, and eating disorders are connected to personal relationships. They may either predate the interpersonal relationship or result from it.

errands for him all night long. Finally I was so exhausted I had to give up my job and catch up on my sleep during the day. The larger I got, the angrier he became. One day he punched me in the stomach. I was scared to death but had no one to call for help. He told me if I left and went home to my parents, he would tell the hospital we wanted to put the baby up for adoption.

"I tried to stay out of Howard's way. I was worried about the health of the baby and asked the doctor to make sure it was okay. I said I slipped and hit my belly really hard on the kitchen floor.

"Things didn't improve after Randy was born. I thought Howard would be happy to have a son. I was scared but didn't think I had any choice now but to stay. He would holler about the bills and slap me around if the house was a mess and dinner wasn't on the table when he got home. Every time I threatened to leave, he threatened to take Randy.

"One night he came after me with a knife but tripped before reaching me. He was so irate that he left the house. I packed a few things for Randy and myself and ran out of there. I was scared for my life and shaking so hard I could hardly hold onto Randy.

"I was lucky we lived near a bus line. Howard sold my car when I stopped working. I was able to get downtown to a pay phone and the police department. I knew I would be safe sitting in the lobby. My folks had to drive all night to get there and take me home. It was my dad who finally called Howard to tell him that Randy and I were fine but that he wasn't to come near me.

"My parents had told me when we first hooked up they didn't want me living with Howard. They could tell right away that he was mean. I didn't see it. By the time I did, I didn't have enough confidence to leave. I never thought I could make it with the baby alone. I was wrong. I can. I should have left sooner."

Wanda's story is a warning to others. At the first signs of abuse, take action. Domestic violence experts will tell you incidences increase in seriousness over time.

Astrological Corroboration: Yes or No?

I am not a proponent of astrological forecasts or birth signs. But you may be. However, before you find hope in the stars, there are a few things you should know.

Chapter 24 ➤ *Getting Out the "For Sale" Sign*

More than 1,800 years ago, an Egyptian astronomer came up with the concept of the zodiac. Eventually this method of divining the future was taken up and further refined by the Greeks. It has remained almost unchanged since, despite the discovery of more stars—even galaxies—and the changed tilt of the earth's axis.

Most astronomers disavow the relevance of astrology. They view it as something related to magic, not the scientific study of the stars. So how did astrology become so popular that it has influenced the decision-making of princesses, first ladies, and thousands of lovers?

Historians claim that newspapers were responsible for the rising importance of astrological charts and predictions. The syndicated daily fortune-telling columns that appeared in newspapers across America became a large part of our pop culture. One of the first such columns appeared in the *Washington Evening Star* in 1924.

I think it is fun to find that the stars may corroborate decisions you have already thoughtfully made. I think it is folly for you to base serious decisions about life and love on the movement of celestial objects. The stars won't be able to free you from the muck you are stuck in if you fail the following quiz. Only you can do the extracting!

Are You Stuck in the Muck?

You aren't a happy live-in partner any longer. You know you should pack your bags or ask your partner to load up his or her belongings, but you just can't make yourself do it. Your days are filled with indecision. Your thought process is cloudy. If the following statements describe your innermost feelings or thoughts, you are stuck in the muck of your own making. Place a check mark by the statement that applies to you.

- ❏ You are willing to settle for less than a terrific relationship.
- ❏ You are naively waiting for things to get better.
- ❏ You are afraid you won't find anyone else to couple up with.
- ❏ You are afraid of being alone.
- ❏ You are dependent on the relationship for your identity.
- ❏ You need help paying the mortgage, rent, or other bills.
- ❏ You are basically insecure without a partner.
- ❏ You are waiting for the perfect moment to leave.
- ❏ You make continual excuses for your live-in's bad behavior.
- ❏ You are afraid of what your live-in might do if you leave.
- ❏ You don't want to admit to your family and friends that they were right: You should not have moved in with this person.
- ❏ You don't know where you would go or what you would do if you left.

Did we miss any of your reasons for staying that carry as little weight as these statements do? If so, add them to your list.

Part 5 ➤ *If the Roof Caves In*

I know it is silly, but I am not leaving because:
_____
_____
_____

Love Stats

Ann L. Weber in her research paper on "Coping with Nonmarital Breakups" says that the degree of "post-breakup distress" is related to emotional connection and involvement of the couple, time they have spent in the relationship, extent to which they have acted as and presented themselves as a couple, and the possibilities of finding other potential romantic partners.

The Least You Need to Know

➤ Live-in relationships don't fall apart in two seconds. Partners divorce themselves psychologically from the union over a period of time.

➤ You are wasting time—and perhaps jeopardizing your life—by staying in a live-in relationship that compromises your well-being in any way!

➤ Time is on your side only when you are completely happy in your live-in situation and when you and your partner continue to share agendas.

➤ Time is your enemy when you live in a world of self-deception and prefer to continue an unsatisfactory live-in relationship rather than burst your fairy-tale bubble.

➤ Ending a relationship is never easy. The incentive comes from knowing why you want out.

Chapter 25

Avoiding Moving-Day Disaster

In This Chapter

➤ The difficulties of breaking up

➤ Creating a separation plan

➤ Emergency exits

➤ Managing painful emotions

➤ Protecting the kids

➤ Recovery tips for ex–live-in lovers

You are about to embark on a new phase of your life and a historically significant moment. Never before has "premarital divorce" been such a common experience in the United States. You are part of the trend of the large number of couples who have chosen to live together and split without marrying one another.

Of course, you aren't the only couple calling it quits these days. The prevalence of divorce and the lack of importance placed on long-term marriages or cohabitation, according to University of Wisconsin professor Larry L. Bumpass, "has to do with ... a decreasing willingness, in general, in our society, and in Western industrialized societies, to make long-term commitment."

The point is, if you are breaking up home and hearth, you have plenty of company. Unfortunately, those who are ending these relationships face the potential for a new kind of disaster on moving day. That is why it is imperative that you carefully prepare for and plan your departure.

Follow the recommendations provided for you in this chapter. Nothing can alleviate the sting of the raw emotions you may be feeling. But being cautious, prudent, and thoughtful will prevent salt from being added to your wounds.

Moving Out Isn't Going to Be Easy

There is sympathy here for your plight. Those who have gone before you will tell you moving out wasn't easy. In fact, the absence of laws and procedures normally associated with divorce preclude an organized and even civilized separation.

> **Love's Hot Line**
>
> Face facts. Your relationship may have been doomed from the start because of a mismatched partnership. It happens all the time. In the professional world, this is called "pre-existing doom." It is manifested by couples whose underlying attraction is insufficient to overcome conflict, because of differences in their backgrounds, goals, or values.

The problem is that when people move in together, they are in love and in a congenial frame of mind. When they leave, the extreme opposite may be the case.

Watch Out!

A study conducted by Jeffrey Coben of Allegheny University of the Health Science of Pittsburgh said that "the period when a relationship ends may be a risky time for women." According to his figures, women who ended a relationship within the last 12 months were seven times more likely to report an incident of abuse.

Women aren't the only victims. Men may find themselves being stalked or harassed in a number of ways. In a San Diego study, 72 percent of individuals who reported being stalked were pursued by estranged husbands, wives, or intimate partners. The primary reason given for the stalking behavior was the desire to reconcile with their partners.

> **Sweet Nothings**
>
> **Obsessive relationship intrusion (ORI)** is intrusive, unwanted behavior into another individual's physical or psychological space, and therefore, an invasion of privacy. The perpetrator is typically an individual who wants, or presumes to have, an intimate relationship with the person whom the perpetrator is, in effect, stalking.

Other forms of *obsessive relational intrusion* (*ORI*) can also signal that you are dealing with a potentially dangerous situation. If the individual repeatedly calls and hangs up, watches you from a distance, visits you at work, leaves notes on your car, spreads personal rumors about you, issues threats, or breaks into your home, you are being stalked.

Planning Your Departure

You may have drifted into this relationship, but you won't be able to drift upstream and out of it quite so smoothly. Look around at all that you have collected together. Now all of that has to be divided.

The things that aren't visible and can't be dismissed so systematically are your emotions. They stand ready to explode with one wrong step, like shells in a mine field. That's why it is imperative to prepare yourself for breaking up and to devise a plan for dismantling home and hearth.

You might want to consider setting a few goals that can benefit you and your ex while going through this ordeal.

Goals that are in your best interest include …

- ➤ Trying to exit with as little conflict as possible.
- ➤ Going for an amicable settlement.
- ➤ Moving swiftly but not haphazardly.
- ➤ Tying up loose ends before, or shortly after, you vacate your shared residence.

A thoughtful split aided by a healthy mindset reduces the stress, strain, and emotional wear and tear present in ending all relationships. The above suggestions should help alleviate a negative aftermath.

A Twelve-Step Separation Plan

In order to meet the goals recommended in the previous section, follow this 12-step plan. Do not omit one single step!

> **Troubles A'Brewing …**
>
> Daphne Rose Kingma, a marriage and family therapist who authored *Coming Apart* (Conari Press, 2000), wrote, "Next to the death of a loved one, the ending of a relationship is the single most emotionally painful experience that any of us ever goes through."

> **Love Stats**
>
> The more miserable person in unrequited love is the individual who does not reciprocate love. The one who gives loves is better for at least having tried to find love.
>
> —From *Breaking Hearts*, Baumeister and Wotman (Guilford Press, 1992)

Part 5 ➤ *If the Roof Caves In*

Your Personal Separation Planner

1. Get organized. Make lists and check off items as you get them done.
2. Determine a time line that includes …
   - ❏ When it would be most convenient for you to break up.
   - ❏ When you plan to move out or when your partner should move out.
   - ❏ When you should tell your partner about your decision.
   - ❏ When your present lease runs out.
   - ❏ When you will have enough money for a deposit on a new home.
   - ❏ When you can start making rent or mortgage payments on a new lease or home.
3. Write out your plan with precision and detail. That includes determining a confidant _____, who will help you move _____, and the best time to tell friends and family members of your plan _____.

   Other details of my plan include: _____

   _____
   _____
   _____

4. Take measures to protect your financial assets and bank accounts. You may wish to withdraw your portion of any joint accounts before you advise your live-in that you want to break up. Keep an accurate accounting for your soon-to-be ex:

   What was ours in the bank _____.

   What portion is my live-in's _____.

   What portion is mine _____.

5. Solidify plans for your new residence and sign your lease.

   New address _____.

6. Make an inventory of household items and check off what you think is yours.

Mine	My Live-In's
_____	_____
_____	_____
_____	_____
_____	_____

Chapter 25 ➤ *Avoiding Moving-Day Disaster*

7. Make a financial ledger showing:

Outstanding Bills	My Share	My Live-In's Share
_____	_____	_____
_____	_____	_____
_____	_____	_____

Money Due from Household Deposits

_____ _____ _____
_____ _____ _____
_____ _____ _____

Other Incidental Accounts to Settle

_____ _____ _____
_____ _____ _____
_____ _____ _____

8. In the event you have to leave suddenly, advise a close friend of your plans to move out.
9. Lay out your plan to your partner. Have your financial ledger ready and your list of household property.
10. Start sleeping in separate beds and forget the sex.
11. Make arrangements to have your name removed from all joint household accounts, utilities, and loans. Complete a list of such accounts.

Account	Date of Name Removal
_____	_____
_____	_____
_____	_____

12. Prior to moving day, separate household items into his and hers. Pack into separate boxes and label to avoid moving-day confusion.

301

> **Love's Hot Line**
>
> The most painful breakups are those that leave one individual confused or without sufficient understanding of why the relationship ended, explained Anne L. Weber in *The Dark Side of Close Relationships* (ed. Brian H. Spitzberg and William R. Apach, Lawrence Erlbaun Associates, 1998). Although it is wise to seek an explanation, it is not prudent to devise it out of rumor or fantasy. To ease the pain, each partner ought to be forthcoming with their feelings and reasons for moving on.

Moving-Day Rules

The day has come at last. You meet it with mixed emotions. You are happy to get the move over with, disappointed things didn't work out, and afraid of what the future holds. But there is no time on moving day to bother with emotions or ponder the future. Follow these rules, and you'll do fine. Later we will deal with the ravages of your emotions.

These rules are ones I have composed for you. Some have room for variations; others do not.

1. Double-check that everything is labeled properly. Only take those boxes and pieces of furniture with your name on them.
2. Whatever you do, don't pick a fight and don't be drawn into one. Don't go for last-minute jabs.
3. Make sure a friend or family member is there to support you emotionally. Do not invite your new love interest to come over.
4. Be civil and courteous. Remember, at one time you thought you loved each other. If you don't think you can maintain this kind of demeanor, consider moving out separately, you in the morning and your ex in the afternoon.
5. If you must cry, go into the bathroom or outside. It is best to show a stiff upper lip. You'll grow into the role.
6. Don't be talked into last-minute changes that you will regret later.
7. Smile. Don't let on that you may be the injured party. Be gentle and sweet if you are the one who wanted out.

8. It takes two to clean up the place. Don't you dare do it by yourself.
9. Wish each other good luck.
10. Walk out with your head held high. Don't look back. Look forward.

There is nothing arbitrary about these 10 rules. Make sure they are enforced by both partners. You'll find it handy to have them to rely on during the upheaval of splitting home and hearth.

Do's and Don'ts for After the Fact

There are a million do's and don'ts that could be mentioned. Many appear throughout this guide in longer sentences and with greater explanations. This list of do's and don'ts should be a part of your common sense and sensible romantic reasoning. It serves as a reminder of how you should proceed, in case you need one. I have deliberately added more do's than don'ts. This is a time to think positively!

Don'ts:

1. Don't be embarrassed or ashamed. You haven't failed the test of love. You simply did not hook up with the right partner for you.
2. Don't engage in obsessive relational intrusion. You could get yourself into serious trouble by annoying or stalking your old honey.
3. Don't go back to sleeping together even though you would make great bed buddies.
4. Don't suddenly decide you want to exchange a couch for a chair, or a table for a lamp. You're probably just being nasty or want to stay in your ex's face.
5. Until you are emotionally detached from your old live-in, don't punish yourself by deliberately remembering the good times.
6. Don't debate the issue. It's over.
7. Don't sit home alone, eating ice cream and getting blue.
8. Don't surround yourself with luxuries you can't afford. They will add happiness only for the moment.

Do's:

1. Do say good-bye to his or her friends and family members whom you liked, but don't think that maintaining a relationship with them will be comfortable.
2. Look on the bright side. No matter how bleak it may seem, happiness can be yours.
3. Take the bull by the horn and tell yourself you are important, deserve happiness, and will find it.

4. Absolve yourself and others from blame and guilt.
5. Explore new options and avenues for growth.
6. Pamper yourself. Go on a vacation, buy that new handball racquet, or enjoy a facial.
7. Redecorate, and be sure to get new bedding.
8. Find pleasure in being self-reliant and alone.
9. If you need more physical distance, move out of town.
10. Start dating as soon as you can go out without talking about your ex or your precious live-in union.
11. Approach your new life with energy, excitement, and vigor. This is a great time to make changes you have been considering.
12. Project the best of you.
13. Break the "emotional attachment" to your ex.
14. Enjoy your freedom.
15. Accept the challenge of a new romantic phase.

If you decide to give live-in love another go, turn immediately to the beginning of this book, start reading, and answer all of the questions before you pack one little bag. Don't make the same mistake twice.

Troubles A'Brewing ...

FBI records indicate that a woman is battered by a lover or spouse every 15 seconds. Domestic violence is the number-one cause of injury for women in the United States. Incidents of battering total more than the combined figures for rape, auto accidents, and muggings.

A Victim's Departure

Bureau of Justice statistics indicate that a woman's risk of violence or death from a batterer increases greatly once she leaves the relationship. Some breakups, therefore, call for extra caution.

Precautionary measure: Memorize the number for the National Domestic Violence Hot Line: 1-800-799-7233.

Find out the local hot line number, and the numbers for shelters or available resources. Shelters provide a safe haven in which you can hide and either talk with a qualified counselor or receive help in locating one.

Devise an exit plan that maximizes your safety. Don't wait until you have to make an emergency exit under the threat of death. Never underestimate a batterer's ability to do you harm.

Seek court-ordered protection if you think it necessary, but be careful not to assume a false sense of security.

Statistics from one study found that as many as 60 percent of the women who got a protection order suffered subsequent abuse. Seventeen percent of women who became domestic homicide victims had already obtained protection orders. Men with prior criminal records will be most likely to violate the protection order.

Once you leave a live-in relationship in which you have been verbally, emotionally, or physically abused, you will experience a period of stress, depression, fear, and doubt. You may miss your partner and consider returning. Give yourself a chance to rebuild your defenses, self-esteem, and clear thinking before you give a second thought to returning home. You may decide that you prefer to build a new life without a partner's abuse.

When Kids Are Involved

Family experts express a great deal of concern over children who live with cohabiting couples. (Review Chapter 2, "The Scoop on Live-In Love," for more-detailed information.) The fact that 40 percent of children are born to unmarried, cohabiting moms makes this a significant issue. These children live in less-stable environments, are more likely to experience family breakups, face a greater risk of abuse, and get bumped around more than other kids.

All in all, their lives are less secure and more emotionally problematic. It would not be surprising to find a child disturbed over the mother's breakup, especially with a man with whom the child has established some degree of closeness and now may never see again.

> **Love Stats**
>
> Studies show that kids from highly conflictive homes in which two parents reside do not fare any better than children from single-parent homes, with respect to educational achievement, behavior problems, or early participation in sex. In the first half of the twentieth century, 80 percent of children lived in homes in which both biological parents were present. That number has dropped to 60 percent at the onset of the millenium.

It is important, therefore, for family members to keep a close watch on children when the breakup involves a home in which their biological parents have been cohabiting or in which a nonparent partner has been living. Taking time to provide an explanation, making sure the children don't blame themselves for the breakup, alerting teachers to the situation, obtaining counseling, and dealing with potential feelings of rejection are wise safety measures to take.

Facing Raw Emotions

There are emotional consequences of *unrequited love* and of ending any relationship, including depression, humiliation, and diminished self-esteem. After all, it is natural to want to belong, connect, love, and couple. However, after living with someone in a public forum and pinning so many hopes and dreams on the positive outcome of this relationship, you may feel an inordinate amount of pain, loneliness, anger, rejection, grief, and betrayal after the union has dissolved.

> **Sweet Nothings**
>
> **Unrequited love** is passionate love that one person feels toward an individual who does not share or reciprocate these feelings and desires for a romantic relationship.

Although it is tempting to engage in an "obsessive review" of the relationship, looking for those "if only" situations isn't healthy. However, an honest review to determine where the trouble lay and how to avoid a rerun of this drama is healthy.

Additionally, continuing to mull over a dissolved relationship in your mind encourages a "persistence of attachment" to one separated partner. That won't help you get over the pain of the separation. Trying to handle the grief associated with disengagement will be more beneficial to the healing process.

Handling Your Grief

Stop recycling your grief! It is time to toss it out. Danish clinicians Leick and Davidsen-Nielsen identify six steps in the process of ridding yourself of relationship grief. Work through each one of them.

1. "Recognize" that the loss is an absolute fact.
2. "Release" or expel emotions associated with grief.
3. "Develop new skills" to accommodate a new life and meet future challenges.
4. Stop fantasizing about reconciliation and instead "reinvest emotional energy" into meeting new people and forming new relationships and attachments.

If you heed this advice, you may successfully lessen the depths of your *emotional loneliness* and quicken your period of recovery.

Chapter 25 ➤ *Avoiding Moving-Day Disaster*

A First-Rate Recovery Tip

The novelist Amy Tan said, "If you can't change your fate, change your attitude."

Major changes needed in your relationship recovery routine include:

> ➤ A major attitude change when it comes to your outlook on being single. Michael Broder, Ph.D., author of *Living Single* (1990), says that one of the biggest mistakes singles make is living "their lives as though it were merely a dress rehearsal, and not the real show. So your first step is to get out of that frame of mind."
>
> ➤ A mindset that expects you to heal.
>
> ➤ A fresh perspective filled with hope and humor.

> **Sweet Nothings**
>
> **Emotional loneliness** is a synonym for isolation. This form of loneliness focuses on the absence of your intimate partner, missing that person and the loss of comforts specifically associated with the relationship.

Close the Door

Without closure, chances are you will suffer the pangs of unfinished business and won't really be able to put your relationship to bed or move forward.

To achieve closure, you must sufficiently analyze the past and reconcile the events of your relationship intellectually and emotionally within yourself. Some relationship experts, unfortunately, have witnessed the process taking up to two years. However, I believe that with the concerted efforts of a new mindset, objectivity, and plenty of stimulating activity, you can beat that time.

Your progress in arriving at a state of closure may be determined by taking the following quiz. Answer with an honest yes or no. To get an A+ on your closure exam requires a no to every question. You flunk the test if a majority of your answers are yes.

My golden rules of closure include: no trial separations, no giving in to sweet talk, no listening to false promises, no straying from future goals, and no fantasizing.

Ask Yourself	Yes	No
Am I waiting for him or her to call?	_____	_____
Did I buy a portable phone in case he or she does call?	_____	_____
Do I race to my answering machine or e-mail when I walk in the door, hoping my ex–love interest left me a message?	_____	_____
Do I find myself talking about him or her with friends?	_____	_____
Am I romanticizing him or her or the relationship?	_____	_____
Have I been going to places where I think I might bump into my old flame?	_____	_____
Do I sit and think about the good times we had?	_____	_____
Do I still wish he or she were here?	_____	_____
Am I comparing each new love interest to him or her?	_____	_____
Do I hang out with my ex's friends so that I'll still feel a part of him or her?	_____	_____

From The Complete Idiot's Guide to Handling a Breakup.

The Least You Need to Know

➤ Ending your live-in relationship will not be easy.

➤ There is a serious need to employ forethought and caution when you move out.

➤ Get your plan in order before you tell your partner or before you depart.

➤ The more organized you are, the more successful your departure will be for you and for your ex.

➤ Don't expect to get out emotionally unscathed. However, the pain does not indicate a terminal disease.

➤ You can recover from heartache and emerge into a better and brighter world.

Part 6
Moving Toward the Altar

You want to be more than spousal equivalents, or you want nothing at all. If that's the case, you are ready for the final part of this book. It is the appropriate moment to test whether your live-in pal is marriage material. This may seem rather silly, since you have been living happily under one roof for a while now. However, what you are after in a live-in partner may differ significantly from the profile of someone who makes a good marriage partner.

In order to assess the situation clearly, you need to know the predictors of marital success, compare your risk factors, upgrade your mindset, and opt for a little relationship education.

Once you are sure you are on the right track, you can proceed to the transition from living-together companions to marriage partners. A smooth transition includes making important changes in behavior, revising expectations, and getting ready for a fresh start.

Whether you follow the sequence in the book or whether your life leads you on another path, I sincerely hope that after digesting all the information provided throughout this book, you will be better equipped to handle the reality of live-in love.

Once you become newlyweds, however, your lives are full of both wonderment and peril. The first few years of marriage are critical to your future well-being and happiness. That is why it is so important to shred the last vestiges of a less-committed live-in love relationship and manage your marital relationship wisely.

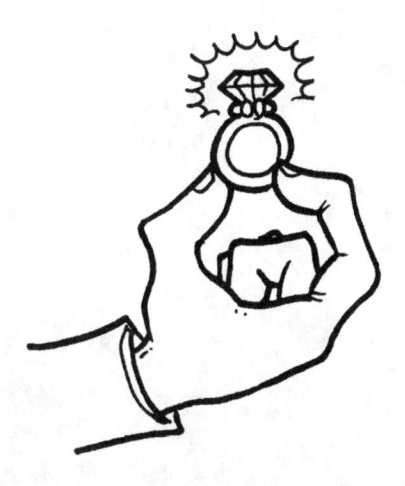

Chapter 26

Marriage Material—His, Hers, Theirs

In This Chapter

➤ Upgrading from significant other to spouse

➤ Facing risks of marital success

➤ Becoming an educated marriage partner

➤ Imperative matrimonial qualities

➤ Protective measures for successful matrimony

Enough of this living-together stuff. You have decided to trade in the title of "spousal equivalent" for the real thing and capture the American dream. If that's the case, you are in sync with most of your countrymen and women. Diane Sollee, founder and director of the Coalition for Marriage, Family, and Couples Education, says that Americans want and value a good marriage above money, work, and health.

Read that sentence again. In my opinion, "good" is the key word. Unfortunately, going from a cohabitation home front to a matrimonial home front has statistically decreased your odds for fulfilling this dream. Population reports by the Bureau of the Census show that young couples who enter into a first marriage have a 40 to 50 percent risk of divorce. Live-ins have a higher rate of divorce, as do second marriages that involve children.

This is all the more reason to look carefully at your live-in partner and at your relationship to determine whether what the two of you have is marriage material and, if not, what you can do about it. This is serious and complex business you are about to embark upon. Not only do failed marriages cost communities and states billions of dollars, but they cause you heartache, stress, disappointment, and despair.

Is Your Live-In Marriage Material?

Although you may have lived with someone for several months or even a year, you may not have a handle on an answer. It's what sociologists call the "selection effect."

When you select a live-in partner, the pool of individuals you select from may be different from the pool out of which you would choose a marriage partner. For instance, before you became involved with your live-in, you could have become romantically involved with someone who (a) would never cohabit, (b) would never live together or consider divorce, (c) would cohabit, or (d) would live together with the potential to marry.

According to Larry L. Bumpass of the University of Wisconsin, those who live together with the potential to marry may actually be the least secure about their relationship. (You may want to recheck Chapter 2, "The Scoop on Live-In Love," if you don't get it.)

Insecurity and indecision make living together sound like a reasonable compatibility test. However, we know for a fact that this isn't the case.

> **Love Stats**
>
> A survey of adults about marriage attitudes came out with these results: 2 percent said it's okay for a wife to be older, 89 percent said it's okay not to want kids, 52 percent said it's okay to live together, and 33 percent said it's okay to have kids without being married.

> **Troubles A'Brewing ...**
>
> It is possible to live with someone who is "on his or her best behavior" and find out after saying "I do" that this person is now a stranger. Cynthia looked like she was going to be a great stepmom. She made breakfast for Carl's son before the boy left for school, was a good pal with his twenty-something daughter, and agreed on no more kids. After she and Carl were married, she slept until 10, lost interest in Carl's daughter, and demanded to get pregnant. The divorce cost Carl a bundle.

Laboratory Predictors of Marital Success

Marriage and love labs have produced definitive predictors of marital success or failure. You are on the road to doom if you roll eyes at each other's comments, act defensively, are critical, and try to stonewall discussion when verbally interacting with one another. Add to those predictors two partners who reciprocate negativity and withdraw during conversations, and the nails are already hammered in the coffin.

Compare Your Marital Risk Factors

These risk factors were gathered from significant, thorough, and major projects completed by the most notable researchers around. You cannot afford to dismiss the importance of this list. As you read through the risk factors, consider carefully whether any might affect your own marital success.

> **Love Stats**
>
> According to information released at a conference of the American Association for Marriage and Family Therapy, marriage benefits both sexes but men more so. Evidence points to the fact that men are protected from depression in marriage; women are more vulnerable to it. Men have a higher level of marital satisfaction than women.

Risk Factors for Individuals and Couples

Although numerous, the following risk factors can be diminished by concerted effort:

- History of cohabitation
- Short courtship
- Problems relating to family and friends
- Negative interaction patterns
- Belief that relationship is dysfunctional
- Inadequate problem-solving abilities
- Communication problems
- Dissimilar attitudes
- Defensive behavior
- Problems in sexual relationship
- More hostility than partnership warmth
- Religious differences
- Maintenance of separate finances

➤ Lack of conscientiousness about the relationship

➤ Low or different levels of education

If any of the above risk factors apply to you, now is the time to attend to these serious matters—all of which can be fixed.

Nonnegotiable Risk Factors

The next three risk factors cannot be changed. They will follow you into any marital partnership. However, that doesn't mean you can't guard against their effects. The first step is to be aware that they do in fact pose significant risk to your marital well-being.

➤ Differences in family origins and values

➤ Divorce history

➤ Problematic personality tendencies

Upgrading Your Live-In Mindset

If you are completely honest, you will nod your head in agreement with this next statement: You moved in with your honey and most likely had an escape plan in the back of your mind in case things didn't go as planned. The notion that this was a permanent relationship that would not go asunder was probably not part of your mindset. And furthermore, that was okay with you. You weren't really ready to think about a relationship that could last a lifetime.

However, Norval D. Glenn of the University of Texas at Austin believes that it is essential for marriage partners to adhere to the ideal that marital permanence is a positive quality and a goal to strive for.

Mental Upgrades

If you and your live-in are going to make good marriage material, valuing permanence alone won't sufficiently upgrade your live-in mindset. You had better increase commitment and love by several notches and lower your autonomy. Love and commitment aren't sufficient for marriage unless you …

➤ Feel comfortable making joint financial investments.

➤ Are vested in the well-being of each other's emotional lives.

> **Love's Hot Line**
>
> "Searching for a definition of 'real love' becomes pointless if one 'feels good' enough about one's relationship. After all, what one is looking for is the 'right place' for oneself."
>
> —Ann Swidler, *Habits of the Heart: Individuals and Commitment in American Life*

- Find satisfaction in making concessions to accommodate your partner's needs and desires.
- Enjoy making life easier and better for your partner.
- Anticipate meeting life's challenges positively and together.
- Want to be viewed by friends and family as a united couple.
- Are able to overlook your partner's minor flaws.
- Put your mate at the top of your list of priorities.
- Derive happiness from pleasing your partner.
- Want to share your mental, emotional, and financial resources to build a secure and better future together.
- Accept your partner as a lifetime companion and helpmate.
- Trust one another implicitly.
- Are willing to expend the time and energy to understand your partner.
- Believe that your life will be better and richer because of the presence of your partner.
- Accept that decisions need to be made jointly.
- Respect and honor your future spouse.
- Are physically attracted and sexually compatible.
- Are willing to forego some of your personal freedom.
- Exchange personal feelings, thoughts, fears, hopes, and dreams.

> **Love Stats**
>
> Autonomy could represent a major gender difference if Joan Borysenko, Ph.D., author of *A Woman's Book of Life* (Riverhead Books, 1998), is right. She believes that autonomy and independence are intrinsic to little boys' development. To achieve this, however, unlike little girls, boys must repress their mother's maternal characteristics of empathy and tenderness in an effort to differentiate themselves from her.

Step back and rethink your decision to move on to matrimony if you are put off or frightened by the preceding list. These items are marriage essentials as far as I am concerned. If you don't agree, you need to go back and reread Chapters 3, "The Facts and Fictions of Living Together," 9, "The Power of Love," and 10, "Is It Love?" for starters!

Reducing Your State of Autonomy

To function with complete autonomy is to be totally independent, emotionally and physically, of other beings. Few folks go to this absolute extreme. However, having just passed through a very "self-centered" era and living in a country that regards dependence negatively, some individuals may find that giving up even a modicum of independence is a stretch. They aren't the ones you want to consider as marriage partners.

Refusing to accompany a live-in to his or her parents' home for dinner or refusing to go to the other's company picnic because it intrudes on alone-time is bad enough. An unwillingness to share time and social lives just doesn't fly in marriage.

A couple who is considering matrimony should function better and more happily because each partner is present in the other's life. Both must demonstrate a willingness to give up certain freedoms in exchange for their partner's company and their gift of love.

If you don't want to spend time together, why be together? Whether or not to marry then becomes a moot point.

But it isn't only the social and physical aspects of your relationship that get shortchanged when your partner wishes to retain a level of autonomy acceptable in live-in love but injurious to marriage. The partner who wishes to remain primarily autonomous is more withdrawn and self-contained. A man or woman with these tendencies has more difficulty creating intimacy through self-disclosure. Intimacy is an ingredient that encourages the growth of love, and love is something that promotes commitment, and good marriages can't get along without that.

The magic formula for each couple mixes comfortable levels of dependence and independence to arrive at a degree of interdependence that enhances a true partnership but allows enough room for individual growth.

> **Love's Hot Line**
>
> To be skilled is to demonstrate understanding, dexterity, great ability, proficiency, or expertness with regard to a skill, behavior, or concept. To be a skilled marriage partner, you must understand and be proficient at using the skills and tools that maintain a marriage relationship.

Going for an Educated Mindset

You don't have to be turned inside out, analyzed from top to bottom, and exorcised of all psychological frailties to become a good marriage partner these days. In fact, most of the experts agree that psychoeducation is a better tool for addressing the "how to" for a better marriage. Psychoanalysis and psychotherapy are out.

The current thinking embraces teaching couples the skills that will help them interact, communicate, argue, and behave in a manner beneficial to their marital relationship. And prevention, rather than repair, is the motto of the premarital counseling movement that has taken over the forefront of contemporary thinking.

The Value of PMC—Premarital Counseling

Good premarital counseling fosters a change in attitudes and beliefs, provides training in relationship skills, and raises awareness of the state of your marital relationship, particularly through critical periods of transition. The transitions into marriage and parenthood offer the greatest challenges.

Trained counselors who assist couples in assessing their relationship, identifying and building strengths, and building good communication can improve the outlook of your marital success.

Dr. Howard Markman, a psychologist at the University of Denver, says good premarital counseling by trained specialists can prevent disappointment in marriage, despair in relationships, problems for society and children caused by failed marriages, physical and emotional stress, and a decrease in productivity.

PMC Isn't Anything to Fear

Premarital counseling shouldn't be threatening. Don't panic about what you might find out sitting across from a premarital counselor. The knowledge could head off trouble at the pass. This is a good time to find out whether the two of you have the right stuff for a lifetime together. In two university-based programs in which engaged couples independently filled out questionnaires and then jointly discussed their answers, no more than 10 percent of the couples broke off their wedding plans as a result of the findings.

"Participating in classes and working on a marriage relationship should not be a laborious task," says Dr. Julianne Serovich, associate professor and director of the marriage and family therapy program at Ohio State University (OSU). "It can be a stimulating endeavor when both men and women take the responsibility for developing intimacy."

> **Love Stats**
>
> Psychologist Howard Markham reports that "Men have more trouble expressing and hearing negative emotions, and are more reactive to them. But our studies show that the critical skill in successful relationships is being able to listen to a wife's concerns and complaints about the relationship."

What PMC Can Reveal About Your Relationship

Through questionnaires and practical discussions, a good PMC professional looks at family backgrounds that could reveal differences in value systems and then helps to establish reasonable boundaries when dealing with in-laws and siblings.

Exploring weakness in the marriages of family members is a good way to avoid repeating mistakes, particularly those of high-conflict couples. Exposing marriage myths, sexual slowdowns, and the changes brought about by the arrival of children all help to establish realistic expectations, Serovich said.

Often a discrepancy surfaces that the couple did not realize existed. However, conflict and differences are inevitable in a marital relationship, explains Dr. Serovich. It is learning how to solve them that counts. As long as couples are actively working toward a solution, are refining the issues, and are trying to compromise—not merely rehashing the same point—they are heading in the right direction.

"Couples know if they can resolve a problem or not," Serovich said. "Some healthy couples can disagree about things for a long time."

Satisfied PMC Newlyweds

A 1997 study found that of those who had taken some form of premarital educational training, 90 percent would do so again.

Julie and John: Julie, 26, and John, 25, went through the program at Ohio State and said it would make a great gift for someone. They were friends in college before they started dating, went through the normal ups and downs of relationships, and fell in love.

Julie relates:

> "John was the first man I had in my life who was stable, committed, and kind, and I took it for granted. I had to prove that I could be trustworthy before we went back together."

> **Love's Hot Line**
>
> Who makes the PMC appointment? At the OSU clinic, Dr. Julianne Serovich found that women didn't feel particularly threatened and made the appointment when they thought their relationship was going well. When men are scared that something is wrong, however, they did the calling.

It didn't long to convince John. Within two months he was down on one knee popping the question. The couple moved in together and set a wedding date.

Despite the length of time they had known one another, the PMC doctoral candidate at OSU uncovered a potential problem between John and Julie. Both wanted a child in approximately five years. What they weren't aware of was their disagreement over whether or not their child would be baptized. Family pressures and religious differences that might have caused a rift were brought out into the open and could be dealt with beforehand.

Melissa and James: Melissa and James found help bridging the wide gap between their spending habits. It's a good thing, too, because studies show that the way a couple handles their money can affect the survival odds of their marriage.

James was the ultimate saver and Melissa the consummate spender. However, they both agreed that as soon as they became engaged, they would start saving for a house. James religiously deposited money into their savings from his paycheck; Julie religiously spent hers. Their counselor got them to compromise on a budget. And in order to control her spending habit, Julie asked James to deposit her paycheck for a while to alleviate any temptation.

A Selection of PMC Opportunities

The selection process is an important one! Not all PMC programs are equally effective.

Diane Sollee, founder and director of the Coalition for Marriage, Family, and Couples Education, says, "Traditional premarital counseling as we have all experienced it and known it, shows it doesn't benefit couples." What a good program does is rely on the research, devise an agenda that addresses the challenges common to all marriages, and supply answers on how to overcome these issues, Sollee says. For her, the exciting development is that researchers are now able to synthesize their findings, and this synthesis enables professional counselors to teach marriage skills to anyone.

Two programs with very high success rates are the Premarital Relationship Enhancement Program (PREP) and Marriage Mentors, among several others.

Among the couples who took the PREP course, which focuses on communication, conflict management, forgiveness, religious beliefs and practices, expectations, fun, and friendship, only 4 percent divorced as compared with 24 percent who participated in standard PMC.

Out of 150 couples who were followed after taking the Marriage Mentors course designed by a husband-and-wife team at Seattle Pacific University, not one divorced. The focus of this program is on actual life stories told by experienced married couples to engaged partners, who can then learn by example.

> **Love's Hot Line**
>
> The optimal time to participate in PMC is five or six months before the wedding. You are already committed to one another, less apt to feel the pressure to say all the right things, and not yet overwhelmed by wedding plans.

Finding a PMC Program Near You

There are several ways to go about finding the right PMC program for you. Good Web sites include smartmarriages.com (the site of Sollee's organization) and www.aamft.org, a site sponsored by the American Association of Marriage and Family Therapists.

If you are near a major university, it may have a premarital clinic in conjunction with the psychology department. This is worth checking out and may be more cost-effective.

The following organizations offer workshops around the country:

Premarital Relationship Enhancement Program (PREP)
303-759-9931

Life Innovations, Inc.
651-635-0511

Relationship Enhancement
1-800-432-6454

Practical Applications for Intimate Relationship Skills (PAIRS)
1-888-724-7748

The Association for Couples in Marriage Enrichment
1-800-634-4325

The Least You Need to Know

➤ Your live-in partner may not represent the best marriage material.

➤ It is prudent to assess your marital risk factors.

➤ Live-in and marriage mindsets are usually different. Marriage calls for an upgrade of love and commitment.

➤ Good premarital counseling is a nonthreatening way to learn skills that will benefit your marriage relationship and make you a better partner.

➤ So far, the research shows that premarital counseling that focuses on education, not psychotherapy, does the most good.

Chapter 27

The Transition from Live-In to Marriage

In This Chapter

➤ Pivotal moments in your relationship
➤ Making the transition from live-in to marriage partners
➤ Distinguishing characteristics of your new union
➤ Revising critical expectations and precedents
➤ Learning about marriage protection
➤ Fun and fresh starts to a new era

You may have been great live-in lovers, and you may both have the potential to be good marriage partners. Nonetheless, the chance for harmonious matrimony could be derailed if you fail to make your move at the prudent moment or fail to pay sufficient attention to the transition between living together and marrying.

Leaving the home you cohabit, standing before a designated official charged with tying the knot, returning to the same unmade bed, and assuming nothing has changed in your relationship is pure, unadulterated folly.

There is work to be done before that wedding date arrives. You should approach this chapter eagerly, vow to give its message serious consideration, and make the necessary preparations that ensure a smooth transition from live-in lovers to marriage partners.

WARNING LABEL: Mandatory Reading

Saying "I do" creates a host of differences! How you look at yourselves, how others see you, and how your families react to you can change overnight. You have entered a new life zone. Trust me. Things in matrimony will be different. And if they aren't, you may really be in trouble.

According to a lot of thorough research, when you were living together, you probably formed some bad habits that could threaten your marital well-being. Cohabitors learn a "low commitment, high-autonomy pattern of relating," which is hard to suddenly "unlearn," explain sociologists David Popenoe and Barbara Dafoe Whitehead. Marriage, on the other hand, is based on long-term commitment. It requires a new pattern of relating, consistent with a higher level of commitment.

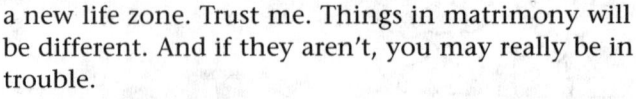

I'm not going to rehash all of the differences between married and cohabiting partners. They are spelled out clearly in Part 1, "Thinking About Living Together." Whether or not these differences are readily apparent in your relationship, don't be foolhardy and think that you and your live-in are the exception to this rule: The transition from living together to marriage is tricky and must be handled with sufficient care.

Ripe and Ready Junctures

Timing is important. You don't want to wait until you or your partner is overly annoyed, angry, or drowning in resentment because of persistent delays in agreeing to wed or in committing to a marriage date. You must determine whether waiting is hurting or helping your relationship and whether your honey needs a judicious nudge.

There are pivotal moments that invite action and provide the opportune time to insist upon a change in status. Watch carefully for them to surface in your relationship. If you arrive at a crossroads that you feel represents a critical juncture, where someone should cross the road or make a left turn, don't stand on the corner afraid to move. You may be wasting a precious pivotal moment.

> **Love's Hot Line**
>
> Men for the most part are hesitant to give up what they consider to be the freedom inherent in single life, and living together is part of their single psyche. Right or wrong, it is likely to be incumbent on the female partner, therefore, to present an image of matrimony that disproves a state of manly bondage.

> **Troubles A'Brewing ...**
>
> Avoiding hurtful relationship mistakes is a whole lot better than trying to make up for them later. Forgiveness for some lovers is hard to come by. It requires foregoing retaliation for understanding and overcoming alienation. In-depth understanding and proof of enduring reform are also required.

Chapter 27 ➤ *The Transition from Live-In to Marriage*

Identifying Pivotal Moments

In case the concept is a little fuzzy, here are some pivotal moments that should not be wasted. They represent the perfect time to press the issue of matrimony.

A pivotal moment may arise when you ...

- ➤ Buy a house.
- ➤ Redecorate an old home.
- ➤ Decide to have kids.
- ➤ Change jobs.
- ➤ Move residences.
- ➤ Get a promotion.
- ➤ Relocate in a new city.
- ➤ Accompany your partner on a business trip and find that you are the only nonspouse in the crowd.
- ➤ Are invited on a family vacation with your partner's folks.

> **Love's Hot Line**
>
> Need another reason to wed? Professor Linda J. Waite analyzed the stats from the National Institute of Aging survey and determined that married folks between 51 and 61 had on the average twice as much money as their unmarried counterparts. Saving wasn't the only reason for the difference. Married men, it seems, earn more money.

This list is by no means complete. Your moment may be unique to your circumstances and just as ripe and ready for your move.

Seizing the Moment

At 21, Shana was rather astute about the nature of men and relationships when she met 31-year-old Paul, who was just recovering from the pain of a broken love affair. Shana recalls:

> "My goal was to marry Paul. He was someone I wanted to share my life with, and that was the bottom line. I knew that he was just coming out of a serious and very passionate relationship and that it would be best for us to become friends before we became lovers."

Shana's plan worked. Paul fell in love with her, and when he took a job out of town he asked her to go with him and move in.

Although Paul's other live-in relationship flunked the test of time, he felt he would be more successful with Shana. Here's what Paul says:

> "We were much more open about what we needed. I knew if I had a problem I could go to her. Shana was my best friend and stronger and more mature than the other women I had had relationships with. Shana helped me out a lot and

323

was her own person, not an appendage I had to take care of. I think we were both very serious and committed to the relationship when we moved."

Shana admitted that she was a traditional girl and that things didn't happen just the way she would have liked them to. Nonetheless, she persisted in the relationship:

"I really kept tabs on what was happening and where the relationship was going. I was not going to let the whole thing run away with me. I think basically we shared the same values and both wanted a traditional life with children. We both firmly believed in marriage. All of that and Paul's goodness made me feel I was doing the right thing."

One day, however, Shana's heart skipped a beat. She was furious and hurt. Paul had had a career setback; his ego was busted and his self-confidence shot. He said he was going back home and announced to Shana:

"Come if you want; if not, goodbye."

Sensible Shana encouraged him to stay, and within a few weeks he got a terrific job offer that opened the door to a subsequently fruitful career climb. Once he was settled into his new job, Shana seized the moment to pin him down to marriage. She was tired of his wavering and felt they were at a crossroads where a new beginning was appropriate.

She handed him a calendar and said:

"'Okay, if we are getting married, pick a date.' I took the bull by the horns and within 15 minutes we had picked a date. Now we laugh at other people's romantic engagements."

Love Stats

Heterosexual couples who live together is only one of several alternative lifestyles that have gained acceptance. According to a 1999 *Newsday* article, gay households, particularly in metropolitan areas, are increasing significantly. Gay men are pursuing the opportunity to become parents and are changing the structure, but not the essence, of the family.

The timing was definitely right for a little nudge. As Paul says:

> "I didn't feel Shana's statement was an ultimatum. I felt she was just being honest about her feelings. If you aren't comfortable enough with the person you want to spend your life with to express yourself out in the open, then something is wrong. It wasn't that I didn't want to marry her; I needed an extra push."

At last count, Shana and Paul had been married more than a decade and numbered a family of four.

Crossing Over the Line

The National Marriage Project reports that matrimony is no longer a significant *rite of passage* into adulthood, sexual intercourse, or a first living-together union. It is now clumped into the overall category of "relationships." Without these distinctions to differentiate matrimony from "intimate relationships" in general, I believe it is imperative and prudent that couples consciously mark marriage as the beginning of a new era.

An elaborate wedding isn't what I am referring to. The line of demarcation must be an emotional and intellectual one that separates the state of matrimony from all other forms of intimate relationships.

> **Sweet Nothings**
>
> A **rite of passage** signifies a transition from one stage of life to another, often with a ritual ceremony of a religious nature as part of the celebration.

The question then becomes, How do you distinguish marriage from living together?

Distinguishing a Live-In Union from Matrimony

The experts have already done their research and supplied us with what they have quantitatively measured as the differences between cohabitation and matrimony. However, you need to be more hands-on and concrete when you make this distinction to your partner.

Marriage must appear to be something better and different. Otherwise, why tie the knot? You must both make that promise, believe in it, visualize it, and fulfill it. It certainly isn't an empty promise. Your vision of marriage should be one that is more …

➤ Loving.
➤ Caring.
➤ Enduring.
➤ Committed.

> Secure.
> Sharing of self.

Each of these qualities is stepped up a notch in marriage and keeps increasing in measure.

What You Can Look Forward To

There is plenty to look forward to in marriage. According to those in the know—couples who have gone before you—here's what is in store:

> A sense of peace, contentment, purpose, and completeness
> Genuine happiness and fulfillment
> A lifetime cheerleader and best friend
> A partner in life's journey
> An upsurge of confidence

> Ego boosting
> Love
> Respect
> Fulfillment of needs
> Sharing goals and dreams

Make sure they are part of your marital relationship if you want the icing on the cake.

> **Love's Hot Line**
>
> Take time to write your own marriage vows and consider how your lives together will change as a result of this pledge. This serious thinking should afford you the important opportunity to thoroughly contemplate what marriage should and will mean to you and your partner.

Revising Expectations

The rewards of marriage don't automatically come your way, particularly if you have been live-in partners. During the time you have cohabited as live-in lovers, you have set precedents that may not fulfill your new and very different set of marital expectations. However, you mustn't assume that your live-in partner will change his or her behavior just because you become Mr. and Mrs.

You would both be wise to state your spousal expectations and analyze which behaviors could be hazardous to a matrimonial union. This revision of partner expectations should be a shared process with mutual willingness to make the necessary changes!

Where it gets sticky is when one partner is not able to bargain from a position of power. The problem is compounded if your live-in relationship was already an inequitable one or ruled by matters of the heart instead of the mind. A real life drama will help illustrate the point.

Chapter 27 ➤ *The Transition from Live-In to Marriage*

An Imbalance of Power and Lopsided Expectations

Cynthia, now 10 years older and wiser, had hoped for marriage. She muses:

> "Who knows what goes through your head when you say, 'I'm going for this one'? I moved in because I hoped the next step would be marriage."

Cynthia explains:

> "It was Ted's idea to live together instead of marrying right away. 'Let's see how it goes,' he told me. "Well, it didn't go well. There were tremendous emotional highs and lows for me. He kept me guessing and called all the shots."

What Ted kept Cynthia guessing about wasn't only marriage but how long he might want her to live with him. Even worse was the uncertainty that he fostered regarding the status of a "former" girlfriend, a young coed with whom he had been involved in a scandalous affair that had closed the door on his first marriage. After the first few months, the pressure got to Cynthia, and she moved out. However, within another two months she was back. She admits:

> "I was really putting myself in a bad position."

Cynthia's fear of provoking Ted into ending their relationship left her with no bargaining power. She could only sit back and watch things unravel.

> **Troubles A'Brewing ...**
>
> Marriage partnerships that last require individuals to learn how to effectively manage their incompatibilities. That's a fundamental principle. Differences in religion, politics, and lifestyle, among others, must be accommodated to each participant's satisfaction. If not, you are dealing with irreconcilable differences that will cause your marriage pot to boil over with trouble.

> "I couldn't stop Ted from running off to a university campus to visit his young girlfriend. In my mind it seemed absolutely ridiculous that a grown man would be entertaining a college coed. My anger grew over these incidents. I was furious that I put myself back in the same precarious situation. When I left the second time approximately six months later, it was in complete anger."

When Cynthia moved in for the third time, it was into a new condo that she and Ted were decorating together. Within a short time, Ted agreed to marry. But this on-again, off-again relationship was to continue to haunt Cynthia for several more years to come. The night before their wedding, the college coed showed up to argue about whether Ted should marry Cynthia.

> **Love's Hot Line**
>
> First off, don't be afraid to express your expectations. Otherwise you won't get anywhere. Second, spout them bluntly. These are important considerations that can't survive whispers and innuendoes. Third, if you feel like it, allow your anger to show; do not let it simmer in the dark. In fact, John Gottman, Ph.D., found that "straightforward anger seems to immunize marriages against deterioration."

Two months after their wedding, Ted moved out. It seems he wasn't over the coed yet. Nor was he when he moved out for the second time. He finally settled down nearly two years and one baby later. A total of five years and another baby were required to put a better set of marital precedents in place.

The live-in precedent that should have gone out the window first was allowing room for a competing coed lover! Of course, that precedent should never have been established in the first place.

Realistic Expectations and Healthy Precedents

To achieve healthy expectations that set the kind of matrimonial precedents capable of serving you for a lifetime, you should …

- Expect and accept that your partner will have some clout and influence over your life.
- Expect to have conflicts and be able to resolve them in a fruitful way.
- Expect to continue learning more about your partner.
- Expect to give up remnants of behavior more typically associated with single than married life.
- Expect household changes, new budgets.
- Expect to be more accommodating to each other's extended family.
- Expect to put one another first.
- Expect to revise your lifetime agenda and plot a new future that involves more than just you.
- Expect marriage to be a new era with different requirements for living together.

Setting expectations is a good exercise. Making sure they are realistic is the sign of wisdom.

Making a Fresh Start

Your goal here should be to mark definite, visible, tangible differences between your live-in days and the married ones to come. This is the place to plan some fun. It is also serious work that deserves your utmost attention, especially if you have been long-term live-in lovers.

1. Create a new era of love and excitement. Plan plenty of love talk (see Chapter 20, "Keeping Love's Embers Warm") and a honeymoon phase that provides lasting memories.
2. Put to bed doubt and indecision by ushering in a new era of matrimonial commitment and security.
3. Take time out away from each other before you marry. Either live with a friend or family member, sleep in separate rooms, or refrain from sex. This adds a dash of wedding night excitement.
4. Go for new traditions. Establish a date night, candlelight dinners, Sunday mornings in bed, fresh flowers on market day, or whatever will be fun, new, and beneficial.
5. Move into a new space neither of you has lived in before.
6. Make plans to vacation or throw a party in a way you didn't before you were wed.
7. Spend greater amounts of time together.
8. Accept the responsibilities inherent in matrimony and start acting like a spouse, not a live-in lover.

> **Love's Hot Line**
>
> Ladies, you may have to use some subtle maneuvering to persuade your transitioning live-in lover to assume the role of spouse. Delicate subjects are always approached more easily after sex, not before, and with dabs and dashes of sincere messages of love. Men are reward-oriented.

Buying Marriage Protection

Buying marriage protection isn't like buying household insurance. You can't take out a policy to protect yourself from a bad marriage. Nonetheless, you can take some positive steps to increase the chances for marriage success and to ensure against potential loss. Throughout this book, I have given you guidelines on relationship success, but Chapter 28, "Newlyweds and Marriage Management," is particularly pertinent.

Part 6 ➤ *Moving Toward the Altar*

For added marriage insurance, psychologist Howard Markham suggests you raise the level of these three protective factors:

➤ Friendship

➤ Interpersonal support

➤ Mutual dedication

I will amend Markham's proposal. Enhancing friendship is great, but it won't be sufficient unless you reach the summit of "best buddies."

Your Personal Transition Worksheet

Reading about the transition between living together and marriage isn't enough. A successful transition requires homework, planning, and implementation. Fill out the blanks in the worksheet provided here for you.

Identify upcoming pivotal moments in your relationship and what action they will call for.

_____
_____
_____

Spell out the distinguishing features that will be present in your married relationship that were not part of your cohabiting union.

_____
_____
_____
_____

List behaviors and precedents that have to go.

_____
_____
_____

Name five qualities you expect a good spouse to display.

_____
_____
_____
_____
_____

Chapter 27 ➤ *The Transition from Live-In to Marriage*

Design several ways you will formulate sound marriage precedents.

_____
_____
_____

Specifically state at least a half dozen ways in which you will give your marital relationship a fresh start.

_____
_____
_____
_____
_____
_____

List two ways in which you will raise the level of your interpersonal support for your spouse and for your mutual dedication.

Increase interpersonal support:

_____
_____

Increase mutual dedication:

_____
_____

Name four ways that will elevate your level of friendship to the realm of best friends.

_____
_____
_____
_____

You have no excuse now but to transition gently, efficiently, and effectively from living-together days to married ones.

The Least You Need to Know

➤ Whether you believe it or not, married life is different from living together.

➤ Some living-together expectations and precedents will have to be abandoned in order to transition into a secure marriage relationship.

➤ There are natural junctures that present good times for moving on to matrimony.

➤ Transitioning from spousal equivalent to spouse takes conscious, concerted, and conscientious thoughtful action.

➤ You will do yourself an injustice if you don't make marked distinctions between your cohabitation and married relationships.

➤ Expectations should be voiced and a fresh start made before you wed.

Chapter 28

Newlyweds and Marriage Management

In This Chapter

➤ Live-ins turned newlyweds

➤ Tackling budgets, babies, and prenups

➤ What it means to manage a marriage

➤ Management theories and secret strategies

You are about to sign a contract that legally binds you and your partner. Whether or not you have been living together, you will still have to face the adjustments and ordinary problems encountered by all newlyweds. Take it from those live-ins who have already traversed this path, you will feel differently after exchanging your matrimonial vows!

Certainly you haven't gotten all the way through this guide without realizing how much time, attention, thought, caring, and wisdom go into building and enjoying relationship decisions. Marriage is simply another link in the chain, albeit the most important link. It is what you have been building up to throughout this book. Now it's up to you to make the most of that opportunity.

Newlyweds vs. Live-Ins

If you want to know what makes live-ins different from marriage, ask the newlyweds:

- Before they tied the knot, they weren't really convinced their relationship was permanent.
- After they married, they felt that keeping track of the loans they had made to one another was inappropriate.
- They encountered a different set of conflicts once they became Mr. and Mrs.
- Some determined that marital compromising was much more important yet more difficult to achieve.
- In this new stage of life together, they focused more on building a future together than they did when living together.
- Men and women experienced greater compunction and determination to work through tough problems.
- After his parents and hers became the "in-laws," they had different family expectations of them as a married couple.

These words of other couples who have taken the leap into matrimony should help you set the stage for your own transition to husband and wife.

Advice for Newlyweds

You are about to embark on a critical period of growth that either sets the stage for mature and enduring love or lowers the curtain on it. Judith S. Wallerstein, clinical psychologist and noted authority on divorce, identified specific tasks that aid couples in building good marriages.

- Invest fully and completely in your marriage by redefining the lines of your connection to one another and by separating from your families of origin.
- Build intimacy yet maintain a balance of essential autonomy.
- Do children arrive, balance attention to them with your need for privacy
- Create partner.
- selves and nd of your relationship slip in the face of inevitable adversity.
- Establish and in which you and your partner can safely express your- both partners.
- Head boredom off a lationship that is satisfying and pleasing for lenging activities.
- Bring laughter and humor
- Provide comfort and support resting friends and finding chal-
- Do not allow the burdens of reality hip. lights of love.

> Continually update and express your partner goals, wishes, and desires together.
> Keep informed about each other's lives and inner feelings.

Love Stats

Most Americans believe that the way to achieve happiness is by having a happy marriage, nurturing a good family life, and providing opportunities for their offspring. What it takes to arrive at this destination is the help of a lifetime partner and helpmate, who, in three out of four cases, takes the title of your best friend.

Before You Take Your Vows

First, make absolutely sure that you are in total agreement that you both want or do not want children. When is another matter. Whether or not to have children is a fundamental issue that can entirely change the hue of your marriage outlook or your attitude toward your would-be spouse.

Second, decide up front which professional or personal last name you will keep or adopt. Changing names to demonstrate male ownership of a wife was a British law brought to this country. Make this decision prior to the ceremony so that no misunderstandings occur later.

Sweet Nothings

A **prenuptial agreement** may also be called an antenuptial. It is a document signed by each partner prior to exchanging marriage vows. The contract describes rights and obligations that both parties agree to abide by in the case of a divorce, primarily the division of financial assets and property and maintenance allowances. The purpose of a prenup is to prevent costly disputes after the fact.

Should You Have a Prenup?

Nearly 1 in 20 couples signs a *prenuptial agreement*. Considering that 41 percent of men and 32 percent of women today who marry are over 30 and have had time to build significant financial assets, a lot more is at stake than there used to be. The three most common reasons given to draw up a prenup were …

- ➤ To protect the financial stake of children from an earlier marriage.
- ➤ To protect business assets, business partners, and family members who share ownership.
- ➤ To protect other assets that an individual did not want the marriage partner to share in after death or divorce.

Averting Financial Disaster

Don't think for a moment that because you filled out a financial worksheet in Chapter 14, "Drawing Floor Plans," your financial work is done. The facts remain:

- ➤ How you handle money now that you are getting married should be vastly different.
- ➤ Money is the number-one thing married couples argue about.
- ➤ Now is the time to combine resources and start building a financial future together.

To accomplish a financial plan with the least wear and tear, family financial expert Joyce Cantrell of the Kansas State School of Family Resources and Human Services advises newlyweds to do the following before they get married:

1. Make a budget. It is important to establish where monies are going and to set aside both an emergency fund and a savings account.
2. Set up your budget so that it is goal-oriented. A portion should be designated for savings. Cantrell's formula is for 25-year-olds to save 7 percent of their overall income. The percentage increases with age and should reach 19 percent when you turn 45.
3. Agree how you plan to handle your money together and establish joint bank accounts. Disclose all debts, and make provisions for paying them off.
4. Whatever you do, avoid credit card debt. Unpayable bills add to the stresses, tugs, and pulls that can crash down on newlyweds.

Love's Hot Line

Dr. John M. Gottman, foremost marriage authority, says that financial issues require teamwork. Before determining your financial plan, lay out your concerns, needs, and fantasies. He warns against creating a budget that turns one partner into a martyr. "This will only build up resentment," he explains.

The Marital Roller Coaster

No matter how well you plan or provide for the unexpected, marriage has its own built-in ups and downs. Your challenge is to endure them and wait them out. Those who fail to do so lose out on the final rewards. Knowing in advance that swings of passion, love, and affection are normal, that happiness rises and falls, and that better times resurface should lessen the whiplash of marital roller-coaster rides. The following figure depicts the most predictable, common ride we take when children enter the picture.

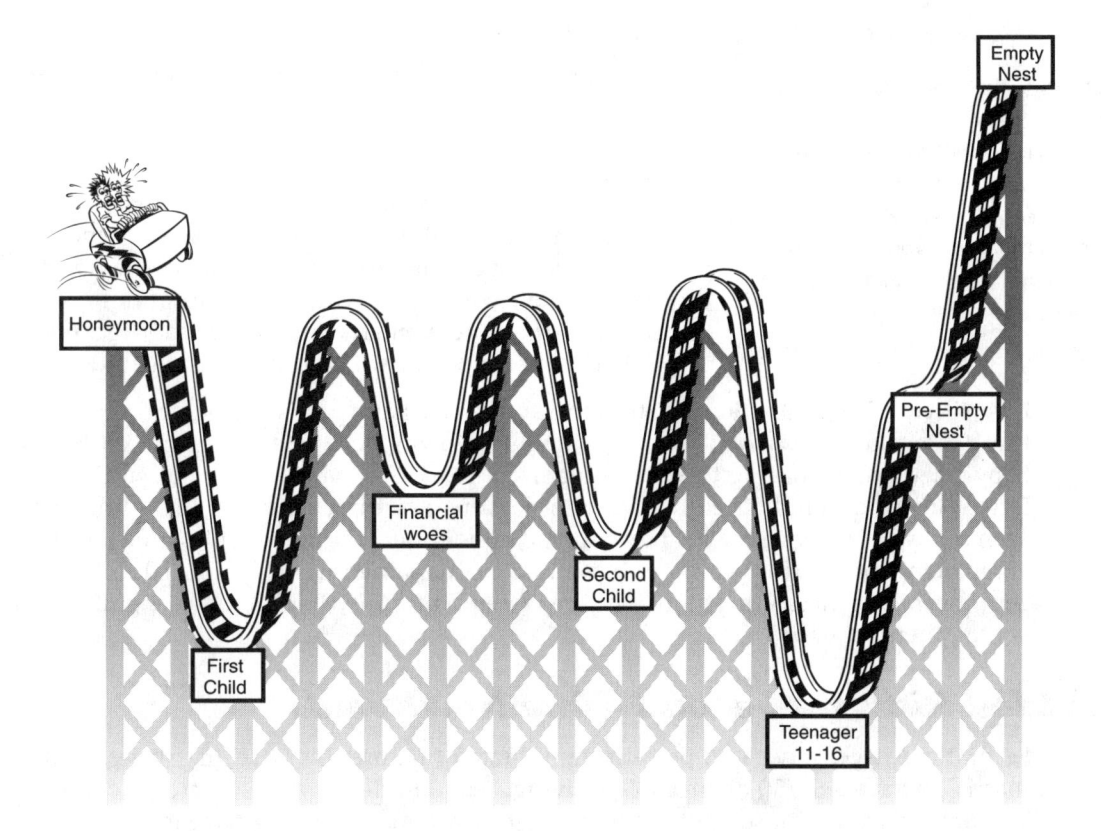

Marital highs and lows.

Along with kids comes a host of complications that impact your marriage. Let's take a look at your sex life first. Sex, after all, is a function of mind and body. A tired body and mental preoccupation with a child spell disinterest. And believe it or not, some experts say new parents feel guilty—consciously or unconsciously—having sex when kids are around. The problem is that sex is also a way to maintain intimacy and show affection. Many husbands feel disenfranchised and jealous with the birth of children and look forward to sex as reassurance that their wives still care about them.

337

Before we conclude this roller-coaster ride, there are several more issues to consider. They, too, may cause fluctuations in your marital barometer of happiness and satisfaction.

> **Love's Hot Line**
>
> Diane Sollee, social worker and family therapist, says that all couples have about 10 issues they never resolve. What you have to do is learn to live with them, accommodating your differences and ignoring the unimportant ones.

Perceived Injustices: A study from the University of Connecticut of two-income family wage earners found that marital satisfaction wasn't determined as much by the fact that women worked more hours for less pay or earned less than men. What did matter was whether the woman felt rewarded for her efforts and perceived her situation as fair.

Women Who Earn More: Equity in breadwinning increased marital satisfaction for men, but the majority of women in a Prudential Securities study believe that earning more than your husband is a cause of marital conflict. Dee Lee, co-author of *Let's Talk Money* (Chandler House Press, 1999), thinks the problem is who gets the say over how the money is spent. Plenty of couples have coped well with this nontraditional situation in which the woman earns more than her spouse. Others have yet to show an enlightened attitude.

Infertility, a Heart Breaker: Historians say that we have passed through the period in the 1960s and 1970's when fewer children were being born and we are currently in a baby-craze era. According to a study reported in a 1997 *Journal of Psychology*, the preferred American family is composed of at least two or three children, including one of each sex with a preference for boys. At the same time, younger couples are fearful of an epidemic of infertility, although the rate has remained right around 10 to 13 percent for middle class Americans. The area where infertility has increased significantly is the American poor.

Added Risks for Second-Time Newlyweds

Second marriages have a 10 percent higher rate of failure than first marriages. First marriages have a 50/50 chance of surviving. Second ones have a 40 percent chance. The first two years for second timers are critical when combining families. The things that you need to watch out for are the same ones that most people find troublesome—different approaches to discipline, conflicting child-rearing practices, and excessive expectations from stepparents.

Marriage Prerequisites

Marriage management takes time and effort. The following conditions are, in my estimation, prerequisites that have to be present in effective relationship management.

1. A worthy partner is someone who has the potential to appreciate and return in full measure the affection, attention, caring, support, and understanding you are willing to give him or her.
2. The willingness to participate is crucial. It takes active involvement by both partners to make a marriage work. A happy marriage isn't a one-sided labor.
3. Accepting a partner's influence, Dr. Gottman found, is particularly important for men, who are more reticent than women to do so. Joint decision making takes into account both parties' opinions and promotes a true partnership.
4. Loving your imperfect mate is imperative. Realities are important here. No one is married to a perfect mate, and no one has a perfect marriage. Marriage is no place to expect the enactment of fairy tales. Measuring your honey against the image of a Prince or Princess Charming and focusing on his or her faults or idiosyncrasies sets you up for disappointments. It shortchanges the real positives in your mate.
5. Unselfish love means letting go of your own ego and not always having to be right, says Dr. Evelyn Moschetta, D.S.W., co-author of *The Marriage Spirit* (Simon & Schuster, 1998). "The marriage spirit is a current of unselfish love that flows through every strong and healthy marriage. And the key word is unselfish ...."
6. The desire and determination to make marriage work is the highest form of commitment. Without that mindset, it is hard to compromise, resolve conflicts, and bend in the way a happy marital union requires.

> **Sweet Nothings**
>
> An **emotionally intelligent individual,** a term Gottman uses, is a person who is in touch with his or her own emotions and those of others. An emotionally intelligent spouse understands, honors, and respects his or her partner and their marriage.

Understanding and accepting these six marriage prerequisites will improve your *emotional intelligence* and positively influence your level of marital satisfaction.

An Active Role

The majority of women I have surveyed believe that they take the more active role in making love and marriage work. My own observations confirm that they monitor and maneuver their marriage through difficult waters, know how to be accommodating without sacrificing themselves, and use all available resources to keep their marriage satisfying. Here are some tips:

- ➤ Have a thoughtful set of established, prudent guidelines but know when and how to be flexible.
- ➤ Expect and demand joint participation.
- ➤ Have a good sense of self-worth, believe in yourself, and respect your partner.
- ➤ Encourage communication and intimacy.
- ➤ Be willing to explore and develop ways to enrich and handle your marital union.
- ➤ Be a best friend, lover, helpmate, and great sexual partner, and attend to your husband's ego regularly.
- ➤ Find pleasure in seeing your spouse happy and satisfied.

A spouse uses all of these talents to provide a better life for herself and her partner. She does so willingly, never begrudgingly.

What Makes Marriage Work?

I like what Dr. John M. Gottman found and wrote about in his book *The Seven Principles for Making Marriage Work* (Crown Books, 1999). Gottman uses the ingredients of happy marriages as the foundation for his model of marital behavior. If both partners emulate these seven conditions, they are fairly certain to be on the road to happiness.

He does concede this isn't always easy, particularly for newlyweds. His findings are a one-step-at-a-time approach to marital success. All seven principles work simultaneously. It takes time and practice to use all of these principles with finesse and ease. Succinctly put, here is what Gottman found after years of study:

1. Happy partners know a great deal about one another, from the big things to the little things. Each knows how the other likes his or her steak and how the other feels about life and death. They prioritize this information in their minds and use it.

2. Not only do partners like and admire one another, but they nurture these feelings by looking for more positive attributes to increase their respect and admiration. They refrain from focusing on less-attractive attributes that disappoint them or are not as appealing.

3. Happily married partners turn to each other for support, engage in self-disclosure, develop intimacy, spend time together, assist each other in solving personal problems, and make time in their lives for one another.

4. Partners with good marriages are willing to be influenced by the other partner and view that as okay. This includes decisions on career paths, going to concerts, or foregoing a football game.

5. These partners know how to solve problems without creating damage to their relationship. They do so by showing tolerance and acceptance and using repair attempts.

6. Partners who make it long-term do not neglect unresolved issues, despite apparent gridlock. Although resolving issues is difficult, in the long run it is beneficial. Couples who have fewer expectations of their marital relationship appear to avoid the more-difficult issues that divide them.

7. Happily married men and women share convictions, thoughts, dreams, and desires in order to create a shared meaning. They blend their ideas into their own patterns, understandings, and rituals.

> **Love's Hot Line**
>
> Couples with long-term, happy relationships have a "shared history." This potpourri of happy, sad, fun, difficult, and cherished moments binds them together and furthers their understanding and compassion for one another. It is this shared history that provides comfort and satisfaction at life's end.

Use Secret Strategies

Don't spill all the beans. That is one of my primary recommendations in *Marriage Secrets: How to Have a Lifetime Love Affair*. Some things may be dangerous when expressed, or even toxic.

Evan Imber-Black, professor of psychiatry at Albert Einstein College of Medicine and author of *The Secret Life of Families: Truth-Telling, Privacy, and Reconciliation in a Tell-All Society* (Bantam Doubleday Dell, 1998), says that "Honesty is the best policy, but that does not mean you have to … tell everything." The professor advises that you are entitled to your secret thoughts, especially those that might adversely affect your marriage relationship or your partner's emotional well-being and those thoughts that are told in spite.

Here are some categories you may find helpful when determining which secrets to tell and which to keep locked up. It is important to distinguish between those secrets that cover up serious marital problems and those that hardly require the risk of exposure.

Ho-Humers: Benign secrets such as an occasional faked orgasm, a fictitious body weight, personal purchases, premarital love affairs, and private fantasies. Sometimes these truths are withheld to avoid hurting your partner's feelings.

Eyebrow-Raisers: Secrets that are a bit more complicated and could have an adverse effect on the marriage relationship should they slip out. On the other hand, keeping these secrets may mean shying away from an issue that your partner has a right to know about and that ought to be confronted. Less than satisfactory sexual performances, money set aside for children of a previous marriage, and a near would-be affair might raise anyone's eyebrows.

Part 6 ➤ *Moving Toward the Altar*

Toxic Tales: Dangerous secrets that can poison a relationship. Without a doubt, the biggest and most potentially damaging secret men and women withhold from one another has to do with extramarital sex. Before voicing a potentially toxic tale of an indiscretion or other serious infraction, you should assess the consequences of telling or not telling, how exposure will damage your relationship, what discovery will do to your partner, and whether disclosing the secret could in some way benefit your marriage.

The critical difference between ho-humers, eyebrow-raisers, and toxic tales is that the last one often signals more trouble in a marriage than is wise to keep hidden. The ultimate decision on which secrets to tell is, of course, left up to your own discretion.

> **Love's Hot Line**
>
> There is no need for secrecy if you answer this question in the right way. What does your marriage relationship really mean to you? The correct answer, "Everything."

Marriage Truths

Marriage truths are bits and pieces of information that give you added insight into marriage and that should help you determine the way in which you interact with your partner.

Marriage Truth #1: "The determining factor in whether wives feel satisfied with the sex, romance, and passion in their marriage is, by 70 percent, the quality of the couple's friendship. For men, the determining factor is, by 70 percent, the quality of the couple's friendship."

(From *The Seven Principles to Making Marriage Work,* John M. Gottman, Ph.D.)

Marriage Truth #2: If there is a quality you look for in your partner but will never find, says Peter Kramer, Ph.D., a solution is to develop that quality in yourself. A marriage partner cannot provide everything his or her spouse needs. Each person is ultimately responsible for his or her own personal happiness and self-satisfaction. We all need our own lives!

Marriage Truth #3: Don't expect to be deliriously happy or in love all the time. However, do not give up on those down days.

Marriage Truth #4: Marriage expert Diane Sollee says irreconcilable differences in matrimony are more accurately termed "irreconcilable disappointments." Disappointments can be handled more easily than differences.

> **Love Stats**
>
> Now here is an interesting bit of data covering 50,000 men and women who were tracked from their senior year in high school to age 32. Those who remained single showed increased undesirable behaviors like alcoholism and use of illegal drugs. There was a marked drop in those behaviors among those who were married.

Marriage Truth #5: Marriage and family life in two-income families is more difficult than in single-income families. There are more stresses and scheduling constraints that intrude on the couples' time for privacy and intimacy. That is why these couples must try harder to set aside moments to maintain and replenish the warmth and feelings of love.

Marriage Truth #6: A good sex life cannot hinder a marital relationship. A bad one can. Men's assessment of a good sexual relationship depends on sexual frequency, fidelity, and emotional investment in the relationship. Women are affected by these factors, too, but marriage adds an extra element of pleasure to sex for women.

What should you do with these marriage truths? Why, use them, of course, to tend to each other's happiness.

> ### The Least You Need to Know
> ➤ Becoming a newlywed requires a new set of tasks.
> ➤ The arrival of children may place your marriage in jeopardy.
> ➤ Marriage relationships require astute and vigilant management.
> ➤ There is no substitute for respect, admiration, or consideration in a marriage relationship.

Appendix A

Men Who Abuse Women

Here is a list of the characteristics of men who batter women:

- ➤ Men who batter women try to control and isolate their partners from family and friends.
- ➤ These men are highly critical of their partners.
- ➤ They accuse their partners of imagining that the verbal or emotional abuse exists.
- ➤ They demean the women they live with and diminish their self-esteem.
- ➤ These men withhold sex and affection as a means of control and inflicting punishment.
- ➤ Men who are frequently abusive blame their partners for everything that goes wrong in their lives.
- ➤ They are motivated by the need to manipulate.
- ➤ They will beg for forgiveness and promise to reform.
- ➤ These men are often from homes in which they witnessed domestic violence.

Abusers are present in all socioeconomic levels of society.

Women who are abused should contact their local domestic violence hot line or the National Domestic Violence Hot Line at 1-800-799-7233 for services in their area.

Appendix B

Stress Busters

Wayne Sotile, Ph.D., and Mary Sotile, M.A., suggest a number of ways couples can work together to alleviate the stress that seeps in and affects the well-being of their love relationship.

Try ...

- Slowing down.
- Resolving stressful conflicts.
- Removing obvious stresses from your environment.
- Making time for the important things in your life.
- Working for greater intimacy.
- Building a life that reflects your joint values.
- Creating a safe resting place to which you can both retreat when making necessary changes.

From *Beat Stress Together,* by Wayne Sotile, Ph.D., and Mary Sotile, M.A. John Wiley & Sons, 1998.

Appendix C

Premarital and Relationship Courses

Here is a list of resources to help you get your relationship on track:

Seattle Marital and Family Institute
The Marriage Survival Kit, by Dr. John Gottman
206-523-9042

Relationship Enhancement
National Institute for Relationship Enhancement
1-800-432-6454

The Association for Couples in Marriage Enhancement
1-800-634-4325

The American Association of Marriage and Family Therapists
www.aamft.org

Practical Applications of Intimate Relationship Skills (PAIRS)
1-800-724-7748

Appendix D

Glossary

agape A selfless, altruistic love style in which giving is thought to be a duty. It is the love style least evident in real, romantic relationships.

alimony Money paid in the form of an allowance to a man or woman by an ex-spouse after the dissolution or divorce of a marriage.

ally Someone with whom you have a relationship and share a united, not divided, front.

anticohabitation laws Laws that prohibit two sexual partners from living together and sharing a home.

aphrodisiacs Substances that arouse sexual thoughts and stir sexual juices. They initiate sexual excitement in the form of an erection for men and lubrication for women.

common-law partners Couples who, having lived together for a specific period of time, are recognized by the law as married, despite the absence of formally exchanged wedding vows.

companionate love Feelings of affection, intimacy, and attachment to an individual with whom one's life is intricately interwoven.

coup de foudre A French term that means literally "bolt of thunder." It is the French equivalent for "love at first sight."

cuddle-buddies A term used to describe a friendly, minutely romantic heterosexual relationship that includes petting and snuggling up tight all night without sex.

cultural narrative The cumulative conventional wisdom encompassed in prevailing social trends that prescribes how individuals and couples ought to think, behave, and measure themselves.

demand withdrawal pattern A common conflict pattern in which one partner wishes to discuss the problem but the other partner prefers to avoid any confrontation and thus withdraws.

destructive conflicts Conflicts that tear a relationship apart, as opposed to ushering in greater understanding and resolution.

diversity In the strictest sense, a variety. It is the buzzword of the new millennium and signifies a positive state and an acceptance of individual differences.

dormant emotions   Feelings that are in a state of inertia but that possess the seeds for love, though these seeds may possibly be underdeveloped or malnourished.

durable power of attorney   A legal term that applies to the power given to an individual who acts on behalf of another person in the event of that person's becoming incapacitated and unable to act without aid.

emotional intelligence   The degree to which an individual is in touch with his or her own emotions and understands those of others.

emotional loneliness   Isolation or loneliness that focuses on the absence of an intimate partner.

empathy   The act of sharing the thoughts, feelings, emotions, and experiences of another individual without actually having the same experience.

first-union relationship   An individual's very first sharing of a household with a romantic partner, whether a live-in or marriage relationship.

fluid life cycle   A less-constricted and -prescribed life cycle that reflects the wider, changing range in which individuals marry and have children today.

friend   A person who offers support and affection to another individual with whom a special bond has been created.

friendship   A relationship between two people who express fondness and camaraderie for one another, share activities together, and experience some level of emotional intimacy with each other.

gridlock   The state in a romantic relationship when it is impossible for a couple to reach an understanding or agreement because one or both partners are unable or unwilling to alter their views.

home base   The mental, emotional, and practical position to which a couple most frequently returns as their lives together change and go through cycles.

I-love-you gifts   Offerings that do not signify a special occasion but are given merely to show affection.

individual narrative   An individual's values, ideas, and expectations and the course of their development.

intrapsychic phase   The period in which one partner feels dissatisfied and begins to search for what is wrong in the other partner and in their relationship.

in vitro   Literally "in a glass," a term that refers to the fertilization process of reproduction in a Petri dish.

live-in bargains   Agreements regarding the sharing of space and household arrangements.

logrolling   The act of trading off, in complementary fashion, concessions or assets between partners.

love junkies Individuals who become addicted to the high caused by bodily chemicals released in the presence of romantic, sexual, or passionate feelings.

love-prone The condition of an individual who habitually falls in love.

monogamy A sexual relationship with only one individual.

obsessive relationship intrusion Unwanted, intrusive behavior on the part of one individual into the life of a love interest or a past relationship partner.

opportunist A person who turns or manipulates circumstances for personal benefit, without regard to basic values or consequences to other individuals.

orgasm A sexual reflex that describes the peak of muscle tension and blood flow to the pelvis and causes the pelvic floor muscles to spasm rhythmically.

prenuptial agreement A document signed by partners prior to exchanging wedding vows. It is a contract that refers primarily to the division of property and assets and stipulates maintenance allowances should the marriage fail.

psychological departure The mental state of a partner who has lost interest in a relationship and is waiting for it to formally end.

regret The expression of remorse over a failure to do something or over actions that have been left undone or unsolved.

relationship negotiation The arrangement of mutually satisfying terms in a transaction achieved through verbal communication.

repair attempts Statements, actions, or behaviors intended to prevent the buildup or residual effects of negative feelings engendered during an argument.

rite of passage A transition from one phase to another, marked by a specific ceremony or act.

romantic love The expression of a spiritual, emotional, and sexual attachment between two individuals.

romantic ultimatum A final statement made or proposed to a partner regarding conditions that must be met if a romantic relationship is to stay alive.

self-esteem The respect, love, appreciation, pride, belief, and confidence that an individual has in him- or herself.

self-respect Liking oneself regardless of personal success or failure. It is the act of liking oneself because of who you are, not who you can be.

serial monogamy A series of sexual relationships with a monogamous sexual partner.

sex Any form of sexual behavior leading up to or including sexual intercourse.

skilled To demonstrate understanding, dexterity, great ability, or proficiency in a skill, behavior, or concept.

stonewalling A defensive measure used to gain time and put off making a relationship decision because of ambivalence, uncertainty, or inadequate love and commitment.

teamwork Joint action between two or more persons who subordinate individual interests and gains to achieve unity and efficiency for the team.

transformational experiences Those experiences that alter the way we see ourselves or situations and that provide unprecedented clarity.

understanding The congruence between two individuals' perspectives and what each other intends and actually thinks.

un-laws A term made up by Miss Manners that refers to the parents of a live-in partner.

unmarried cohabitation partners Sexual partners who share a household but are not married.

unrequited love Love that is not reciprocated by a would-be lover and that often results in feelings of rejection, pain, and anger.

Index

A

abuse (battered women), characteristics of men who abuse, 345
active roles, marriages, 339-340
advanced lovers, reality checkup for love, 128-129
advice for newlyweds, 334
agape love style, 121
agendas
    changing, relationship troublemaker, 268
    decision-making, 88-94
agreements of cohabitation, 161-163
    common-law marriages, 162
    limitations, 164
    necessity, 164-165
    palimony, 162-163
    potential predicaments of not having one, 166-167
    requirements, 165
alimony, 163
alone time, 233-234
Amy Vanderbilt's Complete Book of Etiquette, 220
Andersen, Peter A. (researcher), 197
anticohabitation laws, 167
aphrodisiacs, 256
Art of Living Single, The, 159
Association for Couples in Marriage Enrichment, The, 320
Association Management, agendas, 88-89
astrological corroboration, breaking up, 294-295
attention-grabbers, communication, 145
attraction (love), 110
autonomy, reducing, cohabitation leading to marriage, 315
axioms of love, 190

B

Bacon, Francis (philosopher), 100
bad breakups, 103
bargaining, 154
bathroom etiquette, 222
battered women, 345
bedroom etiquette, 224
befriending your partner's pals and family, 235-236
beginner lovers, reality checkup for love, 124-125
behaviors
    befriending your partner's pals and family, 235-236
    conditions of marital behavior, 340
    expectations, 238-239
    giving time, space and solitude, 233-234
    picking your fights, 234-235
    simple do's, 232
    simple don'ts, 232
    spoilers, 236
        lack of humor, 237
        uncontained stress, 237-238
        whiners, 237
Berschied, Ellen (professor), 251
betrayal, sexual, 197-198
blended families, 214
blending process, couples, 214
Blum, Deborah, Ph.D. (professor and author), 242
Borysenko, Joan Ph.D. (author), 85
Branden, Nathaniel (psychotherapist), 190
breaking up, 102-103, 288
    astrological corroboration, 294-295
    avoiding wasting time, 290
    bad breakups, 103
    children, 305
    emotional consequences, 306
        closure, 307
        handling grief, 306
        recovery, 307
    exposing the issue, 289
    getting stuck, 295
    mental model, 288-289
    moving-day rules, 302-303
    moving out, ORI (obsessive relationship intrusion), 298
    planning departure, 299
    potential losses, 103-104
    real-world examples, 292-294
    "time pieces," 290
        time is on your side, 291
        time is your enemy, 291
    twelve-step separation plan, 299-301
    victim's departure, 304-305
Brehm, Sharon S. (Psychology professor), 86
Broder, Michael, Ph.D. (author), 159
Buckholz, Ester, Ph.D. (psychologist), 233
budgeting, 176-177
business functions, etiquette, 227-228

C

Call of Solitude, The, 233
categories of live-ins, 22
    marriage seekers, 22
    mutual users, 23
    romantic roomies, 23-24
    serious pals and lovers, 24-25
    true believers, 25-26
champions of marriage, 10
    Capitol Hill Republicans, 12
    covenant marriage bill, 12
    educating for marriage, 10
    legislating in favor of marriage, 11-12
characteristics
    compatibility, 134
        empathy and understanding, 135
        friendship, 134
        passion, 135
        respect, 135
        shared values, 136
    couples, 213-214
charting your partner's love graph, 150
cheating. *See* sexual betrayal
checks and balances, relationships, 284-285
children
    effects of break-ups, 305
    influence of live-ins on, 27-28
    making a place for children in live-in homes, 180-181
Clarkberg, Marin (sociologist), 68, 71
Cleopatra (love idol), 115
closure, breaking up, 307
Coben, Jeffrey (researcher), 298
cohabiting, 17. *See also* live-in loves

agreements, 161-163
  common-law marriages, 162
  limitations, 164
  necessity, 164-165
  palimony, 162-163
  potential predicaments of not having one, 166-167
  requirements, 165
marriage, 68
  buying marriage protection, 329-330
  decision-making, 69-71
  disadvantages, 69
  distinguishing cohabitation and marriage, 325-326
  expectations, 326-329
  factors leading to, 71-72
  games to avoid, 72-77
  laboratory predictors of marital success, 313
  making a fresh start, 329
  mature relationships, 77-78
  misunderstandings, 74-76
  pivotal moments, 322-325
  psychoeducation, 316-320
  reducing autonomy, 315
  risk factors, 313-314
  rite of passage, 325
  safety, 77
  "selection effect," 312
  sociological views, 68-69
  theories, 68
  transition worksheet, 330-331
  upgrading your live-in mindset, 314-315
  what awaits you, 326
  men, 70
  women, 71
cold feet, 159
Coming Apart, 299
commitment, 33
  joint investments, 33
  making concessions, 34-35
  recheck for troubled relationships, 269
  role in marriages and live-ins, 35
  trading assets, 33-34
common-law unions, 18, 162
  versus live-in loves, 17-18
communication, 142-143
  agreement list for would-be live-ins, 156
  attention-grabbers, 145
  how to express frustrations, 282-284
  misunderstandings, 74-75
  preventing shutdowns, 144

rules of engagement, 153-154
  bargaining, 154
  ultimatums, 154-155
  sexual, 260
  skills, 143-144
companionate love, 110
compatibility, 134-136
  characteristics, 134
    empathy and understanding, 135
    friendship, 134
    passion, 135
    respect, 135
    shared values, 136
  sexual, 136-137
    misinterpretations, 137-138
    real-world story, 140
    self-test, 138-140
Compiling a Live-In Time Line worksheet, 183
complacency, marriage decisions, 74
Complete Idiot's Guide to Handling a Breakup, The, 275
concessions, defining commitment, 34-35
conditions of marital behavior, 340
conflicts, 141-142
  relationship strengtheners, 281
conscientiousness, 188
consideration, 187
contradiction and betrayal stage (three-stage cycle of relationships), 213
counseling, premarital, 317
  satisfied customers, 318
  selection process, 319
  sources and Web sites, 319-320
coup de foudre (love at first sight), 209
couplehood
  blending process, 214
  characteristics, 213-214
  development of the relationship as an identity all its own, 211
  interdependence, 215
  recheck for troubled relationships, 271
  sequences, identifying, 214-215
  three-stage cycle, 212
    contradiction and betrayal stage, 213
    expansive stage, 212
    resolution stage, 213
  vocabulary
    becoming "we," 208-209
    "ours," 210

Couples: Exploring and Understanding the Cycles of Intimate Relationships, 211
coupling styles, factors accounting for changes, 18
  delayed marriages, 19
  liberal sexual ethic, 19
  prevalence of divorce, 19
  working women, 19
courses, premarital and relationships, 349
covenant marriage bill, 12
cultural narrative, 208

D

daily love planner, 191
Dangerous House on Main Street scenario, risks of living together, 54
Dealing with My Ex worksheet, 182
Dealing with My Ex-Spouse and My Live-In worksheet, 182
decision-making, 84
  agendas, 88-94
  cohabitation versus marriage, 69-72
    games to avoid, 72-77
    mature relationships, 77-78
    misunderstandings, 74-76
    safety, 77
  deciding to become live-ins, 153
    agreement list for would-be live-ins, 156
    cold feet, 159
    readiness quiz, 158
    rules of engagement, 153-155
  financial matters, 175
    developing a live-in budget, 176-177
    selecting a financial plan, 175
  implications, 86
  inaction versus action, 84
  motives, 86-88
  reversibility thinking, 85
  where to live, 172
    Pick an Address worksheet, 173-175
    real-world examples, 172
    recommendations, 172
decision/commitment component (triangular theory of love), 83
delayed marriages, factor accounting for coupling style changes, 19

Index

desperation, women at risk for being hurt by love, 47
detecting lies, 279
dining room etiquette, 222
direct perspective, 75
disequilibrium, transformational experiences, 281
disparity, 196
    distrust, 198
    family disapproval, 200
    foundation safety checklist, 202-203
    jealousy, 197-198
        avoiding unfaithful partners, 199
    "love busters," 201
    negative vibes, 199
    precedents of live-ins carry over to marriage, 201
    previous relationships, 196-197
    sexual betrayal, 197-198
distrust, 198
divorce, factor accounting for coupling style changes, 19
domestic violence, 345
    battered women, characteristics of men who abuse, 345
    precautions for moving out, 304-305
dormant emotions, 246-248
Dumped at Bedside scenario, risks of living together, 64-65
Durable Power of Attorney, 169
Durable Power of Attorney for Health Care, 169
Dym, Barry, Ph.D. (family therapist), 209

E

economics, effects on marriages, 6
educating for marriage, 10
Effective Emotional Management (Sotiles product), 285
ego-building, improving home atmospheres, 284
emotional consequences of breaking up, 306
    closure, 307
    handling grief, 306
    recovery, 307
emotional intelligence, 339
empathy, compatibility characteristic, 135
erotic lovers, 120
    mixed with ludic, 121
    mixed with storge, 121

etiquette, 220-222
    bathroom, 222
    bedroom, 224
    dining room, 222
    interacting with families, 226
    introductions, 226
    kitchen, 223
    laundry room, 224
    living room, 223-224
    regulative, 221
    ritual, 221
    rules, 225
    social and business functions, 227-228
    symbolic, 221
    unsettled issues, 225
    writing your own rules, 228-229
Etiquette in Society, in Business, in Politics, and at Home, 220
Everything You Always Wanted to Know About Sex, 251
ex-spouses, 181
    disparity in current relationship, 196-197
exercises. *See* self-tests
expansive stage (three-stage cycle of relationships), 212
expectations
    behavioral, 238-239
    cohabitation leading to marriage, 326-329
    significant others, 178-179
exposing the issue, breaking up, 289

F

families
    disapproval, 200
    influence of live-ins on families, 27-28
    patterns, 13-14
fatal attractions, 113-114
    obsessive lovers traits, 114-115
    verus romantic love, 114
Felmlee, Diane (researcher), 267
females. *See* women
fighting, picking your fights, 234-235
financial guidelines, 175
    developing a live-in budget, 176-177
    home buying, 169
    list of "nevers," 169-170
    selecting a financial plan, 175

mishaps, relationship troublemaker, 268
    plans, 336
first-union relationship, 19
foundations
    avoiding disparity, 196
    avoiding unfaithful partners, 199
    distrust, 198
    family disapproval, 200
    "harsh setups," 199
    infidelity, 197-198
    jealousy, 197
    "love busters," 201
    previous relationships, 196-197
    safety checklist, 202-203
friendship, 186, 272
    compatibility characteristic, 134
    recheck for troubled relationships, 272
Fuller, Richard Buckminster (synergy), 273

G

gender
    interpretations, love talk, 244-245
    issues, sex, 253
        female turn-ons, 255
        male turn-ons, 255
        self-consciousness of women, 254
        tastes and practices, 253-254
    relationship to love style, 121
Glenn, Michael, M.D. (family therapist), 209
Glenn, Norval D. (professor), 314
Gottman, Dr. John (The Marriage Survival Kit), 349
gridlock, 196
grief, breaking up, 306
growth cycle of love, 110-111
    intimacy, 111
    mutual dependence, 111
    rapport, 111
    self-disclosure, 111
Guerrero, Laura K. (researcher), 197

H

Habits of the Heart: Individuals and Commitment in American Life, 314

357

happiness in relationships, 266
    self-test, 266-270
        troublemakers, 268-269
            assessing coupledom, 271
            changing agendas, 268
            evaluating love, 270-271
            financial mishaps, 268
            friendship factor, 272
            household heavies, 268
            incompatibility, 269
            meddling outsiders, 268
            rechecking level of commitment, 269
"harsh setups," flooding your partner with negative vibes, 199
healthy relationship signs, 193-194
history of relationships, 150
    charting your partner's love graph, 150
    interpreting your partner's love graph, 151-152
    secrets, 153
Hollander, Dory, Ph.D. (author), 76, 279
home base, 213
home buying, 168
    financial guidelines, 169
    "tenants in common" agreement, 168
home front
    children, 180-181
    deciding where to live, 172
        Pick an Address worksheet, 173-175
        real-world examples, 172
        recommendations, 172
    ex-spouses, 181
    financial guidelines, 175
        developing a live-in budget, 176-177
        selecting a financial plan, 175
    significant others, 177
        expectations, 178-179
        rating your significance, 178
honor, 188
house meetings, mending troubled relationships, 281-282
House with No Windows scenario, risks of living together, 50-51
House with the Locked Door scenario, risks of living together, 51-52
House with the Trapdoor scenario, risks of living together, 52
household heavies, relationship troublemakers, 268

human motivations. *See* motives
humor, 237

I

idols of love, 115-116
    Cleopatra, 115
    Orpheus, 115
    Romeo and Juliet, 116
Imber-Black, Evan (professor), 341
impersonal profiles (live-ins), 21
inaction, 84
incompatibility, relationship troublemaker, 269
individual narrative, 212
individuals, risk factors, cohabitation leading to marriage, 313-314
infertility, 338
infidelity. *See* sexual betrayal
insignificant others, 41-42
interdependence, couples, 215
intermediate lovers, reality checkup for love, 126
international live-ins, statistics, 22
interpreting your partner's love graph, 151-152
intimacy (growth cycle of love), 111
introductions, etiquette, 226
issues of love, 112-113

J-K

jealousy, 197-198
    avoiding unfaithful partners, 199
joint investments, defining commitment, 33
Jumping Over the Threshold scenario, risks of living together, 62-63

Kingma, Daphne Rose (marriage and family therapist), 299
kitchen etiquette, 223
Knight in Shining Armor scenario, risks of living together, 63-64

L

laboratory predictors of marital success, cohabitation leading to marriage, 313
last century of marriage, 4-5
laundry room etiquette, 224

lavish attention, 243
legal issues of cohabitation, 161
    anticohabitation laws, 167
    cohabitation agreements, 163
        limitations, 164
        necessity, 164-165
        potential predicaments of not having one, 166-167
        requirements, 165
    common-law marriages, 162
    home buying, 168
        financial guidelines, 169
        "tenants in common" agreement, 168
    palimony, 162-163
legislating in favor of marriage, 11-12
liars, detecting, 76-77, 279
liberal sexual ethic, factor accounting for coupling style changes, 19
Lieberman, David J., Ph.D. (author), 76, 278
Life Innovations, Inc., 320
limerence, 113-114
    obsessive lovers traits, 114-115
    versus romantic love, 114
limitations of cohabitation agreements, 164
live-in loves, 17. *See also* cohabiting
    agreement list, 156
    categories, 22
        marriage seekers, 22
        mutual users, 23
        romantic roomies, 23-24
        serious pals and lovers, 24-25
        true believers, 25-26
    children, 180-181
    cold feet, 159
    conscientiousness, 188
    consideration, 187
    deciding where to live, 172
        developing a live-in budget, 176-177
        financial guidelines, 175
        Pick an Address worksheet, 173-175
        real-world examples, 172
        recommendations, 172
    ex-spouses, 181
    factors accounting for change in coupling styles, 18
        delayed marriages, 19
        liberal sexual ethic, 19
        prevalence of divorce, 19
        working women, 19
    friendship, 186
    honor, 188

influence on family and
    children, 27-28
measuring happiness, 266
men as serial live-ins, 65
misconceptions, 40-41
profiles, 20
    impersonal, 21
    personal, 20
readiness quiz, 158
respect, 187
role of commitment, 35
satisfaction assessment, 26-27
sharing, 187
significant others, 177
    expectations, 178-179
    rating your significance, 178
statistics, 20
    international, 22
testing relationship builders, 188
time lines, 183
tolerance, 187
tool kit, 186
troublemakers, 268-269
    assessing coupledom, 271
    changing agendas, 268
    financial mishaps, 268
    friendship factor, 272
    household heavies, 268
    incompatibility, 269
    meddling outsiders, 268
    rechecking level of commitment, 269
    revaluating love, 270-271
versus common-law unions, 17-18
versus marriages, 35-38
    differences, 36-37
    prelude to marriage, 39-40
    similarities, 37
    substitutes for marriage, 38
versus newlyweds, 333-335
    advice for newlyweds, 334
    financial plans, 336
    marital roller coasters, 337-338
    prenuptial agreements, 335-336
    second marriages, 338
living room etiquette, 223-224
logrolling, 36
losses, 103-104
    bad breakups, 105
    minimizing, 105
love, 109-110
    at first sight (*coup de foudre*), 209
    attraction, 110
    axioms, 190

companionate, 110
confusing with lust, 60
daily planner, 191
decision-making, 84
    agendas, 88-94
    implications, 86
    inaction versus action, 84
    motives, 86-88
    reversibility thinking, 85
dormant emotions, 246-248
growth cycle, 110-111
    intimacy, 111
    mutual dependence, 111
    rapport, 111
    self-disclosure, 111
healthy relationships, 193-194
idols, 115-116
    Cleopatra, 115
    Orpheus, 115
    Romeo and Juliet, 116
issues, 112-113
junkies, 150
limerence, 113-114
    obsessive lovers traits, 114-115
mutual exclusiveness versus mutual necessity, 130-131
nutrients, 111
play, 243
recheck for troubled relationships, 270-271
responsive love acts, 248-249
rewards, 112
styles, 119
    agape, 121
    erotic, 120
    gender influence, 121
    ludic, 120
    ludic and erotic mix, 121
    ludic and storge mix, 121
    manic, 120
    pragmatic, 121
    self-test, 122-129
    storge, 120
    storge and erotic mix, 121
talk, 241-243
    gender interpretations, 244-245
triangular theory, decision/commitment component, 83
unrequited, 102
versus lust, 131
versus romance, 245
"love busters," behaviors that break up marriages, 201
low self-esteem, women at risk for being hurt by love, 48

ludic lovers, 120
    mixed with erotic, 121
    mixed with storge, 121
lust, 60, 131

M

Making a Place for Kids worksheet, 180
males. *See* men
manic lovers, 120
marriage
    active roles, 339-340
    champions, 10
        Capitol Hill Republicans, 12
        covenant marriage bill, 12
        educating for marriage, 10
        legislating in favor of marriage, 11-12
    cohabitation leading to, 68
        buying marriage protection, 329-330
        decision-making, 69-71
        disadvantages, 69
        distinguishing cohabitation and marriage, 325-326
        expectations, 326-329
        factors, 71-72
        games to avoid, 72-77
        laboratory predictors of marital success, 313
        making a fresh start, 329
        mature relationships, 77-78
        misunderstandings, 74-76
        pivotal moments, 322-325
        psychoeducation, 316-320
        reducing autonomy, 315
        risk factors, 313-314
        rite of passage, 325
        safety, 77
        "selection effect," 312
        sociological views, 68-69
        theories, 68
        transition worksheet, 330-331
        upgrading your live-in mindset, 314-315
        what awaits you, 326
    common-law, 162
    conditions of marital behavior, 340
    crosswinds of change, 12-13
    delayed, factors accounting for coupling style changes, 19
    effects of social change, 5
        economics, 6
        "postponed generation," 5-6
    family patterns, 13-14

359

financial plans, 336
last century, 4-5
marital roller coasters, 337-338
men, 70
new millenium projections, 7
  national movement to promote marriage, 9
  negative predictions, 7
  positive hopes, 7-9
  prenuptial agreements, 335-336
  prerequisites, 338-339
  role of commitment, 35
  second marriages, 338
secrets, 341-342
seekers (live-ins category), 22
truths, 342-343
versus live-in loves, 35-38
  differences, 36-37
  misconceptions, 40-41
  prelude to marriage, 39-40
  similarities, 37
  substitutes for marriage, 38
women, 70
Marriage Secrets: How to Have a Lifetime Love Affair, 238, 341
Marriage Spirit, The, 339
Marriage Survival Kit, The, 349
mature love. *See* companionate love
measuring happiness, 266
  self-test, 266-270
  troublemakers, 268-269
    assessing coupledom, 271
    changing agendas, 268
    evaluating love, 270-271
    financial mishaps, 268
    friendship factor, 272
    household heavies, 268
    incompatibility, 269
    meddling outsiders, 268
    rechecking level of commitment, 269
meddling outsiders, relationship troublemaker, 268
men
  as serial live-ins, 65
    self-test to evaluate risk, 65-66
  cohabitators, 70
  confusing lust with love, 60
  divorced, time requirement before cohabiting again, 59
  domestic violence, 345
  identifying women who spell trouble, 60
  interpretations of love messages, 244-245
  marriage, 70

risks of live-in loves, 61
  Dumped at Bedside scenario, 64-65
  Jumping Over the Threshold scenario, 62-63
  Knight in Shining Armor scenario, 63-64
  Runaway Mutual User scenario, 61-62
sexual turn-ons, 255
traits
  least success of cohabiting, 58
  successful cohabiting, 59
mending troubled relationships, 284
  conflicts that strengthen relationships, 281
  ego-building, 284
  house meetings, 281-282
    expressing frustrations, 282-284
  objectivity, 278-279
    detecting partner's lies, 279
  personality-based problems, 279-280
  reducing stress, 284
  situational-based problems, 280-281
mental model, breaking up, 288-289
metaperspective, 75
misconceptions (live-ins), 40-41
misinterpretations about sex, 137-138
misunderstandings, 74-75
monitoring the course of a relationship, 284-285
monogamy, 41
Monogamy Myth, The, 198
Moschetta, Dr. Evelyn, D.S.W. (author), 339
MoSex. *See* Museum of Sex
motives, decision-making, 86-88
moving-day rules, 302-303
moving out, ORI (obsessive relationship intrusion), 298
Mullen, Paul (researcher), 197
Museum of Sex, 252
mutual dependence (growth cycle of love), 111
mutual users (live-ins category), 23

N

National Domestic Violence Hot Line, 304
National Marriage Project, 325

national movement to promote marriage, 9
necessity of cohabitation agreements, 164-165
negative
  predictions, new millenium marriages, 7
  vibes, 199
negotiation in relationships, 89
Never Be Lied to Again, 278
newlyweds versus live-ins, 333-335
  advice for newlyweds, 334
  financial plans, 336
  marital roller coasters, 337-338
  prenuptial agreements, 335-336
  second marriages, 338
nonnegotiable risk factors, cohabitation leading to marriage, 314
nutrients of love, 111

O

objectivity, mending relationship discontentedness, 278-279
obsessive love, 113-114
  obsessive lovers traits, 114-115
  versus romantic, 114
obsessive relationship intrusion. *See* ORI
opportunities, 97-98
  disadvantages, 102
  evaluation of, 99
  exercise, 99-100
  qualifiers, 98-99
  real-world examples, 100-102
  tools for rethinking, 105
orgasms, 259-260
ORI (obsessive relationship intrusion), 298
Orpheus (love idol), 115

P

PAIRS, 320
palimony, 162-163
passion, compatibility characteristic, 135
Peele, Stanton (author and psychotherapist), definition of love, 116-117
personal profiles (live-ins), 20
personality-based problems, mending relationship discontentedness, 279-280

Index

PGs ("postponed generations"), effect on marriages, 5-6
Pick an Address worksheet, deciding where to live, 173-175
Pittman, Frank (psychiatrist and author), 198
pivotal moments, cohabitation leading to marriage, 322-323
   seizing the moment, 323-325
planning departure (breaking up), 299
   do's and don'ts after the fact, 303-304
   moving-day rules, 302-303
   twelve-step separation plan, 299-301
poor foundations (relationships), 196
   distrust, 198
   family disapproval, 200
   foundation safety checklist, 202-203
   jealousy, 197-198
      avoiding unfaithful partners, 199
   "love busters," 201
   negative vibes, 199
   previous relationships, 196-197
   sexual betrayal, 197-198
positive signs, new millenium marriages, 7-9
Post, Emily (etiquette), 220
post-breakup distress, 296
"postponed generation." *See* PGs
pragmatic lovers, 121
predictors of marital success, cohabitation leading to marriage, 313
prelude to marriage (live-ins), 39-40
premarital
   counseling, 317
      satisfied customers, 318
      selection process, 319
      sources, 319-320
      courses, 349
Premarital Relationship Enhancement Program. *See* PREP
prenuptial agreements, 335-336
PREP (Premarital Relationship Enhancement Program), 320
prerequisites for marriages, 338-339
Private Lies: Infidelity and the Betrayal of Intimacy, 198
profiles of live-in loves, 20
   impersonal, 21
   personal, 20

projections, new millenium marriages, 7
   national movement to promote marriage, 9
   negative predictions, 7
   positive hopes, 7-9
psychoeducation, cohabitation leading to marriage, 316
   premarital counseling, 317-320
psychological departure (breaking up), 288
purchasing a home, 168
   financial guidelines, 169
   "tenants in common" agreement, 168

Q-R

qualifiers (for opportunities), 98-99

rapport (growth cycle of love), 111
Rating Your Significance worksheet, 178
readiness quiz, deciding to become live-ins, 158
Rebound Duplex scenario, risks of living together, 52-53
recommendations, deciding where to live, 172
recovery, breaking up, 307
regrets, 105
regulative etiquette, 221
Relationship Enhancement, 320
relationships
   behaviors
      befriending your partner's pals and family, 235-236
      expectations, 238-239
      giving time, space, and solitude, 233-234
      picking your fights, 234-235
      simple do's, 232
      simple don'ts, 232
      spoilers, 236-238
   blending process, 214
   breaking up, 102-103, 288
      astrological corroboration, 294-295
      avoiding wasting time, 290
      bad breakups, 103
      children, 305
      closure, 307
      do's and don'ts after the fact, 303-304
      emotional consequences, 306

      exposing the issue, 289
      getting stuck, 295
      mental model, 288-289
      moving-day rules, 302-303
      moving out, 298
      planning departure, 299
      real-world examples, 292-294
      recovery, 307
      "time pieces," 290-291
      twelve-step separation plan, 299-301
      victim's departure, 304-305
   builders
      conscientiousness, 188
      consideration, 187
      friendship, 186
      honor, 188
      respect, 187
      sharing, 187
      testing, 188
      tolerance, 187
   categories of live-ins, 22
      marriage seekers, 22
      mutual users, 23
      romantic roomies, 23-24
      serious pals and lovers, 24-25
      true believers, 25-26
   characteristics of couples, 213-214
   checks and balances, 284-285
   commitment, 33
      joint investments, 33
      making concessions, 34-35
      role in marriages and live-ins, 35
      trading assets, 33-34
   communication, 142-143
      attention-grabbers, 145
      preventing shutdowns, 144
      skills, 143-144
   conflicts, 141-142
   confusing lust with love, 60
   courses, 349
   decision-making. *See* decision-making
   development of a life and identity all its own, 211
   disparity, 196
      distrust, 198
      family disapproval, 200
      foundation safety checklist, 202-203
      jealousy, 197-199
      "love busters," 201
      negative vibes, 199
      previous relationships, 196-197
      sexual betrayal, 197-198

361

divorced men, time require-
    ment before cohabiting
    again, 59
etiquette, 220-222
    bathroom, 222
    bedroom, 224
    dining room, 222
    interacting with families,
        226
    introductions, 226
    kitchen, 223
    laundry room, 224
    living room, 223-224
    regulative, 221
    ritual, 221
    rules, 225
    social and business
        functions, 227-228
    symbolic, 221
    unsettled issues, 225
    writing your own rules,
        228-229
factors accounting for change
    in coupling styles, 18
    delayed marriages, 19
    liberal sexual ethic, 19
    prevalence of divorce, 19
    working women, 19
first-union, 19
history, 150
    charting your partner's love
        graph, 150
    interpreting your partner's
        love graph, 151-152
    secrets, 153
identifying women at risk for
    being hurt, 45-46
    desperation, 47
    low self-esteem, 48-49
    self-test, 46
insignificant others, 41-42
interdependence, 215
live-in loves
    influence on family and
        children, 27-28
    international statistics, 22
    versus common-law union,
        17-18
    versus marriages, 35-38
love, 109-110
    attraction, 110
    axioms, 190
    companionate love, 110
    defined by Stanton Peele,
        116-117
    dormant emotions, 246-248
    growth cycle, 110-111
    healthy relationship signs,
        193-194
    idols, 115-116

issues, 112-113
limerence, 113-115
mutual exclusiveness versus
    mutual necessity, 130-131
nutrients, 111
responsive love acts,
    248-249
rewards, 112
styles, 119-129
talk, 241-245
versus lust, 131
maturity, 77-78
measuring happiness, 266
men
    least success of cohabiting,
        58
    as serial live-ins, 65
    traits for successful cohabit-
        ing, 59
mending, 284
    conflicts that strengthen
        relationships, 281
    ego-building, 284
    house meetings, 281-284
    objectivity, 278-279
    personality-based problems,
        279-280
    prioritizing priorities, 284
    reducing stress, 284
    situational-based problems,
        280-281
misunderstandings. See mis-
    understandings
negotiation, 89
potential losses, 103-104
profiles of live-in loves, 20
    impersonal, 21
    personal, 20
risks of live-in loves, 49-61
    Dangerous House on Main
        Street scenario, 54
    Dumped at Bedside sce-
        nario, 64-65
    House with No Windows
        scenario, 50-51
    House with the Locked
        Door scenario, 51-52
    House with the Trapdoor
        scenario, 52
    Jumping Over the
        Threshold scenario, 62-63
    Knight in Shining Armor
        scenario, 63-64
    Rebound Duplex scenario,
        52-53
    Runaway Mutual User
        scenario, 61-62
satisfaction assessment of
    live-ins, 26-27

sequences, identifying,
    214-215
sexual compatibility, 136-137
    misinterpretations, 137-138
    real-world story, 140
    self-test, 138-140
stress alleviation, 347
synergy, 273-274
    exercise evaluation, 274
    runaway, 274
three-stage cycle, 212
    contradiction and betrayal
        stage, 213
    expansive stage, 212
    resolution stage, 213
troublemakers, 268-269
    absolute breakers, 275-276
    assessing coupledom, 271
    changing agendas, 268
    evaluating love, 270-271
    financial mishaps, 268
    friendship factor, 272
    household heavies, 268
    incompatibility, 269
    meddling outsiders, 268
    rechecking level of
        commitment, 269
    signs and signals, 275
vocabulary
    becoming "we," 208-209
    "ours," 210
resolution stage (three-stage cycle
    of relationships), 213
respect, 187
    compatibility characteristic,
        135
responsive love acts, 248-249
Reuben, David, M.D. (author),
    251
reversibility thinking, 85
rewards of love, 112
risks
    cohabitation leading to mar-
        riage, 313
        individuals and couples,
            313-314
        nonnegotiable, 314
    live-in relationships, 49-61
        Dangerous House on Main
            Street scenario, 54
        Dumped at Bedside sce-
            nario, 64-65
        House with No Windows
            scenario, 50-51
        House with the Locked
            Door scenario, 51-52
        House with the Trapdoor
            scenario, 52
        Jumping Over the
            Threshold scenario, 62-63

Index

    Knight in Shining Armor scenario, 63-64
    Rebound Duplex scenario, 52-53
    Runaway Mutual User scenario, 61-62
rite of passage, cohabitation leading to marriage, 325
ritual etiquette, 221
romance versus love, 245
romantic love, 190
    versus obsessive love/limerence, 114
romantic overtures, 245-246
romantic roomies (live-ins category), 23-24
Romeo and Juliet (love idols), 116
rules
    engagement, 153-154
        bargaining, 154
            ultimatums, 154-155
    etiquette, 225
    sexual, 261
Runaway Mutual User scenario, risks of living together, 61-62
runaway synergy, 274

S

safety, precautions for victims of domestic violence moving out, 304-305
satisfaction assessment, live-in loves, 26-27
Schoen, Robert (researcher), 67
second marriages, 338
Secret Life of Families: Truth-Telling, Privacy, and Reconciliation in a Tell-All Society, The, 341
secrets
    marriages, 341-342
    past relationships, 153
"selection effect," cohabitation leading to marriage, 312
self-consciousness of women, sex, 254
self-disclosure (growth cycle of love), 111
self-esteem, women at risk for being hurt by love, 48
self-tests
    deciding to become live-ins, 158
    decision-making agendas, 92-94
    evaluation potenial losses, 104
    fact and fiction about live-ins, 31-33
    interdependence rating, 216

love styles, 122-123
    advanced lovers, 128-129
    beginners, 124-125
    intermediate lovers, 126
measuring live-in happiness, 266-270
opportunity evaluation, 99-100
relationship builders, 188
risk of men as serial live-ins, 65-66
self-esteem, 49
sexual compatibility, 138-140
synergy, 274
women at risk for being hurt by love, 46
serial live-ins (men), 65
self-test to evaluate risk, 65-66
serial monogamy, 41
serious pals and lovers (live-ins category), 24-25
Seven Principles for Making Marriage Work, The, 340
sex, 252
    alleviating boredom, 257
        changing maneuvers, 257
        creating sexual surprises, 257
        tactile sensations, 259
    communication, 260
    complaints, 256
    facts, 252-255
    gender issues, 253
        female turn-ons, 255
        male turn-ons, 255
        self-consciousness of women, 254
        tastes and practices, 253-254
    orgasms, 259
    rules, 261
    transaction, 275
Sex on the Brain: The Biological Difference Between Men and Women, 242
sexual betrayal, 197-198
sexual compatibility, 136-137
    misinterpretations, 137-138
    real-world story, 140
    self-test, 138-140
shared values, compatibility characteristic, 136
sharing, 187
shutdowns, communication, 144
significant others, 41, 177
    checklist, 42
    expectations, 178-179
    rating your significance, 178
signs of a troubled relationship, 275
    absolute breakers, 275-276

Sillars, Alan L., 74-75
situational-based problems, mending relationship discontentedness, 280-281
skills, communication, 143-144
social change, effects on marriages, 5
    economics, 6
    "postponed generation," 5-6
social functions, etiquette, 227-228
sociological views, cohabitation leading to marriage, 68-69
Sotile, Mary O., M.A., Ph.D. (author), 285, 347
Sotile, Wayne M., Ph.D. (author), 285, 347
sources, premarital counseling, 319-320
spoilers (behaviors), 236
    lack of humor, 237
    uncontained stress, 237-238
    whiners, 237
spouses
    equivalents, 177
    ex-spouses, 181
Sprecher, Susan (researcher), 267
statistics, live-in loves, 20
    international, 22
stonewalling (breaking up), 291
storge lovers, 120
    mixed with erotic, 121
    mixed with ludic, 121
stress
    alleviating, 347
    effect on relationship, 237-238
    reducers, improving home atmospheres, 284
styles of love, 119
    erotic, 120
    gender influence, 121
    ludic, 120
    ludic and erotic mix, 121
    ludic and storge mix, 121
    manic, 120
    pragmatic, 121
    self-test, 122-123
        advanced lovers, 128-129
        beginners, 124-125
        intermediate lovers, 126
    storge, 120
    storge and erotic mix, 121
substitutes for marriage (live-ins), 38
Supercouple Syndrome, 285
symbolic etiquette, 221
synergy, 273-274
    exercise evaluation, 274
    runaway, 274

363

T

tactile sensations, alleviating sexual boredom, 259
Tannen, Deborah, Ph.D. (linguist and author), 85, 145, 215
"tenants in common" agreement, home buying, 168
testing relationship builders, 188
Then, Debbie, Ph.D., 275
theories, cohabitation leading to marriage, 68
three-stage cycle (relationships), 212
    contradiction and betrayal stage, 213
    expansive stage, 212
    resolution stage, 213
time lines, 183
"time pieces," breaking up, 290
    time is on your side, 291
    time is your enemy, 291
tolerance, 187
tool kit for live-ins, 186
trading assets, defining commitment, 33-34
transaction sex, 275
transformational experiences, 281
transition worksheet, cohabitation to marriage, 330-331
triangular theory of love, decision/commitment component, 83
troublemakers (relationship discontentedness), 268-269
    absolute breakers, 275-276
    assessing coupledom, 271
    changing agendas, 268
    evaluating love, 270-271
    financial mishaps, 268
    friendship factor, 272
    household heavies, 268
    incompatibility, 269
    meddling outsiders, 268
    mending, 284
        conflicts that strengthen relationships, 281
        ego-building, 284
        house meetings, 281-284
        objectivity, 278-279
        personality-based problems, 279-280
        prioritizing priorities, 284
        reducing stress, 284
        situational-based problems, 280-281
    rechecking level of commitment, 269
    signs and symbols, 275
true believers (live-ins category), 25-26
trust, loss of, 198
truths, marriages, 342-343
twelve-step separation plan, 299-301

U

ultimatums, 154-155
uncontained stress, 237-238
understanding, compatibility characteristic, 135
unrequited love, 102
    emotional consequences, 306
        closure, 307
        handling grief, 306
        recovery, 307
upgrading your live-in mindset, cohabitation leading to marriage, 314-315

V

values, shared, compatibility characteristic, 136
Vaughan, Peggy (author), 198
vocabulary, couple
    becoming "we," 208-209
    "ours," 210

W-Z

Web sites, premarital counseling, 319-320
Weber, Ann L. (psychologist and researcher), 99, 296
Weinick, Robin M. (researcher), 67
whiners, 237
White, Gregory L. (researcher), 197
women
    cohabitators, 71
    domestic violence, 345
    interpretations of love messages, 244-245
    marriage, 70
    risk for being hurt by love, 45-46
        desperation, 47
        low self-esteem, 48-49
        self-test, 46
    risks of living together reported by women, 49-50
        Dangerous House on Main Street scenario, 54
        House with No Windows scenario, 50-51
        House with the Locked Door scenario, 51-52
        House with the Trapdoor scenario, 52
        Rebound Duplex scenario, 52-53
    self-consciousness during sexual practices, 254
    sexual turn-ons, 255
    traits that are trouble for men, 60
    working, factor accounting for coupling style changes, 19
worksheets
    Compiling a Live-In Time Line, 183
    Dealing with My Ex, 182
    Dealing with My Ex-Spouse and My Live-In, 182
    Live-In Budget, 176-177
    Making a Place for Kids, 180
    Pick an Address, 173-175
    Rating Your Significance, 178
    transition from cohabitation to marriage, 330-331

You Just Don't Understand: Women and Men in Conversation, 145, 215